A Guide to
Healing the Family Tree

A *Guide to*
Healing the Family Tree

by Dr. Kenneth McAll

PUBLISHING COMPANY
P.O. Box 220, Goleta, CA 93116
(800) 647-9882 • (805) 692-0043 • Fax: (805) 967-5843

Most Bible quotations are taken from the Revised English Version of the Bible, published by Oxford and Cambridge University Presses.

©1996 Queenship Publishing

Library of Congress Number # 96-69338

Published by:
Queenship Publishing
P.O. Box 220
Goleta, CA 93116
(800) 647-9882 • (805) 692-0043 • Fax: (805) 967-5843

Printed in the United States of America

ISBN: 1-882972-64-3

Contents

ACKNOWLEDGMENTS

The one most involved with the production of this book from its beginning was the one time Adult Education Officer, Sheila Richards. She bravely took it on herself to unscramble the spaghetti like writings which I had been producing over the past five years, adding much from her own experience. She now runs her own clinic using this approach. Without her help this book would hardly have got off the ground.

Once unscrambled, the manuscript was passed to Moira Pullen, the "ghost" writer of my previous two books. Her understanding and skills of perfection will be evident to the reader.

Thirdly, there is my wife Frances, a retired general practitioner who, with unswerving loyalty, brought her critical faculties and experience of general medicine to bear on the work.

Many of the patients whose stories appear in these pages, look forward to using this book themselves in helping others. Their willingness to be exposed is covered by slight alterations in details of place and age.

From the religious world I have received great support and encouragement from Morris Maddocks, former Bishop of Selby, Bishop Genders, formerly Bishop of Bermuda, the late Bishop Cuthbert Bardsley and Archbishop Malingo of Rome.

Outstanding supporters from the psychiatric world are Professor W.P. Wilson , formerly of Duke University, USA, Professor Philip Ney of Victoria, British Columbia, Professor Bill Wilkie of Brisbane, Australia, and Professor D. Wu of Taiwan.

Finally, I owe much to my local "team" who have helped with the work of production, especially Revd. Steven Kyle, who is also a consultant accountant and Tom Stenning, a former IBM troubleshooter.

Kenneth McAll M.B. Ch.B. (Edin.) July 1994

INTRODUCTION

This book contains a collections of true life stories taken from over fifty years of medical practice. Coming from three generations of missionaries, Dr. Kenneth McAll trained, as his father had done, in Edinburgh University and followed him into medical missionary work in China in 1937. His father, in the 1890's had begun to create Chinese medical literature and his name is still to be found in some of these books. Dr. McAll married another medical graduate, Frances, having met as students. Their wedding took place in Beijing in 1940.

As a surgeon in a Chinese guerrilla war area and then for four years in Japanese internment camps, life was not all that easy. The story of these times is told by his wife with over three hundred illustrations of his own in the book *The Moon Looks Down*. Though his surgical work was much needed – the eighty-bed hospital served a densely populated area the size of Wales – he was challenged by the work of a diminutive Chinese Bible woman who, with prayer or simple exorcism, produced cures in severely disturbed people. He remembered her in the internment camp where, to his surprise, several patients were healed after prayer. He was to remember her again many years later when practicing as a psychiatrist.

At home in post-war England, with no prospect of returning to China, Dr. McAll worked for a few years in general practice until he felt God was calling him to learn "all that man could teach about the mind." Then followed eight years of study and work in mental hospitals. Even during this time of training he experienced unexpected healing which, in spite of the results, caused some friction with his seniors.

In 1961 Dr. McAll left hospital work to set up as a private psychiatric consultant and in 1994 is still working. His first book, describing his present work in which he is regarded as a pioneer, *Healing the Family Tree*, is now in eleven languages and a best seller.

The purpose of this present book is to provide the reader with a "D.I.Y." guide to exploring the lives of patients and , in particular, their ancestors. Here, commonly, will be found very disturbed souls with unfinished business or who had suffered violent death or rejection, who now appear to be living out their hurts and frustrations in the life of one of their descendants. These are usually the most sensitive of the living family and the pattern may often be repeated in succeeding generations. This exploration may lead us to our ultimate goal of finding the root of the patient's problem. Then comes the therapeutic approach, quite often initially using recognized medical means as these can be useful in giving temporary relief though they cannot achieve cure. The cure, once the origin of the trouble has been identified, lies in confession, forgiveness and a new spiritual discipline based on daily morning quiet times with God and attendance at the Eucharist.

In the course of this exploration many wide dimensions of responsibility have been revealed so there is much world-wide adventure ahead. Bishop Maddocks said of Dr. McAll's work, "You have found a lacuna in the healing ministry of the Church and Medicine and you have filled it."

R.L. Stevenson wrote:
"I keep six honest serving men, they taught me all I know.
Their names are What and Why and When
and How and Where and WHO?"
In listing out all the patient's symptoms and signs and asking all the above questions, one ultimately may identify the pattern of life and the problems of a previously living person. This is not necessarily the patient's ancestor, but some definite individual wandering in the "borderlands," lost and alone in the darkness complaining of their last memories. They have no words with which to ask for help or prayer but, in psychiatric terms as used by Carl Jung, they "possess" the patient, badgering and inflicting their miseries on them or, as the Old Testament would have it, they "visit" the patient, in the New Testament they "trespass."

Psychiatry has coined the expression, "The Passivity Syndrome." Unfortunately, using this term tends to label disturbed patients as schizophrenics and the danger of that label is that they may face long periods of incarceration in hospital with no further questioning. Recently a London professor of medicine said that he reckoned 96 % of his patients' illnesses were psychosomatic in origin. Using his own approach Dr. McAll has seen release in 70-84%, depending on which label had been used to identify the illness. So one naturally asks, "What else is going on?" Some disturbed people have been treated by surgical means which has left them non-disturbing cabbages, some, it is true are ill for congenital reasons or as the result of infectious diseases to which we are all prey, but while we continue to look only for material reasons for our "dis-ease" our health services will continue to be over stretched. We need to look deeper for the underlying causes of illness, both mental and physical, and to recognize the real purpose of life here as a spiritual training for the life to come.

About the Author

Born in China in 1910, Dr. Kenneth McAll graduated in medicine from Edinburgh University. On his return to China in 1937 his experiences there led to interest in the powers of possession and he has devoted his life since to the curing of psychiatric illness through divine guidance. Hi unique book on the subject *HEALING THE FAMILY TREE* has become an international bestseller

His second book *THE MOON LOOKS DOWN* is a unique illustrated record, with a commentary by his wife, of their gruelling experiences in Japanese internment camps during the Second World War.

He has practised as a Consultant Psychiatrist in England for twenty-five years and is an Associate Member of the Royal College of Psychiatrists.

PART I
MEDICAL DISEASES

Abscess

The natural course of an abscess formation and its treatment is well understood and today's antibiotics and dressings seldom need any other concern. But there is a psychogenic factor which needs to be considered and when found there is an entirely different approach.

The first example was in a business man aged fifty-five who developed a large foot abscess on the dorsum (above the instep). When the doctor was called his temperature was 106°, the site was open $2^1/_2$ x 1 inch and the crater $^1/_2$ inch deep.

Antibiotics and dressings failed to alter the situation. On the third day of treatment a psychotherapist and spiritual healer saw him on his own initiative, merely saying, "You used to play football and you want to kick all the men in your office in the pants because of your temper, so purely subconsciously you have held this part of your foot in spasm and the circulation has ceased and this area has rotted. I will show you that forgiveness is more powerful and is God's gift to us." The patient got even more angry and told this visitor to get out, but before he turned to go he took hold of the foot and said, "Please God this man does not know you have forgiven him, but please help him to understand." The patient snatched his foot away and the healer left.

Early the next morning the nurse went in to do the dressing and on opening up saw an absolutely normal area of skin. There was not even any discoloration. They phoned the doctor who came. The patient reported that at the moment of the healer touching him the whole foot immediately became burning hot, that was why he had snatched it away. The following Monday he went back to work and at lunch time phoned the doctor to say that on the Monday morning when all the office had gathered, without any forethought and to his own surprise, he had stood up on his chair and publicly apologized for having lost his temper.

The second example was of a factory worker in the midlands who under family pressure decided to go south to enter a seven-year training to become a priest. The circumstances were spartan and the training rigorous. By the second year, he had developed a deep pit-like abscess on the tip of his left shoulder. It was big enough to hold the end of a finger. He came daily to the surgery for dressings, but is still enlarged. It was gently suggested that he was carrying a "chip" on his shoulder and deeply resented his training. At this he flew into a violent temper and accused the doctor of trying to teach laws of theology that were none of the doctor's business. However, the next day he came again a little more willing to listen. In fact, he was told that he should go home to his family and work in the Midlands. That night he talked it over with the tutor priest. The next morning there was no sign of the abscess. He came to the surgery to say thank you as he was on his way home, but he had been given a warning that, because it was only a doctor who had given the advice, he was not to witness his healing to anyone, as he belonged to the "wrong" church!

We quote, "How beautiful are the feet of those who walk in the paths of peace" (Isaiah 52 verse 7).

When extraneous unwelcome thoughts enter our subconscious we may try to suppress them, but they have to have an outlet in the end. As we see in the two quoted cases the right side represented what he wanted to do as compared with the other with the "chip" on his left shoulder our receiving side.

The subconscious thought always has to have a physical outlet. We may say it aloud, swearing or cursing; or by action hitting out; or if we are covering up, then it will be expressed as symptoms or so called dis-eases in the most appropriate end organ, for example the foot or the shoulder.

Absorption, Adiposity, Assimilation

Some people have difficulty in absorbing foods; this is particularly common after prolonged starvation, for instance, in areas of famine. The gut then is unable to process normal food, having become used only to coarse substances or having been damaged by diseases such as the dysenteries or sprue. Other people may not produce sufficient digestive juices, as in achlorhydria of the gastric mucosa, pernicious anaemia or some cancers. Alternatively, some absorb everything they eat and "layer it on." They may be very lonely people who eat too much either from boredom or frustration. To break the cycle and to achieve results, discipline is always required plus, usually, the firm support of others; and the basic cause must be faced and dealt with. It may be necessary to examine all of the patient's relationships, especially those of infancy including the possibility of breast deprivation in the first weeks of life.

In psychosomatic understanding, overeating may be a compensatory mechanism – putting something into the mouth, sucking the thumb, chewing gum, smoking a cigarette or frequently tasting tidbits when alone. In some monasteries, although the vows of chastity, poverty and obedience are taken and observed, mealtimes may provide compensation by over-zealous cracks and jolly fellowship!

Obesity has many causes, from glandular hormonal imbalance to simple overeating, indulgence or disease. Each requires medical diagnosis. One must be aware of pituitary disturbances in some patients; these show an exact pattern and should be treated by a doctor. Some medicines, prescribed for various conditions, may cause retention of water while others cause diuresis.

People who are anergic, lazy or incapable of using up their carbohydrates tend to store them as excess fat and appropriate physical exercises are necessary to enable them to do so. Most western nationals eat too much animal fats, including those from dairy products which are readily available. Nature provided them for the benefit of children and they should be balanced accurately with calcium and vitamin D. They are acceptable in the active years of life, but frequently may be damaging in older, more immobile people who store the fat rather that use it.

Overeating or obesity certainly may be a buffer against the outside world. People are not like the animals that lay in stores and hibernate; we are intended for positive action. America has developed a characteristic urge for speed. The original settlers there were often refugees from disasters; they had run away, grabbed what they could and rushed on to escape and survive. Many of their descendants live in a similar way – with fast food, quickly gobbled, in a throw-away society, "keeping up with the Jones's" and always demanding whatever is new.

Excess food has a soporific effect on the eater. Spiritually, the opposite is true – thus, the saint fasts and prays, his mind clear. In prisons in the Far East during the last world war, it was found – and confirmed by personal experience – that in a starvation situation the mind became extraordinarily clear so that to pray, listen and observe presented little difficulty. There were two sayings in a Japanese prisoner-of-war camp: "there's almost enough for our need, not for our greed" and "waste not, want less." The famous runner of the film *Chariots of Fire*, 1921 world record holder Eric Liddell, had only one rule concerning his dietary discipline in training – he ended each meal feeling that he could eat it all over again.

Obesity Anonymous is an international fellowship of like-minded people with the same problem. Excluding those with thyroid or pituitary problems, often a common denominator is found to be the fact that their siblings or their own babies have been aborted and they are seeking subconscious satisfaction in satiated appetites. There are those who eat double amounts because of subconscious pressure from others (see Part V: Possession Syndrome).

A single woman, aged thirty-two years who weighed nearly twenty-four stone, was said to be an epileptic from childhood. She often fell and would lie for about twenty minutes in a state of stupor, but would never hurt herself. Medicines did not affect the frequency of these attacks. She was not incontinent and ECG tracings were normal. Recently, she learned about her twin brother who had miscarried at five months and had been disposed of in an incinerator, while she herself was born at term. Now she understood that she should name and commit her twin to God. In doing so she realized that she had been saying subconsciously, "I dropped dead" and that, also, she had been compensating by eating for two.

A fourteen year-old girl, weighing nearly sixteen stone, was released from her eating addiction when her sibling, who had been aborted, was prayed for and apologized for by her parents.

In one family, the parents and their six children were all over-weight. For three generations they had been bread makers and bakers but one uncle's occupation was exterminator for a gang; he had killed many people and finally killed himself. Also, there had been sixteen miscarriages, two abortions and two still-born babies. Then, one member of the family became a "born-again" Christian and began a new pattern of prayer and fasting. She prayed for the whole family situation including everyone's greed, and when in prayer she heard the words, "They can't find the bread of life." Now she is teaching her siblings individually; one of her sisters and three of her own children are joyful "born-again" Christians.

A thirty year-old man who weighed over twenty-one stone was found to be fat as a result of enormous beer consumption and, thus, excess intake of calories. He adopted the simple expedient of not visiting pubs and was very successful in overcoming his problem. Three cases of obesity have been cured by self-discipline and eleven by Eucharistic approach for ancestors.

There is thought to be a "satiety" center in the mid-brain that controls eating habits. For instance, most people are able to eat a considerable amount of white bread or mashed potatoes. If, however, these are replaced with whole-meal bread or potato skins, the actual volume consumed is reduced because the essential B vitamins, needed for the absorption of starches in the body, have been taking in with the white in the brown pericarp or skin. The "satiety" center then switches off.

The Victorian Prime Minister Gladstone, who lived for over eighty years, obeyed a lifelong rule that every mouthful of food must be chewed thirty-two times. His food was certainly well digested and, also, he could not discuss politics during mealtimes; therefore, his mind would be refreshed. The modern "business lunch" – a rushed meal while talking "shop" throughout – damages the overfed who have a high cholesterol intake; it is often followed by a bout of indigestion. Yet a child will give undivided attention to its plateful of food at mealtime. Family conversations during meals should be simple enough to include even the youngest member, thus ensuring adequate time for proper digestion.

God said through Moses, "I will take them into this rich and fertile land... there they will have all the food they want and they will live comfortable. But they will turn away and worship other gods" (Deut 31.20). "Their houses are full of deceit; that is why they are powerful and rich, why they are fat and well fed. There is no limit to their evil deeds. They do not give orphans their rights or show justice to the oppressed. But I the Lord will punish them for these things..." (Jeremiah 5.27-29).

AIDS

AIDS   (acquired cellular immune-deficiency syndrome) is caused by the HIV virus which attacks key white blood cells concerned with the immune process. The body then loses its resistance to invading organisms; the patient is open to any passing infection.

The virus is passed from one person to another mainly through sexual intercourse, particularly homosexual anal intercourse as the mucous membrane of the anus is delicate and easily damaged not having been designed for this purpose. The condom is not regarded as adequate protection. The virus can also be transmitted through blood – through injury or transfusion with infected blood. It is also present in saliva, but the risk of transmission through kissing or through using the same chalice during Communion is nil as long as the mucous membrane of the lips is intact.

Four thousand years ago, men knew that to behave in a homosexual way meant death; gradually, their observations became public health laws. Disobedience to these laws was regarded as sin and this brought early death. In today's so-called "liberated" society, "sin" is largely ignored, but such indulgence precipitates disaster. These laws were made to protect people who have no guidelines, boundaries or consciences, so to ignore them is fatal. Those who have moral standards, exercise their consciences and develop spirituality as free people who can enjoy life and not fear the law.

A scientist in San Francisco said, "It seems that they have induced a self-destruct system." This is the modern version of, "The wages of sin is death" – both physical and spiritual.

Allergies

Allergy is an overworked diagnosis. Correctly used, it covers certain skin problems, asthma and bowel disturbances. When tissues are traumatized, they produce histamine very easily, then swelling and irritation develop. If this is of the skin it is known as urticaria; if it is of the bronchi, then breathing is blocked by the swelling and the spasm and can result in asthma.

Foreign proteins entering the body through the lungs, bowels or blood are fought against by the creation of antibodies. If this is excessive, there can be an allergic reaction and adrenalin may have to be injected to control it. Antihistamine drugs are used for long term treatment. Homeopathic remedies work on the theory that minute doses of toxic substances stimulate the body's reaction so, therefore, to imitate the noxious substance in minute form for administration ultimately will overcome the actual threatening disease. Considerable suggestion into the subconscious is added to this method of therapy.

Usually, the body system achieves an amazing balance by its team-work. All depends upon the human dominating spirit working through mind, brain and nerves to control distant areas; without this ordered control, target organs express trauma – we use the terms psychosomatic, psychogenic or somatopsychic.

A mother and her three children were all asthmatic. Her father's asthma began at the age of six when he witnessed the death of his three year-old sister. A tub of water, which was boiling on an outdoor fire of olive wood, fell on her and he was blamed for the accident. Three generations of the family subsequently had allergic sensitivity to olive wood plants or oil. The final therapeutic approach was a repeated Eucharistic service for the three year-old child whose funeral had been conducted in anger.

A depressed and sleepless sixty year-old woman was sensitive to household dust, mould and plastic. She had lost one stillborn child, had undergone an abortion and had disposed of two miscarriages in her house. Maybe the unborn were saying, "We lie moldering in the grave," so this was taken to a Eucharistic service. The woman was healed and her allergies disappeared.

A woman's face, neck and one hand were affected by urticaria. This was a "shown up" reaction because these areas of her body could be seen by other people. She had been abandoned by her mother when she was just four years old but hoped, as an adult, that no one would know that her mother had not wanted her. At a Eucharistic service, the words in the Lord's Prayer "as we forgive those who trespass against us" proved curative for her.

A three year-old boy was overactive and very bright, but was allergic to all white flour products and to white sugar. His mother's siblings were all girls but, in three generations, every male had died from alcoholism. Thus, the boy became the target for their demands for attention. His parents, knowing that alcohol is a ready source of sugar, related this in prayers for the release of these male relatives and their son was healed.

A married woman of fifty years had nannies as a child and servants throughout her life. She did not know that her twin sister had been still-born. As a five year-old she developed a "mirror" friend who accompanied her everywhere until, about three years later her parents teased her out of the pretence. Allergies then began, followed by numerous investigations, even continuing into middle age. One test revealed that she was sensitive to everything from her own countryside, even water. From infancy, her son was a similar sufferer. Her most serious allergic attacks began after her first miscarriage – she had eight before his birth and two afterwards. These ten miscarriages, not having been admitted into the conscious acceptance as family members, were lost and wandering, visiting their most sensitive and closest relatives. They were saying, "We never enjoyed dairy products, or the harvests of our country. We were never fed or cared for or given a drink of water."

As our subconscious picks up such voices, we may develop a negative reaction to the various substances. This is partly proved by the fact that food from abroad did not produce allergic reactions in this woman – rice, millet, maize, certain potatoes and some meats were quite safe for her to eat. The ultimate test came after the Eucharistic approach with the naming of all the children and their inclusion by the family. Healing of both the woman and her surviving son was evident within a week.

North American Allergies

One of the main memories of my visits to America is that people seem to revel in their allergies. Their conversations are frequently about their latest complaint and they carry small bottles of tablets around with them. In looking into this phenomenon I have found that the earlier their families arrived in the New World, the more likely they are to complain. Does this fact correlate with another fact discovered during my most recent visit? American Indians, other than those who are Christians, do not want their dead, who have died at the hands of the white man, committed to God or to have any form of funeral for them, as they want the resentful dead to continue to haunt the descendants of the guilty immigrants.

The symptom complexes can range from sleeplessness and depression of the reactive type, to gastro-intestinal upsets. Many have skin allergies – eczema, urticaria or edema while others have respiratory problems such as chronic sinusitis, asthma or hay fever. They seem to be illustrating the saying that "The sorrows with their unshed tears make organs weep." In cases of bulimia (induced vomiting after binging) or colitis, for example, it would seem that the organs are trying to rid themselves of some unpleasant secret. The skin may blush in self-defence or shame. The psychosomatic approach to these conditions is therefore helpful, the cure we will discuss further on.

One of these cases is recorded in the book *Healing the Haunted* in the chapter headed "The Ranch." A couple was living on the site where a massacre of Indians by the Spanish had occurred centuries before. The wife suffered from multiple allergies. On investigating the case we found it also involved the slaughter of the cavemen by the Indians when they arrived and then the driving out of the Spanish by later arrivals from Europe.

When thirty-eight year-old Meg moved to a new ranch, her whole body became swollen by urticaria. She developed breathlessness, palpitations and general fear, complaining of a pervading smell of burning hair. The previous occupants of the ranch had been ill, also, and had been hospitalized. They had the added complication of marked fluid retention and cortico-steroids were prescribed. It was discovered that in 1820, on the site of the ranch, one hundred and twenty-five Red Indians had been burned to death. Three people, including Meg, were relieved of their symptoms at a service seeking forgiveness for this massacre.

Another case, so far unrecorded, was that of a woman in her fifties, who, for many years, had suffered from an urticarial rash on the upper part of her body from a straight line transversely across her breasts. The rash only appeared when she was in public. It was bright red, scalding and unresponsive to treatment. The symptoms suggested to me that a female had been buried alive. Prayers brought relief almost immediately.

After weeks of research it was found that, in the eighteenth century, an ancestor had married a native woman. The tribe shot the white man then took the woman and buried her in sand up to her nipples in a tidal estuary. They tormented her by day and she was attacked by wild dogs at night. Finally, she died when they lit a bonfire over her. The family were able to identify her by name. After a service of committal my patient was completely healed.

Another woman had been hospitalized many times for her total allergy syndrome. She was now living in isolation far away from other human habitation in a caravan raised up on stilts. She could only tolerate wild rice and spring water which her husband delivered daily at the end of a long causeway so that she had no other human contact.

We met in a small bungalow, again, completely isolated, which they had built for their holidays many years before. I could fine no fault in their family tree so enquired into the circumstances surrounding the onset of her problems. They confessed to having built this bungalow in Indian reservation land without seeking permission. They reckoned they could get away with this as court cases against whites who do this sort of thing have a "thirty-five year delay in the courts in Washington."

My response to this was to suggest that the Indian women who had lived and died there were angry with them and so annoyed at the total pollution of their land that they were haunting the wife's subconscious, making her believe that everything was polluted and dangerous. I said, "Tonight you will apologize to God and to the Indians for offending them and stealing their property. You will promise to destroy this bungalow and return to your own home in the city."

This they decided to do and the following day, when I was due to speak in another town and before I had said a word, this lady came up on to the platform and asked to show her healed self and tell her story.

Another family was descended from immigrants in 1653. Today, seven of the family have hay fever or asthma and recently three have died from this.

A man suffering from colitis found that, around 1800, his family had bought land from an earlier settler who had taken Indian land. When he put this right, he was healed.

Because of these earlier stories, I was asked to visit America again to meet families of settlers who had looked into their origins. These included Armenians, Hugenots, Plymouth Brethren and Irish who had fled from the potato famine. They were to take responsibility for those of their ancestors who had been left behind and, as far as they knew, never had any funeral or committal. Those we met experienced healing from a variety of conditions including alcoholism, schizophrenia and diabetes.

But, because this year saw the 500th anniversary of the "discovery of America" which to the native American was the anniversary of a disaster, we tuned in especially to the Indian way of life. We visited their villages and were shown many things. Social clubs, churches, schools, houses, had all been built for them. We had the very strong feeling that we, the Whites, were trying to force running deer into pig sties, fine sties though they might be.

With eight other people including a priest, I visited Wounded Knee. Here there is a netted enclosure on a small knoll surrounded by rolling hills. It is approached by a gravel track and marks the burial place of the three hundred fifty men, women and children shot by the American cavalry in 1890. We had decided to hold a service on this spot and, as it was cold, we stayed inside the minivan.

As we began the services, a rain storm blew up which violently rocked the van. The priest interpreted this as an attack by the haunting dead Indian braves. To me, the black clouds seemed to be the Indian women rushing past us in their fury. It all seemed so disturbed that I asked God for a sign that we were doing the right thing. At that moment the clouds opened and a strong ray of sunlight shone through the windscreen right on to the chalice and the wine glowed with a rich red light, then the clouds closed over again and the rain went on pouring down. Then we ended the service, having confessed to the slaughter and committed the dead to God, the rain stopped and we were able to go out and walk to the actual burial enclosure with its high heavy netting, an area of 10 by 20 feet. We also looked at more recent simple graves, some of them of babies.

As we drove away, we saw two Indian men approaching us. They walked with a menacing cow-boy swagger and both wore long white feathers in their head-bands. Our driver warned us not to open the van windows, but to drive slowly past without stopping. He told us they were probably on patrol to see that no one interfered with their dead. Apparently the Smithsonian Institute had earlier intended to provide a proper funeral for the victims of the massacre, but the Sioux tribe had refused to allow this as they wanted their dead to continue to haunt the white people.

We stopped to pray in the Black Hills where, again, Indian land had been abused by farming and the heads of American Presidents had been carved into the hillsides. Then we drove through the Badlands, a terrifying stretch of desert country with high towering columns of powdery white rock, ideal country for ambushing the wagon trails of the early settlers. It stretches north and south like a great barrier to the West. Further on we were to attend a three day conference in Pierre. Here we hoped there would be Indians too. It had been a difficult conference to arrange as these people are wary of the many sects who have good intentions, but are rather more keen on their message than on helping individuals.

The conference had been arranged by an amazing Methodist who had had the vision of it for a long time. He intended that every national group and church philosophy should be represented. I was to speak with Dr. Doug Schoenenger on the healing of the family tree. About one hundred fifty people turned up on the Friday evening and again on the Saturday morning. We were preparing them to draw out their family trees, noting especially glaring faults and unfinished business amongst the dead to present at the Masses which were to be held later.

Over five hundred turned up for the Roman Catholic Mass on Saturday afternoon. In the evening we were seated in a very dimly lit gymnasium facing a large stage which was kept in total darkness throughout. This was to create an atmosphere of morning. There was a lot of restlessness and people, especially children, wandered at will. The program was planned to include both worship and entertainment so there were poetry readings, prayers, songs and strangely beautiful Indian humming. Then there was the Indian drumming on eight drums, sometimes quite deafening. We traced the history of these American natives as they had faced invasion, the loss of their lands and homes, their suffering from new diseases, their humiliation and finally, pollution. We talked of killings, torture and scalping, the wrongs of both sides. The service ended with candle ceremonies, new vows of forgiveness and love over the shared peace pipe. Many community leaders and clergy, including the Anglican Bishop took part.

The service over, we were all treated to an Indian feast which consisted of a large bowl of meat stew, a small bowl of rich, spicy gravy and another small bowl of a thick fruit jam. This was to be eaten by breaking off chunks of bread and using it to scoop up the various ingredients. It was a jolly meal as we all moved round talking to all and sundry. As we parted, we were each given a small ring of woven scented grass as a sign of friendship.

On the Sunday morning we held a Eucharist in the Anglican church attended by about two hundred people. We had prepared specific prayers for different people to confess aloud their sense of shame and to accept forgiveness from God and from others. Whites in the congregation confessed the wrongs of invading the country, introducing diseases and alcohol, bribing Indian tribes to fight against each other, abusing nature and the pollution which followed. The Indians on their part remembered their own original arrival in the north west, their wiping out of the even earlier cave dwellers and their cannibalism.

At this point in the service, an Indian man and his wife stood up at the back of the church and said they wished to confess the truth about Wounded Knee. The true story had never before been told, but it was now possible to do so. This man told us that his uncle had been one of the Indians there. The American cavalry, on Government orders, were to put a stop to the tribes performing what were known as Devil dances. In these they drank heavily and took part in wild war dancing which, the Government feared, could lead to violence. The army was ordered to disarm the Indians, forming a ring of cavalry round the camps while they did so. They were specifically ordered not to shoot.

While this was going on, his uncle suddenly heard a woman screaming and in one of the American tents, found an American soldier raping a teenage Indian girl. In his fury, he picked up the soldier's rifle and shot him. The sound of the shot caused the American commander to believe that the Indians still had hidden weapons. He, therefore, ordered the soldiers to open fire killing all the men, women and children. His uncle in his anger shot many Americans from behind running away. He fled to South America until he was about to die. Then he returned home and revealed his secret to his own tribe. He had died two years ago.

We were all deeply moved by this story and immediately turned it into a prayer of confession for us all. We prayed for the shot soldiers, the three hundred fifty massacred Indians and especially for the soul of the uncle himself. This incident proved a rich climax to all we had prepared. The Lord was very good and gave many people visual insights confirming the origins of other family problems. The Indians present felt it was one of the most important days of their lives and the news of it spread rapidly so that, within a month, I had heard about it from my sister-in-law who is in close touch with the Pueblo Indians of New Mexico.

The story of Black Elk was with us from the beginning. He was a Sioux Indian and on becoming a Christian had made huge efforts to be an example to his people. He talked of the "hoop" of life which was never complete and, as he neared death, he was terribly sad that he had not accomplished his work. We prayed about him thanking God for his life. In our minds we could see that he was free, free to be himself, and could visualize him galloping his horse across the sky, holding a cross before him, shouting to all the Indian settlements that the "hoop" was now complete and that they could all join with him. We could see thousands of warriors on their chargers galloping after him in a "V" formation like the great formations of migrating geese. They were no longer earthbound, but free to advance into Heaven.

Blindness and Vision

Some people claim to be blind – the result of hysterical overlay – in order to gain sympathy and attention, abrogate their responsibilities or receive charity. Others do not want to "see" their situation, so there is a subconscious shut-off; many are only "blind" when other people are around. The sensory area of their vision becomes the target end organ. (In this chapter, we are discussing neither congenital blindness, senile blindness caused by cataracts or vitamin deficiencies, nor blindness from abrasions and infections in Eastern countries.)

Nob, a little man of eighty-four who lived alone, came complaining of failing sight. I "cured" him by cleaning his glasses!

A middle-aged woman, Greta, always wore very large dark glasses whatever the weather, insisting that any light hurt her eyes. Wealthy and beautiful, she would boast of the men with whom she had intercourse. When she began to attend Eucharistic services regularly and was able to confess and accept forgiveness, Greta felt that she had in some way "come home." Her eyesight returned to normal.

Mollie, a middle-aged spinster, was a science teacher in a large school in the north of England. She expected promotion and to become the head of her department but suddenly a very young man, no better qualified, was appointed instead. Mollie shut her eyes, unable to even lift her eyelids; at home she moved only by touching familiar objects with her hands. Feeling slighted, she became depressed and sleepless and was on sick leave from school on account of her "blindness." Her own doctor asked me to visit her. There were no immediate problems in the family tree, so together we helped her to face the hurts, rejection and ingratitude. We prayed through this situation, bringing her to the realization that Christ had carried far greater loads for us. She returned to school to apologize to her Headmaster for her resentment. Church activities are now central to her life and her visual ability is quite unimpaired.

A Christian brother and sister in their forties (both with high IQs and considerable insight) suffered from photophobia and kept their eyelids partly shut. They were descendants of Oliver Cromwell who was a narrow, bigoted, theological literalist – anti-royalty and anti-Roman Catholicism. Many citizens were forced into his army which destroyed castles and monasteries, statues and stained glass, killing indiscriminately throughout Britain and Ireland. Desecrated ruins still lie unrepented of and unattended. Cromwell was "blinkered" in the narrowness of his vision. He thought he was doing God's will, lived a sexually clean life and died in old age – but his evil deeds followed him. This was the issue and the intention of the family prayers that were brought by the brother and sister to the Eucharistic celebration. Their outward appearance improved as they were able to objectify the cause of their eye problems.

About this time, a German therapist and artist, Eugan Vinnai, was working with me and involved in Christian healing. During his stay, Kathy (age thirty-six) was brought to us by her husband as an emergency. She had gone "blind" suddenly that morning. I had known the couple for several years. When they came in, Eugan hardly looked up and merely said, "What is this man doing here?" He replied, "I am Kathy's husband, Hal." "Oh no, you are not, get out," said Eugan. After a long pause the man said, "Actually, you are correct." (She had walked out on her real husband.) It was arranged, finally, that Kathy should return to her real husband with his child. Everything was apologized for on the phone and in prayer but her husband used the moment of meeting again to humiliate her in front of the neighborhood. With much noise, he threw her and her possessions into the street. Divorce proceedings were completed and she married Hal who had joined us in prayer. He adopted her little daughter and they became a very united Christian family.

Eugan Vinnai had experienced several such healings. He explained, "Their lives were contrary to God's laws. Kathy's guilt and sheme made her want to hide: if nobody could see her then she could not see them. Also, she felt that when she walked outside, the surfaces of the streets were irregular, any lamp-post or telegraph post wobbled and slanted, her "standards and right angles" were all awry. Therefore, it was easier to shut off vision. Kathy agreed with Eugan and , after prayers, she was able to see immediately.

A forty-six year-old woman had peripheral vision only – that is, all her central vision was weak and she could read best from the sides of her eyes. In this condition, known medically as "central scotoma," a neurological examination of the interior of the eye will reveal a white spot in the visual center (the macula) indicating degeneration of the nerves there. As the patient's eyes did not show this, a psychosomatic cause was sought. (Tunnel vision is exactly the opposite condition where there may be neurological damage in the occipital visual centers.) She experienced a general sense of fear, especially in public and at night, with an intense fear of all animals. This suggested that their family had not faced the truth about some event in a previous generation. In fact, the patient's ancestors had raped and slaughtered women and her symptoms prompted the thought that one had been buried alive and left to die. The family agreed that this might have happened and took the case to a Eucharistic service, after which the woman recovered her sight fully.

A single middle-aged man was attending a medical conference. After the meetings he never joined in any of the discussions or celebrations, but just sat or stood with a stony forward stare. He did not speak to those around him and if addressed was immediately suspicious and self-defensive demanding, "What is it to do with you?" He would not accept another's opinion and the slightest fault brought a dismissive, condemnatory remark. The man was difficult to help because of his narrow, restricted vision.

A fifty-five year-old man often "saw red." He was a macho stocky type, the descendant of a family of deported criminals, and always had lived by the gun. Whisky helped him to ignore any self-critical ability so he regarded everyone else as "crooked" and ready for a fight. In a temper he would stalk through his house, gun in hand, "booting out" any visitors. Finally, his wife and sons left; only then did he slow down and face himself. His wife and children became Christians but, as yet, he has refused to join them.

At fifteen years old, a girl developed encephalitis which apparently caused complete blindness and she said she was paralysed. After spending two months in hospital she recovered, being left only with spots of numbness. She had two disastrous marriages before she was twenty-three and four years later was back in hospital, blind and paralysed again. The families of both her parents were involved with Curanderos (Mexican witch doctors); there were also two murders, two vehicle deaths and two people who disappeared, all in three generations. After a hospital visitor prayed with the patient, she began to improve. Three years later, she met and married a caring Christian man and now lives a normal, happy life.

An ophthalmologist and a neurologist diagnosed an inflamed optic nerve in a woman who had a sudden onset of dim vision (blurred) in her left eye. A C.A.T. scan of her brain proved negative. She had failed to organize herself for a college course and felt blamed despite being the most sensitive sibling and the favorite of her grandmother who spoiled her until she died. The woman had been sexually abused by a man who claimed to have telepathic control over her. The psychosomatic position was that she failed to face the feelings of being battered and yet smothered as a helpless child. Her eye problems ensured shelter in the parents' home where her "tiredness" enabled her to spend much time in bed. Spiritually there was no discipline. Change, therefore, had to begin with personal decision on her part and then with the parents, removal through Eucharists of ancestral ties – especially those of her dead grandmother. This brought deliverance from evil, and her ancestors' progression into God's kingdom. The woman was healed.

Every example of such types of "blindness" is different, as I have found in about forty cases. Father Hampsch of California describes six complete and sudden healings; Neill in *Psychosomatics* records many more.

In evolutionary progression, the furthest development is the spiritual human being. Following the primitive instinct for self-preservation and a defensive attitude, finally we grasp the concept of moral sensibility and the idea of family loyalty. Our furthest forward goals lie within our present determination and decisions – the more spiritually orientated, the more tenuous, for they are not yet laid down as permanent hereditary factors. Obviously, the ancestral, moral and divine attributes are more easily assimilated by our descendants, for whom they become blessings.

Alcohol and hallucinogenic drugs, however, adversely affect these tenuous controls so that the "censor" to our thoughts and actions is cut and conscious restraints are removed. We then revert to a lower – even primitive – level of behavior.

Visual imagery is one of the greatest human attributes. We can recall the sights of places and of people. Most can see these in color and are able to describe them verbally; others can transpose them manually on to paper in writing or pictures. There is a further development, proven more recently by the many recorded, life-after-life experiences or life-after-death experiences. These are confirmed by the "visionaries" in the books of BC 2000.

We know that there are other wavelengths that humans cannot register; beyond us are all the telepathic, television and radio impulses. Cats can see infra-red rays, dogs can see ghosts, bats can hear vibrations far beyond our reach and experiments have proven the porpoises can communicate on nine different systems at once.

The human spiritual/visual ability has been highly developed by the Chinese in "reading" people's characters. Some Tibetans, by "reading" the intentions of visiting delegations, learned all the details of China's plans to conquer.

In times of silence, many Christians visualize divine beings. The proven results of seeing and hearing within the spiritual medium of the Christian Church, demonstrate that here is a real gift which should be developed. Through it many illness have been healed. We can see and hear now and can begin to live eternally.

Brain Damage, Autism and Dyslexia

After an attack of encephalitis or meningitis, the brain can suffer residual damage. The severity of scars in brain tissue varies with the extent of the original damage. Some patients need to live in mental hospitals and may resemble schizophrenics in their unpredictable behavior; others suffers epileptic attacks. During birth, the fetal head comes under great pressure from the uterine muscles; finally, other abdominal muscles push it through a restricted canal, somewhat limited by the size of the female pelvis. Within the skull, of course, is the brain, the substance of which is very soft, almost jelly-like, but it can withstand considerable pressure.

There is a theory that the cause of the trouble in children with learning difficulties may be that during this time of intense compression, it is not the brain substance itself which is damaged, but the minute developing blood capillaries therein, so that they fail to receive an adequate blood supply. Vasodilators of the vitamin B complex have been used to test this theory – especially B3 (nicotinamide) together with B6 (pyridoxine) – resulting in a seventy per cent success rate. For example, a ten year-old child on B3 plus B6 daily became normal within a month. Most such children do not require further treatment beyond six weeks – only one patient has needed a continuation. Some have progressed well using eltroxin, a thyroid substitute. Administration of this drug should be under experienced medical supervision.

When growing children are found to have learning difficulties, they may be lacking in verbal expression (autism), in memorizing or in reading ability (dyslexia). Sometimes they may show gradual improvement with special instruction. A twenty-six year-old girl in a mental hospital had been given various labels from hysteria to paranoid schizophrenia and had undergone several courses of electroconvulsive therapy. She was regarded as a nuisance. The onset of her illness followed a severe attack of "influenza" but her history had not been recorded adequately. When this was realized, the changed diagnosis and relevant treatment (with vitamins) resulted in considerable improvement.

Similarly, a post-vaccinal encephalopathy in a child left much brain scaring but with the help of mega-vitamins she made progress.

It was difficult to pin point the origin of a middle-aged man's attacks in which he curled up and fell forward with head-jerking. He was a religious man and it was thought that it might be a possible possession syndrome resulting from the sudden death of an unmourned ancestor, so he took this unknown person to the Eucharist for committal. The outcome was a remarkable lessening of the attacks to fewer than one a year (after a five-year follow-up).

Initially, leukotomy was a drastic operation but now it is quite safe and very localized. It was developed after an accident in which a pickaxe entered the frontal lobe of a Spanish laborer's brain. In this operation, which took place under full anathesia, a cut was made through the frontal lobes. The man lived, but there was a complete character change from a rambunctious, tough individual to a docile husband. Later, leukotomy was tried out on uncontrollably mad patients, thirty per cent of whom died from hemorrhage, thirty per cent improved partially, but became mere "cabbages" and thirty per cent became docile, yet without initiative. The other ten per cent showed no change.

In the 1940s, leukotomy became common practice within the enclosed environments of mental hospitals and, gradually, more localized operations were devised when it was realized that the frontal lobes of the brain initiated mental and physical activity. The target of the operation was the actual tracks, focusing on specific lines of communication related to the symptoms. This procedure succeeded; using local anathesia and a probe, on the end of which could be sparked a minute cautery, the right track was located by questioning the patient at the time, resulting in great accuracy in cutting the established route of an obsessional pattern.

An exceptional example of a failed frontal leukotomy of the first dramatic type was a lady in her forties who had spent a disastrous thirty years of life as a schizophrenic. Her filthy body, blasphemous speech and lack of insight had not been helped by any therapy. A leukotomy was performed; there was a hemorrhage and she should have died. She was now blind, dumb and bald and became a large flabby mass of flesh. After eighteen months her sister and brother-in-law intervened and sought help. During the subsequent interview, the only suggestion made was that interfering humans (the doctors) had precipitated this tragedy and that, therefore, we should apologize to God. Quite unaware of whether or not the patient registered the conversation, twelve people joined in a three-minute prayer session, including the Lord's Prayer. The interview ended after twenty minutes with, "Sorry, there's no other solution, good-bye," and the family left.

Next morning when the patient wakened, she could see herself in a mirror. She shouted, "Come and look at my hair." Overnight a quarter of an inch of hair had grown, she could see and speak and asked for her husband. Not knowing that she had lost thirty years of her life, she expected to step back into her own house, but her husband had divorced her, remarried and lived in another town with his wife and children. Gradually, she was introduced to the cruel truth – there was no home and no husband, although he came to visit her. A very depressed period ensued, but she was supported by her sister and brother-in-law. After some months, she slowly recovered and was welcomed back with open arms to her church. Several people were transformed by this miracle, especially the pastor. The hospital doctors did not doubt the change in the woman, but for them the label "spontaneous remission" was more acceptable than a "miracle." Five years later, the "patient" is living in a flat near her ex-husband's home. She has become an "adopted aunt" to his children; they are all very happy.

Four more examples of the sudden cure of failed leukotomies through prayer and the Eucharistic are recorded. Miracles do occur, the why's and wherefore's of which we do not understand. Faith the size of a grain of mustard seed is needed, not necessarily on the part of the patient but, perhaps, by a close relative or friend who trusts in the faith of the Lord Jesus Christ in His father, God.

Breathlessness and Asthma

Breathing is the body's natural system for the exchange of gases, via the lungs. Oxygen is absorbed for the tissues to use in their metabolism and carbon dioxide is expelled. To cope with situations of fear, anger or any form of exertion, the body demands increased oxygen.

Over-breathing is caused by a lack of balance of these gases in the blood in a small mid-brain center which is the controller of the autonomic nervous system. Fortunately, our conscious mechanism does not have to think about this process. Over-breathing can occur if the blood volume, or red cells, are inadequate either from their formation or from their loss. Of course, any block to the breathing system, any constriction or diminution in the area of lung tissue, or any heart problem is operative in this balance, including external circumstances such as lack of oxygen in a confined space or its rarity on a mountain top.

A hysterical person may over-breath (or hyperventilate) merely as part of attention-seeking; if this is deliberate, the giddiness and fainting can be induced. Firm handling should break the cycle. At the other extreme, little children can withhold their breath until they turn blue if, for instance, they are punished excessively. In a game of hide-and-seek, they may say to each other, "Do not make a sound; do not breathe!" as adults, we hold our breath with sudden pain, "choke over our words" or become "speechless with anger." To learn to whisper the Lord's Prayer is very therapeutic.

A forty-five year-old minister suffered from spasms of breathlessness – but only when in the pulpit of his church. The attacks began when he heard of his father's "drowning" from the police who had found the body, head downwards in the mud at low tide in the docklands. As his father had been alcoholic, it was presumed that he had been drunk at the time – it had taken twenty years to identify him. Finally, the minister realized that his father had suffocated and that when he was in his pulpit, he was in the ideal position to confess his father's sin of suicide and to commit him to God. This he did with another minister and he was immediately released from all attacks.

Thirty-eight year-old Betty always reacted breathlessly and fearfully to the sight of stinging nettles and sand and, therefore, never took her children to the seaside. In therapeutic sessions, analysis released the memory of an incident when, aged three years, she was in an air-raid shelter with her family. It was wrecked by a bomb and they found themselves shut in by a fall of sand and stinging mettles. Betty's breathlessness was cured by the conscious awareness of the origin of her fear and her ability to replace it with a deliberate acceptance, through Jesus Christ, of the love and security of beginning the eternal life now.

The breathlessness Jesus Christ Himself suffered on the Cross was man-induced. He had suffered thirty hours of physical torture and could not even carry His own Cross as a man of His size was expected to do. Hanging by the arms, His autonomic breathing was unable to function, so voluntary breathing had to be used but the muscles involved cannot work for long. Already exhausted, He died earlier than the soldiers expected. Their usual procedure was to induce immediate asphyxia by breaking the legs, but Jesus was already dead and, as foretold, His bones were not broken.

Although He died from suffocation or cardiac rupture, the attitude of His spirit was to weep for His accusers' ignorance – because they did not know what they were doing – not for His own physical pain. Even on the Cross, He was able to think for them, praying that they should be forgiven, and to make provision for His mother and His favorite disciple, John. He also appointed His mother as the mother of all humankind for future generations.

Asthma (bronchial) is a condition in which there is spasm of the bronchial tubes with increased thick mucous secretion. It is characterized by paroxysms of breathlessness, often at night with wheezing and special difficulty in breathing out. It is brought on through an over-production of certain antibodies normally used to combat irritants of various kinds, e.g. pollen, house dust, mites etc.

Asthma often seems to represent a "frozen rabbit" reaction where, faced with a threatening situation, the patient can neither fight nor run away and, returning to a situation associated with fear, an attack may be triggered.

A lady in her late forties could "smell" even the past presence of a cat in a room, this would trigger an asthmatic attack. Analysis revealed that as a small child she had been given a kitten which slept on her pillow. That night, burglars broke into the house. Thirty-five years later, this memory was re-opened and prayed over. Her asthma was healed, for God's love casts out all fear.

At twenty-seven years of age, Ken returned to live in the city where he was born. Soon he began to waken every night at 2 a.m. with an asthmatic attack associated with flashing lights on the ceiling. Many medical trials failed to help him. His mother remembered that as an eighteen months-old baby, Ken had been disturbed at 2 a.m. one night by intruders carrying lamps. This memory was relived into full consciousness and prayed over. The claim that Jesus Christ is always present released him from further attacks.

Breathing is a necessary physiological function, but it can be affected by others who have died. This is known as the "possession syndrome" and happens when lost beings of the earth-bound world are trying to draw attention to the traumatic circumstances of their deaths, for which there had been no confession or apology. Their release depends upon those who are alive and will pray for them.

Cancer

The uncontrolled over-multiplication of living cells can occur in all animal life and even in the vegetable kingdom. The varieties in humans are usually classified according to the tissue functions – for example, glandular or connective tissue. Vast research programs go into finer and finer detail resulting in control by the manipulation of cell-destroying drugs or radiation for some, and for others cure by early surgical removal. This section shows another aspect.

Every living cell is developed according to genetic patterns and fulfills a specific function. Cells multiply as part of a definite program, living as members of a team in harmony with all other cells of the body. When their work is done, they shrivel and die. Our bodies are the temporary hosts of this amazing organization. If we demand extra multiplication, for instance to combat infection, the white cells multiply, inactivate or engulf organisms, then die – this is called pus. When foreign substances are put on the fingers, such as tar from cigarette smoking, more an more skin is formed as protection. If in any way we over-stimulate these areas, the cells' teamwork is lost and they begin to multiply out of control; they become rogue cells, revolt and spread, regardless of their true function, into the lymphatic system and the blood stream, so secondary growths are established. There is no limit to their activity until they die by killing their host.

What then is the ultimate controlling force? Has each cell a self-determining factor and does it, both individually and in conjunction with other cells, hold a balance for the sake of the total organism or human frame? Perhaps it comes under the central control of all the body's organizations from the subconscious area. Have we the ability consciously to take control? The ultimate solution lies in who we are.

When we abuse our bodies, for instance with nicotine, then the cells may revolt and become cancerous, out of control and beyond all reason. If we can relate to these cells, adopt a genuine attitude of apology and confession, analyze our motives and correct them, then there is a basis for an evidence of cure.

The long medical debate on the relationship between tobacco and cancer in Britain is now finalized and a ban on smoking is implemented in more and more places. Literature abounds with statistics showing lung and heart diseases attributable to smoking and the consequently enormous cost in medical attention and death. Psychosomatically, the smoker is labelled "narcissistic, nipple sucking," probably was not breast-fed so craves mother figures, and frequently plays with the lips or chew. There is a need to occupy the mind and hands and to dampen the subconscious demand for attention; nicotine puts the blood vessels in spasm. Cigarettes are white, black or brown – no one smokes green, red or picture-painted cigarette papers – because they seem to represent the nipple and emanate a "milky" substitute. The action of selecting a cigarette and the performance of lighting-up becomes a ritual, a covering-up in awkward or exposed situations, with a certain amount of face covering – the point of conflict and of elimination being exteriorized by the burning to ash of the distant tip.

One patient who chain-smoked always finished each cigarette only half-smoked by bending it violently in the ash tray with his thumb. He had been responsible for several miscarriages, abortions and three broken marriages.

The smoking habit is formed partly by its ritual and partly by the drug itself. The starting-point is often a wish to keep up with one's peer group. In all habits that should be broken, the motive behind the will to do so is paramount. If we hope to achieve merely the loss of a habit, then we continually face and battle with it and even hypnotic treatment is very temporary. To make a conscious choice and train the mind into new affections – perhaps, for the sake of fiancee, spouse, child or parent – is a very loving motive and can invite an expulsive power. Becoming a pure instrument as a channel of God's grace carries with it the gift of a new power. We choose to switch our thoughts to become a candle of the Lord, so that our prayers may rise like incense and change situations in the troubled world around us. This is emotionally very rewarding.

The cancerous reaction of the cells of the bronchial mucous lining is like a frightened horse galloping regardless of its own eventual destruction. These cells, originally perfectly balanced, were designed to provide a moist, efficient tube conducting gases to the alveoli's capillaries to exchange gases for our metabolism. If irritated for long by tar products they finally revolt, multiply out of control, break away and spread. It does not seem relevant whether a person smokes only one or many cigarettes a day, whether they have given up smoking years earlier or, even, whether the damage comes from the inhalation of others' cigarettes – the disobedience remains. This is very hard on the victims of passive smoking.

Fifty-eight year-old Charles smoked in the office throughout his life. He had a lung resection of his cancer tumor and radiation to control quite extensive secondaries; he was dying and terrified. He had never been religious, but asked me what was the point of life, what would be his end and whether he should increase his dosage of pain-killing tablets. I introduced him to the knowledge that Jesus Christ represented another pattern of life, fear-free training for eternity. Charles began morning prayers, quiet times and Bible study; he was transformed. The secondaries which had been seen in the lymphatic glands of his neck disappeared, he breathed easily, slept well without any discomfort and abandoned all drugs. In his home environment, he took an interest in many charities and in church work so enthusiastically and joyfully that he was nicknamed "Lord X" (the town's name) for he chaired many committees. Two years later, his wife discovered that he had died in the night without struggle; he had just passed on. A post-mortem examination showed no evidence of cancer, only the scarred areas of the original disease, but on the death certificate the cause had to be written as "myocardial degeneration."

The subconscious mind acts out on the body the unexpressed areas of conflict, either consciously, verbally or physically by selecting a target or end organ which can deal with them most appropriately. Every thought has physical outlet. When an organ is so disrupted and demanding of attention from the whole body, the reverse process obtains and a somatopsychic situation develops.

Mabel had been hospitalized for years with colitis, which controlled her life. A cancerous growth was suspected, so a resection operation and a colostomy were performed. A depressive illness with sleep disturbance developed, for which medication gave only temporary relief. Psychological analysis established that Mabel had been brought up in an orphanage and nothing was known of her parents. She had always longed for family love, wondering whether she had any brothers or sisters and she mourned this. The orphanage was efficient and in her teens she took up domestic service and emigrated. She married an excellent man and their children were normal except for shyness. Life was good, but the awareness of her unknown ancestry dogged her thoughts and frequently her conversation. Joseph's "bowels did yearn upon his brother" Benjamin (Genesis 43.30, AV) and likewise, Mable's bowels became the end organ of her unresolved grief. Late in life, twelve years after the operation, she found that she could mourn, apologize, and commit her unknown family to God. Of course, this did not alter the colostomy, but it did bring her great joy and peace.

A forty year-old woman's rapidly growing breast cancer, with spinal and cranial secondaries, precipitated a search by her family and friends for the cause. Whereas in most cases early recognition of a breast lump leads to immediate operative removal, this woman's developed too quickly. (She had not breast-fed her four children, this being the mistaken fashion at that time.) Medical care seemed to arrest the growths twice but, after team prayer and fasting, all her symptoms and lumps were gone. The family tree was drawn up, revealing some very early disasters, the most notable being an "affair" of her great-grandmother's with a nobleman, which had resulted in the birth of her grandfather. This lord had revolted against his own King and led a rebellion. A curse had been put upon this earlier family – that if they visited the family grave then they would die within a year. This cased much fear and, indeed, several members had died doing so. These problems were brought to a priest who quite willingly held a Requiem Mass for both family and patient. For a few weeks afterwards, all seemed resolved, but the woman's secondary symptoms built up again and she died – peacefully and without fear.

It was found that none of the intentions had been spoken at the Mass. This showed that the efficacy of the Mass does not depend upon the priest – he represents the Lord. The intentions are those thought by the family. With their stated family love they should have confessed the sins of their ancestors aloud, named the people and committed them to God, with several members each taking different facets of the problem. The unspoken sins concerned conflicts and revolts in the ancestry – "keeping my guilt hidden within my breast" (Job 31.33). Not having breast-fed her children, there were now too many trying to "feed on her breast." The woman was an active member of a prayer group and people depended on her but, "in the bosom" of the group were found subversive elements determined to wreck the whole fellowship. All of these problems were unresolved at her death and the resultant anger, frustration and mourning became a challenge for all concerned and a lesson for the future.

A man of eighty-two years was at home dying from cancer of the prostate and secondaries. His wife had left him for she could not cope with the disease, but one of his daughters stayed to look after him. In despair, she came to a cathedral healing service and asked, "Is it possible to proxy another for healing?" The answer was, "I don't know, but I can try." We prayed for the old man and the priest gave a blessing. When the daughter arrived home, her father was dressed and cooking their evening meal, feeling perfectly well. Three weeks later, his wife came home. He lived for a further eight years in great peace and with no sign of malignant disease.

Tumors of the brain have many classifications according to the area affected and the type of cell. Some grow very quickly – from the first symptoms to death may only be a month. Others are very slow to develop and are operable by a neurosurgeon. There is much confusion in this field, for people sometimes think that they have such tumors and claim healing without medical facts.

A thirty-year-old man was in a London hospital awaiting an operation for a brain tumor. Routinely, he was visited by the hospital chaplain who laid his hands upon him and prayed during a very short visit. Next morning, in the operating theater, the surgeon claimed that the wrong patient had been brought. X-rays were repeated and there was no sign of any tumor; the man returned home, all symptoms gone. Strangely, the chaplain belonged to a different denomination from the patient, whose own church had neither prayed for him nor even thought of a healing.

Paula was in her twenties when she sought help for backache and was found to have a primary cancer in her breast with secondaries in her spine and neck glands; she also suffered from confusion and loss of concentration. For weeks she lay at home terrified, sleepless and depressed. She felt that she was getting worse, but no one had told her the truth. One morning she demanded and received an honest answer from her doctor, whereupon she stopped all her sedative drugs immediately, called in her parents and family and led them in prayer. That night she felt great joy and peace, prayed with her parents and fell asleep like a child. Next morning they found her in the same position. She had died in the night. The various branches of her family not involved in prayer were stunned to shame but then resolved to reform.

In some cancer patients there is a darkness, a death wish, an escape mechanism. Psychosomatic evidence of this was seen in a man who was in hospital awaiting an operation for oesophageal carcinoma. His priest helped him to examine his lifestyle and to acknowledge that his work as an estate agent often involved convivance and dishonesty. Wanting to escape, he literally could not "swallow" the situation. He faced this, confessed vowed to be honest and with prayer was healed. Two days later he was sent home.

A problem is the varying measure of healing; we do not understand why some people are cured, some are not, some linger, while in others the onset and the end are sudden. Sometimes a patient is blamed for having too little faith. This is very unkind for faith is merely the substance of things hoped for, the evidence of things unseen, an intangible temporal attitude. It can be our faith in Jesus Christ, or the faith of Jesus Christ in His Father. In either case, ours is a surrender, a handing over to God for whatever He intends and an acceptance that we should respect our human frames and not permit the body cells to develop their own rebellious control. Where there is no decision, there is no victory.

St. Paul said, "The law kills, judgmental sin destroys; the spirit makes alive." A lawyer himself, he meant that if we live only within the bounds of laws, then we are miserable, restricted, uncreative beings, subject to "judgmentalism." God shows us that, through Jesus Christ, He took over the battle between our eternal spiritual development and the inherent animal nature within us, so that we might rise to another level of creative activity, freedom and joy.

For diseases like cancer, a new criterion of cure must be found, based on wholeness of body, mind and spirit. The body will stop living, the mind may become senile, yet the spirit is eternal. Fear, pain and disease are earthly; peace, love and joy are everlasting.

Cardiovascular System

From the days of primitive man, it was thought that life existed in the blood since, the "being" died if the blood were drained. Additionally, the pumping heart varies in rhythm and power according to circumstances, so it was regarded as the seat of the emotions. We know now, however, that the heart is a self-limiting organ with four muscular chambers that pump blood and, if over-exerted will cause a person to stop an activity or to lie down. Dietary or alcohol abuse or smoking increase the risk of damaging the heart.

After years of psychological demand with, as it were, "clenched fist" determination, arteries can remain in spasm and become hardened. The blood pressure then rises to force blood along rigid tubes that should be elastic. With hardened arteries, the heart may pump more rapidly and even the coronary arteries (the heart's own blood-supplying vessels) will become hard and may even block causing a heart attack. A partially blocked coronary artery may be cleared by passing a balloon catheter or, if this is ineffective, a bypass operation may be performed, replacing the damaged vessel by one taken from another part of the body.

Teamwork of the parts of the heart is important. This is coordinated by the autonomic nerve conduction between the chambers. For many years, the basis of heart medicines was digitalis which is derived from the leaves of the foxglove flower. This was discovered by an old Scottish peasant who effectively used it to slow and strengthen the heart-beat.

Throughout most of our lives we are unaware of our heart-beat; we are used to it. In the womb our ears were upon the mother's aorta, the largest and noisiest blood vessel in the body, and we registered every emotion that she experience. Sonic scans record a fetus' momentary alarm if, for instance, a pregnant mother hears her front door open, only relaxing when she knows it is her husband or friend. Such a rapid reaction to alarm is protective, preparing the body for "fight or flight." When we have been frightened we say, "my heart pounded" or, if it was excessive fear, "my heart stood still." We refer to someone we love as "my heart-throb" and a moment of complete surrender is described as "I gave my heart."

A very sensitive person may faint upon seeing blood, having correlated the loss of life with fear of the unknown. The blood pressure falls suddenly, becoming inadequate for the brain, so the person collapses to the ground. Thus, the pressure is evened up and blood is restored to the brain which, unlike other areas, cannot do without blood for more than a few seconds. Such a situation can be imitated but the pulse rate will not alter and, invariably, the hysteric will fall upon a comfortable landing place with, preferably, a responsive audience.

As with all musculature, the heart responds to graduated exercise, but if there is negligence by over or under-exertion, then it become vulnerable. The heart's sensations are referred along the left upper thoracic nerve routes, where the heart was formed, and along the inner surface of the left ear, which has the same nerve supply. Later, they descend into the lower chest area, therefore, pain experienced around the heart region is probably not connected with the heart but with other organs-the lungs, pleura, ribs or, most commonly, the fundus which is situated at the top of the stomach. (This is a symptom of indigestion.) After exercise, a big meal or an emotional shock, we may be aware of our heart-beat bumping against the chest wall.

The heart is the target organ of many emotions, so personal faults are blamed upon it and an attempt is made to objectify those faults. It is an amazingly efficient temporary servant which should be cared for and its immediate response to our every emotion serves as a monitor which, in itself, makes us aware of, and able to objectify our subjective experiences. Thus, it is also a warning system. Although modern technology can relieve many tense situations, prevention by a lifetime of discipline is best. Change is possible and there is healing through prayer. Exploring this area entails an accurate, medical, fact-finding diagnosis beforehand, and careful checking afterwards.

When Gertrude was forty-three years old, her husband died suddenly. As she felt so lonely, she removed her eight year-old son from boarding school to live at home with her. She began to complain of "heart symptoms" and palpitations and was told by her physician, a professor of medicine, that her cardiograph showed some coronary occlusion. He prescribed vitamins and iron; a few years later, another physician treated her with thyroid. In her sixties, having done the rounds of many doctors in Scotland, Gertrude went to Harley Street in London where one specialist dared to tell her that there was nothing wrong with her. She became very angry and so consulted yet another physician in Hampshire who confirmed that nothing was physically wrong. He told her, however, that her relationship with her son, whose life she obviously possessed, was much amiss. (The son, now labelled schizophrenic, lived in a mental hospital in Edinburgh, while his wife was ill in a tubercular unit.) Again Gertrude became very angry, stormed out of the surgery and slammed the door. She walked up a nearby hill and, feeling breathless, went into a church to rest. Suddenly, she heard a voice saying, "You have never cut the umbilical cord of your youngest child." On her knees, she then apologized to God. Her anger vanished and the palpitations stopped. Throughout many years of follow-up, there has been no recurrence of her "heart symptoms."

Her son and daughter-in-law were healed on the same day, despite living four hundred miles away. Both were released from hospital and their child, who had been fostered, was returned to them. God had intervened and these three people were each cured. Often, cases of healing are quite unrelated to time and distance.

A sixty-six year-old widow was dying from coronary heart disease. While the priest was administering the last rites, she had a vision of Jesus Christ and asked us to interpret what the Lord was saying. In my own mind, I was sure that He was commanding, "Feed my sheep." The woman recovered full consciousness and, when everyone had left her room, she rose and dressed herself. She adopted a new, outgoing attitude and lived for another eleven years. This, again, was an unexpected intervention by God.

A man in his early seventies, with no previous ailments, was rushed to the hospital's intensive care unit with coronary symptoms. A large aneurism on the font wall of his heart was found. His wife thought she heard him murmur my name and asked me to visit him. The resident doctor told me, "I am waiting for the final flicker on the screen over there to pronounce him dead; there's no point in going to him as he is quite unconscious." I felt duty-bound to go to his bedside, however, especially as his wife was sitting in the corridor waiting for the doctor's word. I knew the man, a retired shopkeeper who had been all around the world and was now a very keen gardener – but an avowed atheist. I stood beside him saying nothing and touched his left hand which was blue and very cold. Suddenly he spoke: "Isn't Jesus wonderful!" He looked virtually dead; I could find no pulse, so I slipped away.

Next day, hardly daring to contact the family, I called at the hospital. There was my man sitting upright reading an Agatha Christie novel, with all the tubes and wires removed from him and showing a normal cardiograph. He greeted me cheerfully with, "You've brought your daily reading with you, haven't you?" I read "I shall give you a new heart of flesh and remove your stony heart.". He exclaimed, "I knew it!" He lived for another fourteen years, active and extremely happy, dying very suddenly with no premonitory symptoms a few weeks after his wife.

We seek to learn "what is at the hear of the matter" but many unanswered questions remain. We know, of course, that life ends when the heart stops beating and out flies the eternal spirit from the body although, with modern resuscitation methods, many people are brought back to life. If they, as with the patients in the previous examples, begin a spiritual development, then something is achieved; if not, there seems little point in bringing them back.

Evidently, whatever intervenes and precipitates a cure does not depend upon our own decisions. We may conclude, therefore, that the source of life and the giver of life is the Holy Spirit preceding from the Father and the Son – mysterious but adequate appellations that are viable because they are proven realities and produce visible effects.

Medical students are taught, "Man is as old as his arteries." Village physicians in China feel the pulse from the radial artery in both left and right hands, understanding that the right side is a person's performing, outgoing side, while the left is the receptive side. If the arteries on the right hand are hard, the patient may be a forceful materialist, easily angered, given to thumping the table, treading on other people and kicking them out of the way.

A businessman worked hard to accumulate sufficient money to enable him to retire and play golf, which he achieved by fifty years of age. He built a bungalow on the south coast of England but, within a month, died from coronary heart disease. His wife was a very resentful woman who, thereafter, complained of heart pains – neither of them, however, had sought advice. They had even refused to have children. The woman finally turned to the church and there found fellowship and a measure of release.

A forty-eight year-old divorcee suffered acute hypertensive reaction when she felt she had been cheated in a court case. After several counseling sessions over two months, she was "cured" and, thereafter, became active and outgoing in her nursing position.

Anger, resentment, frustration, or a purely materialistic attitude forces the target organ, the blood vessels, to carry the strain. Many people use a medical diagnosis as an escape route, excusing their bad behavior by hiding behind labels such as "my high blood pressure"-thus blaming anything other than themselves. Stress results from resistance to the pressures and challenges of life so, where there is no resistance, there is not stress. To learn to relax, therefore, is essential. Although often under pressure at work, we should establish a daily period of exactly the opposite – for example, enjoying the silence and restful greenery of a garden, playing golf, or the productive activity of gardening. The discipline of a convent or the monastic life, where periods of intense activity – often among other people – are balanced by times of silent devotion, gives both the heart and body the best foundation for the achievement of spiritual maturity. Moderation in all things is the ideal.

Dermatomyositis

This is a rare disease which can occur at any age including childhood. It may be acute leading to rapid death or run a chronic course with spontaneous remissions. It is one of the auto-immune diseases in which the immune system destroys the body's own cells. In this case it is the muscle cells which are attacked causing weakness and pain with muscle atrophy and calcium deposits. There may also be a mild inflammatory arthritis. In many cases there will also be skin rashes with a typical purple coloring round the eyes. Treatment is with steroids.

In two families with affected children, there had been widespread family involvement in occult practices with suspected curses and doll-needling. In one family there had also been incest in three generations. As the children had certainly not invited this disease, it is worth looking at patterns of ancestral behavior.

Dermoid Cyst and Hydatidiform Mole

This cyst, varying in size from a quarter-of-an-inch upwards, sometimes develops rapidly and , therefore, has to be removed. Since it has no attachment, there is no damage to the host when it is cut off. Such a cyst, opened after excision, is seen to contain hair, bone, teeth and various other human tissues, although they are quite undeveloped. Some medical opinion suggests that this indicates a twin but mostly this theory is discarded as nonsense.

A beautiful woman in her early fifties had been a depressive. She was married, but her mood swings kept her on the edge of divorce for years. An unsightly swelling developed on her thyroid but, not having any symptoms from over or under-functioning, she did nothing until the swelling became very awkward and surgery was requested. To the surgeon's surprise, it shelled out very easily – it was not thyroid tissue, but a dermoid cyst. When the patient was told, she decided to pray for, and name her twin. At once her long-term depression lifted and she felt light and joyful. Subsequently, her marriage became one of great delight and now, three years later, she witnesses to this dramatic change in her life.

A so-called schizophrenic woman heard "voices" whenever she was alone in a woodland near her home. During a D & C operation four years previously, she was found to have a hydatidiform mole. (This is an abnormal growth of the placenta or afterbirth. It is associated with an abnormal pregnancy. It can grow very large and become malignant so the pregnancy has to be terminated and the mole removed.) Ten years prior to that operation, the patient had an abortion. Now twenty-six years old, she was able to pray for the two lost souls and, from the first day of doing so her "voices" have not recurred.

Since infancy, a thirty-two year-old woman suffered from uncontrollable minor fits, without damaging herself. Drugs did not help. She always felt aware of another presence around her and she developed depressive mood swings. After her mother's death, she discovered a newspaper cutting concerning her own twin who was miscarried at four months because of a hydatidiform mole. She prayed specifically for it and gave it a name. This brought relief from all her symptoms and fits.

Diabetes

Diabetes is a condition in which there is an inability to control carbohydrate, fat and protein metabolism due to an absence or deficiency of insulin. This results in too much sugar circulating in the blood and can have serious and life-threatening results. There are two main types of diabetes – (1) in which the cells in the pancreas which produce insulin are destroyed by the body's own immune system and (2) in which, though the cells are not damaged, there is an inability to utilize insulin. The first type occurs mainly in younger people and may start in childhood and this kind is dependent on injections of insulin to keep the patient alive. The second type tends to occur in people over forty and can be controlled by diet or special drugs. It can have the same effects on the body, but has a longer survival rate.

A doctor must be aware of the possibility of temporary blood sugar changes and glycosuria (sugar in the urine), resulting from thyroid or pituitary abnormalities or from kidney disorders. A diabetic man once said, "I can use only my own sweetness. I refuse to take any sugars. No one has ever been sweet to me or accepted me – not even my own mother, although she miscarried my brother."

Dr. William Wilkie, a Brisbane psychiatrist, maintains that there is a common factor in the psychosomatic origins of diabetes. He thinks that when diabetics come up against a life-threatening situation, which mobilizes massive carbohydrate release into the blood, they burn up the carbohydrates very quickly in the supposed emergency; then they lose control and the threat seems to continue. Thus, it becomes essential to examine the common denominator of the threatening pattern.

A divorced forty-eight year-old woman was a psychologist and lived with a much older woman friend who also worked. This was not a lesbian relationship. The elder woman developed a disease and died, leaving the psychologist alone except for her father to whom she was very attached. He died suddenly within a week. She was able to mourn both of them but, at her father's funeral, which she organized and at which she was responsible for presenting the eulogy, she felt an epigastric spasm, just as she had when her friend died. This continued and the pressure was so severe that her meals and sleep were disturbed, accompanied by symptoms of weariness and loss of weight. A blood sugar test confirmed the diagnosis of diabetes. The woman dieted and injected insulin, also beginning a new discipline with a better spiritual control of her resentment at losing two loved ones in a short space of time. She now requires smaller dose of insulin.

Grace was a married woman, just fifty years old, who developed diabetes when her father died from diabetic gangrene of the feet, as did her grandfather and two uncles all of whom had amputations. As an eight year-old child, Grace's great-grandmother, who also died from gangrene, had been sent by her parents from Europe to New York in 1860. She then had to find her own way to the "orphan train," to be adopted by a farmer in the West, having been told that there were too many children in her own family. She must have felt as though she had been dealt a body blow to the stomach; she was unable to cry, or even to be sick. Such a "punch in the stomach" in reality had paralyzed the insulin production in the pancreas. This physical restriction, together with deep resentment and sadness, had been passed down to each generation. Grace is quite able to control her blood sugar by dieting and has been able to forgive and release the past. Hopefully, therefore, the diabetic abnormality will not continue into any future generation. In the Mass setting, Grace saw the Lord lifting her ancestors from a pool of light before the altar; after the service she identified each one from photographs. Six months later, she knew that she was cured and, after laboratory tests, stopped taking insulin.

A similar "punch in the stomach" was recorded by a man of thirty who, twelve years before, had been removed from college in order to support his mother and his younger siblings. He became a diabetic and remembers his deep-felt bitterness at that situation.

A married woman of thirty-six years, with no children; complained of a constant sense of grief – not depression; she felt torn apart and wanted to vomit. As a teenager she had been diagnosed as diabetic and controlled her own insulin intake. Her sister, father and aunt were also diabetic, as were her grandparents. The latter had escaped from Ireland at the time of the potato famine in 1845. They were children at the time and, after walking for many miles, finally came by boat to England. Anyone able and fit enough to flee the situation either sailed to America, thirty per cent of them dying on the journey, or walked across country to take ship to England, thus leaving behind the old, ill and dead who had neither funeral nor burial. (Even today, farmers sometimes uncover human bones when ploughing.) Their descendants are learning to attend Requiem Masses where they themselves pray specifically for these ancestors. The present patient married a man of similar origin. She reported that her only relief from epigastric tension and moods of grief was to be found in a potato baked in its jacket!

A divorced forty-eight year-old woman came from a family of strict Scottish Calvinists who had emigrated in 1760 to America, a third of them dying on the journey. The patient developed diabetes at sixteen years of age when her diabetic mother died. For over thirty years she endured her grief but now, for the first time in her life, she realized the truth and that she need not continue to weep for unknown reasons. The Lord said to Isaiah, "I shall add fifteen years to your life and deliver you and this city" (2 Kings 20.5-6). Also, she discovered that the male figure who had always haunted her was a Calvinist ancestor who had died on that sea voyage. She felt that at least she belonged to a family that was freed from its Calvinistic strait-jacket. She found a new sense of peace and the idea that other people were depressing her disappeared.

Two grandparents who had married and brought up their family, discovered, later in life, that they were cousins. They felt very guilty about this – both developed diabetes.

A family who had emigrated to America had been involved in witchcraft. Two members had been murdered, two had died in traffic accidents and two had disappeared. There were four diabetics in the family but only one of them sought – and received – spiritual help.

When a grandmother drowned in the Ukraine, her daughter emigrated to America and became a completely irresponsible prostitute. Her eight year-old daughter was left to bring up a younger brother. When the woman produced three more children, the girl was given full charge of them. She became a diabetic and did not seek help until she was twenty-six years old.

There are many other precipitating stress factors that induce diabetes, e.g. a teenager became diabetic when her sister disappeared; a forty year-old man became diabetic after his wife died, leaving him with eleven children. The oldest male in each generation of a family became diabetic. The family was descended from a seventeenth century judge responsible for many hangings.

Diabetes is possibly no longer considered to be a "life sentence." Exploration of the original stresses in the context of the family tree often can identify its cause. Twelve cases have been seen whose histories clearly indicate the origin of the disease and six of them now have their own control, unaided by artificially used insulin. Three others have reached a four-year follow-up and all are using the Eucharistic morning pattern. Several other doctors have reported similar findings. In the Eucharistic family approach, Dr. Wilkie is obtaining results but, as yet, it is a private communication and more time is needed for the data to be considered conclusive.

Down's Syndrome

In this disability, once known as mongolism because of the shape of the eyelids, every cell in the body has an extra chromosome. As yet, there is not treatment, although research into the cause has made progress, but statistics show that suffers are frequently the off-spring of older parents. There are undoubtedly varying grades of the syndrome.

Habits of cleanliness are not natural to them as children and they may have a tendency to protrude the tongue, which is often abnormally large, and sometimes rub the upper chin until it is sore. They seem to develop further when they are among other children who, with patience, can teach them essential disciplines.

Children with Down's Syndrome often have innate abilities and are very loving and musical. Considerable success has been achieved with those who have been placed in small private Christian institutions, where their loving nature has fostered an objective aim in the care of others. Their singing, spiritual discipline and aptitude for housework proves that there is definite potential in brains with an initially low IQ and many live useful lives well into their sixties.

With the development of cytogenetics, pregnant women nowadays are encouraged to have an amniocentesis test; this is possible in the sixteenth week, although it can be carried out at the sixth week, using a minute chorionic villus test or needle specimen. If the twenty-first gene is seen to be abnormal, the mother has the choice of termination or not. Then, a child's prospective life must be weighed against the different psychological adjustments to be made within the whole family. The world of materialism speaks of strain, trauma and cost: the loving family of opportunity, discipline, unselfishness and much joy.

It should be noted that during pregnancy four-fifths of all Down's syndrome babies are spontaneously aborted. The change or "flip" of the genetic structure probably occurs at the moment of conception and does not appear to be caused by any abnormality in parental genes, nor can it be traced to parental indiscipline.

Headaches and Migraine

"Home Erectus" developed a high observation post – his HEAD. This makes a contact with the outside world and is his most vulnerable area and the first place to show response. Areas of pain are multiple and have many cases. Following muscle tension in the jaw after considerable stress, the muscle origins of the temporal region in the head will be painful. There may be pain also along the line of blood vessels and along the nerves from root pressure.

When a patient presents with headaches, a doctor must observe all the orifices – look into the ears, tap the mastoid, examine eyes, sinuses, nose, teeth, mouth and tonsils. One carious tooth can send a referred pain over the corresponding eyebrow. There can be infections in each of these areas which, thus, use a warning or alert system to draw attention to the fact that something is wrong. Antibiotics, increased vitamin intake, heat, rest or even surgical intervention may be needed. If a person puts a hand flat on the top of his head saying, "Oh, my headache" then a doctor is aware of the fact that it is not just one nerve supply that ends there but branches of nerves from either side. The "headache," therefore, is not an actual pain but a psychogenic worry or stress pattern, which no medication will stop.

Pain can be referred, also, along cervical nerves that are trapped, as they leave, between cervical vertebrae as a result of accidents or twists. This can be relieved by extension – that is, standing behind the seated patient and lifting his head with a slight rotating movement. This simple manipulation released a priest who had suffered from a "wry-neck" for years after an accident. Another man, an engineer, had to give up work after machinery fell on him damaging his neck and affecting his balance. Eventually, five years later, he made his own neck extension apparatus and the abnormality was corrected.

A headache is a symptom of some underlying condition and may be associated with loss of appetite, nausea, vomiting, visual disturbance, sensory, motor and mood changes. Fifty per cent of people have a headache a year; a few will visit their doctors. A small proportion of patients will show actual neurological signs and be referred to a neurologist.

Women's headaches occur twice as frequently as men's. In their premenstrual phases, the complaint is most common and, therefore, the frequency diminishes rapidly after the menopause. Even in older age, however, the occurrence in women is more that twice that in men. People of lower intelligence suffer from fewer headaches and many less, proportionately, seek advice. Just over one per cent of patients report three carinal symptoms – unilateral pain, nausea and various warning signs that precede an attack. In children, headaches usually are associated with other symptoms such as stomach aches and fever. (This information is a summary of a lecture on *The Epidemiology of Migraine Headaches* given by Professor E. Waters of Southampton University in 1987.)

Most sufferers know that a headache will clear by itself and many understand that it arises from stress and, therefore, will deal with the stress. Some people will use a "headache" as an excuse for isolation, privacy or avoidance of trauma. The psychosomatic origins of these pains are numerous; if all therapy including analysis is instituted, then the ultimate diagnosis is different for each case.

A headmistress complained of stabbing headaches for years. During this time, she had carried many psychological burdens from the school children and governors, her church and parents and, from her own occult activity. She was released gradually by analysis, antidepressants, E.C.T., manipulation and, ultimately, a new spiritual discipline. She even became a lay-preacher; this was the happiest period of her adult life.

A mother seeking help for her anorexic daughter admitted the fact of an abortion, apologized to God and in prayer committed the baby by name. Not only was the girl's anorexia healed, but the mothers' constant headaches suddenly ceased. She had not mentioned these headaches previously to her doctor.

A refractory headache in an elderly married woman, finally labelled post-encephalitic in origin, was cured in a Eucharistic healing service. Another fifty-five year-old woman's headaches were cured when she faced her judgmental attitude and anger towards her Victorian domineering mother who had opposed her marriage. She dealt with this in a small prayer group.

Several examples have a combined therapy, where there are family patterns of migraine. One such, a forty year-old woman, was the fourth generation of sufferers. The proof of origin came after Eucharistic confession and absolution because family members in each of the previous three generations had dabbled in the occult.

A young married woman required extension of her neck to relieve her migraine. Her great grandfather had been a grave-digger who, after being missing for many hours, was found dead at the bottom of a grave which had collapsed on top of him. His brother died accidentally: his throat was cut by a barber when someone had burst into the shop. The woman's grandfather, an alcoholic, had died of cancer of the tongue. She attended Eucharistic services for these three relations and was completely cured.

A woman in her mid-sixties suffered from exactly the same migraine as her son and parents. The latter were now dead, but she and her son were cured when they prayed, in the Eucharistic setting, about a family murder of three generations back.

It has been estimated that seven per cent of all people have experienced migraine at some time, with flashing lights or vomiting. Usually, this is associated with changes in caliber of the blood vessels, common premenstrualy. For some adults it follows the ingestion of tyramine-containing foods – cheese, chocolate, citrus fruit or alcohol. Often, there are mood changes. One variation is known as cluster headaches because they occur daily for a few days.

Many headaches are referred pain from the neck where cervical discs have worn thin or become wedge-shaped, resulting in the nerve roots being pinched. This can be caused by whip-lash injuries, dislocations, sports accidents or even awkward lying positions in bed where one side of the neck is warm and relaxed while the other is cold and in spasm. Traction, manipulation, collars, support, or just the loving hands of someone who will take the weight off the head in a gentle vertical lift for a few seconds, have given relief, sometimes years after a slight dislocation.

The simple phrase, "a stiff-necked people" (Exodus 32.9) applies adequately to those who are proud and haughty, or those who are narrow-minded and unbending-staring straight ahead and unable to make allowances for, or even acknowledge others; such people have stiff necks. The muscles are held in spasm and the vicious circle of pressure, pain and poor circulation follows. Descriptions of "a pain in the neck" or "he gives me a headache" come under mechanical disturbance and mostly are psychosomatic, caused by tension. Honesty and apology within relationships is usually the quickest way to bring relief and release.

The human frame has developed a very good warning system for the protection of the head and its receptive organs; we "put our heads down," "keep out of sight," or "cover up."

Pain from arterial inflammation, known as "arteritis," is always on the line of a blood vessel and is very localized. It may be associated with general illness and is treated with steroids. For acute headaches, an accurate medical examination is essential; without it – ameningitis or a subdural hemorrhage might be overlooked.

Homosexuality

Homosexuality is the sexual preference for one's own sex. It is common to everyone in the growing up period. If continued into adult life it is no longer regarded as a mental disorder, but is officially considered to be sexual deviant behavior, although there is growing pressure for the term "deviant" to be dropped.

In human development from infancy there is a genetic, hormonal bonding between children and parents and between siblings. This is a protective measure within the family unit. At puberty, boys are usually the first to mature in heterosexuality, girls developing rather more slowly. In a proportion of the population this maturing is delayed and if the individual then becomes sexually active with a homosexual partner, the process of maturation may be halted. Although, nowadays, homosexuality is regarded by many in society as normal and is actually encouraged, possibly as a form of population control, it can be "cured."

Two types of homosexuals are found. The larger group, sometimes called "secondary," are those who, after puberty, learn active homosexuality, remaining absorbed by it and failing to mature. A higher incidence of this type occurs commonly in boarding schools, prisons or the armed services, anywhere where people are separated from normal family or social relationships. They are regarded as "sufferers" because they are curable. A deliberate moral and spiritual decision can alter their whole direction. A transformation can occur bringing release from guilt and insecurity – homosexual relationships are notoriously brittle – into normal heterosexual development.

The second type include those who say they were born like this. This in known as primary homosexuality. They consider they cannot change, often resenting the suggestion. "Why should I? This is the way God made me. I can't help it." They do not necessarily become active. Many wish to escape from their state, but feel powerless. They are often lonely and withdrawn and may, like one young schoolmaster in a boy's school where temptation was strong, find their sexuality a threat to their job.

For this group the question is why are they like it? Under hypnosis, or light anaesthesia, a process known as abreaction, questions can be asked probing back into the patient's early life. Subconscious memories have been recorded on tape going back as far as intra-uterine life. In six cases, conversations or wrong sexual behavior indulged in by the parents at this time have apparently determined the child's attitude towards the parent at fault. The fetus, already aware of its own sex, will record, "I will never trust men," or "I will never trust women." These tapes were played back to the conscious patient and even taken to the parents for verification of the recorded facts. There followed apology to each other and to God. In each case, there was healing and the emergence of a heterosexual personality.

Examples

A thirty-two year old male was cured when his mother, a hospital nurse, confessed that, while pregnant with him, she had repeatedly had intercourse with a patient while on night duty. This behavior had gone right against her own moral standards; she felt deep guilt.

The mother of a lesbian patient had had intercourse with eight other men during pregnancy.

A thirty-three year old male, revolted by his mother's abortions, his father's cruelty and attempt to drown his brother, sought new father figures. He spent five years on the street as a "pimp." Now, seeing all this in perspective, he is making courageous decisions to change.

A male of forty-two was a primary homosexual, but non-active. He had always been isolated at school, never playing games or joining in any team activities. He married and had children, but was obsessed with feelings of guilt. He himself was an unplanned child, unwelcome and always put down. He was born when his mother was approaching the menopause and had siblings fifteen and thirteen years older than himself. He admitted his immaturity and was urged to build a team of men to work together in his profession of counseling and include his wife, herself a psychologist. Putting this into practice, he matured and grew through the homosexual phase with wider targets and intentions in his life.

The younger schoolmaster, referred to earlier, whose mother had "controlled" him from the age of two when his father had been killed, decided to return to his Catholic faith and found release.

Multiple Sclerosis (and allied diseases)

The complexity of the body's defence mechanisms becomes increasingly apparent as modern research reveals that ever wider factors are involved, each opening up further ramifications. At one time, only white and red blood cells were identified; then the white cells were differentiated; now it is recognized that these, in turn, have various routes of development. The precursor cell, according to demand, makes other cells with entirely different functions: one travels over cell walls identifying danger areas, one produces antibodies to deal with toxins or antigens, another becomes a killer cell that can destroy tumor cells and cells infected by viruses.

The final controlling trigger that starts the disorders, however, or the trigger that begins the immune process, is still unknown. In utero, the cells of the immune system learn to recognize their own tissue cells but, when born into the world, foreign toxins entering the body have to be combated. The attacks of organisms in infections is understood and, also, the multiplication of commensal organisms that, usually, are held in abeyance, but it has not been proven that multiple sclerosis results from any infection.

The material factors at fault have been analyzed scientifically, but attempts to correct them have been unsuccessful. For some reason, the neuronal cell and the cellular covering of its axon become damaged so that the myelin in the sheath is exposed and lost and is not replaced by increasing the intake of lipids by mouth. It changes to grayish plaque-like scars and the messages do not travel along the nerves. Post-mortem microscopic examination showed that such scars become widely scattered throughout the whole central nervous system, thus, the illness was named disseminated sclerosis. The excessive production of T cells has not halted the progress of the disease. The administration of interferon has not helped the natural anti-viral processes; glut-free diets, hyperbolic oxygen, spinal stimulation – all have failed to cure. There may be fluctuation – in some people a spontaneous remission has been known to last for thirty years. We do not know why a scar may disappear and normal function be regained or why this condition is rare in the tropics; and it has been observed that people who emigrate from the tropics to temperate zones, usually do not contract the illness even after about fifteen years – perhaps, the adult has then acquired an immunity.

In many so-called illnesses, multifactorial causes and repair systems come into play. In the process of spontaneous remission and release or cure, as in Divine Healing, this can be so sudden that we have no concept of what actually happens. Some "patients" tell of intense heat over the affected areas, or a suddenly enhanced mood, weightlessness, peaceful sleep, or a change of orientation in life's purpose. The marked frequency of multiple sclerosis, anklylosing spondylitis and ulcerative colitis in some families suggests a common denominator of unknown origin. In Divine Healing these, too, can be cured suddenly. The areas that are transformed or changed are fundamentally those of the soul which has been dictating to the mind; what has been subconscious is brought into the light. Hence, the original fear in the asthmatic's subconscious control is removed and replaced with confidence and love.

In the arthritic and rheumatic, spasm and the consequent stagnation of an area may be caused by anger and resentment; if this is then replaced by forgiveness and confidence, suddenly the central controlling impulses are released into normal balanced functioning. We do not understand how the cells and hormones all behave normally within a few hours but we know, for example, that red blood cells are replaced every nine days and all these metabolic motor neuron diseases have been thought of as nutritional or from metallic poisons, viral infections or failure of the auto-immune system, but also one may postulate that a more fundamental cause lies in spiritual indiscipline, since reversing it has brought immediate cure in many different illnesses of this group. Of twenty-one patients recorded, fifteen are presently in remission.

A forty-five year-old woman's symptoms began after her husband became paranoid. He had tried to have her killed and had alienated her two children against her. After several years, he was admitted to a mental hospital and she to a private residential home where she needed nursing care and used a Zimmer frame. After several Eucharistic services with confession of her past sins and forgiveness towards her family, she walked and moved normally for several months. To her this was a conversion but she "stepped overboard" into spiritualism and the ouija board and became even more disabled than before. Thus, the remission was short-lived and she has shown no willingness to correct her errors. We are warned against these in Deuteronomy 18.10-12.

Madge, a thirty-one year-old married woman, antagonized her family by involving herself with several other men. The symptoms of multiple sclerosis had been developing over five years but, on her confession, apology and decision to change to a fully Christian life, there was spontaneous remission. This has lasted for thirty-three years.

A prisoner, aged twenty-eight years and suffering from multiple sclerosis, asked for an interview with the chaplain who heard his confession and prayed with him. To their astonishment the man was transformed, his symptoms disappeared and his prison sentence was remitted.

A middle-aged woman in a wheelchair had been very angry with God ever since her only two pregnancies had miscarried. In a church Eucharistic service, she apologized for her anger and prayed for the two children. Suddenly, a hot glow penetrated her whole being, she rose to her feet and then walked all the way home. She had not waited to go up to the altar-evidently, her intentions were sufficient.

A divorcee in her mid-thirties lived with a male artist, but never trusted men. She had suffered from multiple sclerosis for several years and needed constant reassurance. Her parents had been very contentious; she could remember that, at the age of three, she would go to bed and put her head under her pillow to avoid hearing their shouting and slamming of doors. When they went abroad, the child was sent to her grandparents. (Her grandmother admitted to having two abortions.) In the Eucharistic setting, together with the woman's parents, all this was apologized for and, in the subsequent discipline, the symptoms of her disease disappeared.

A spontaneous remission of multiple sclerosis occurred when a married forty-two year-old woman confessed at Mass the traumatic battles of her dead parents. Weeks later, the neurologist she attended wanted an explanation but, when she mentioned the word "prayer," he became very angry, showed her the door and told her never to return. She had no need to do so.

In the allied auto-immune diseases such as ulcerative colitis, we are aware psychosomatically, that the subconscious mind is trying to get rid of an unpleasant situation within personal relationships, even to the extent of trying to vomit it up. In ankylosing spondylitis, the subconscious may be carrying burdens "on the back"; secrets and family problems may never be talked through so that the burden grows "heavy" and paralysing. The back is held very still and bowed, the circulation stagnates and the bone "over-repairs" by laying down more and more calcium deposits until the bones are locked.

As in multiple sclerosis, the person becomes ultra sensitive and vulnerable, with more exposed "nerves." These express the woundings in relationships, either within the immediate family or in past generations, that never have been resolved, and thus, destroy nerve function. A common factor is a backlash of bitterness over traumatic family relationships, but resolution within the soul of the whole family can bring about healing. It is generally agreed that this disease is nether genetic in origin, nor endogenous (growing from within). It is, therefore, exogenous (coming from without) possibly by infection from another relative or relationship. Each frictional event is unpredictable in time and place. Each wounded nerve has a similar scatter wounding, scarring and loss of function. This results in regression, a giving up and a total suppression of the functioning axons of nerve cells.

A seven year-old child was never handled, constantly hushed and not allowed to cry. She was often told that she was "not planned." Her father had no time for her and was the authority in every circumstance – even taking away her presents so that she was afraid to step out of line. Just before he died, when she was ten years old, there had been a big family row – no tears were shed at the father's funeral. The child's right leg and foot were the first to be affected – and the most severely. By twenty-five years of age, multiple sclerosis was apparent. Nearly forty years later, the woman began to find the answer in the Eucharistic setting.

Patients often assume that the incidence of euphoria is the result of a longed-for identification of their disease, when they have suffered from a series of seemingly unrelated symptoms and consequent diagnostic confusion. The relief of knowing that they have a "real disease" and are not malingering, lazy or weak-minded may produce another set of reactions. They may say, "Now you have to take care of me" or "Now you have to listen and look at me," meaning "Now you will have to love me." The diagnosis can be used and abused to demand the desired attention. Medical opinion differs – some doctors connect the states of euphoria and atonia with the onset of depression and others with advancing intellectual deterioration.

In twenty-one cases from eighteen families, the patient was the target and main recipient of bickering family battles that caused bitterness. As far as could be assessed, they were the most vulnerable members of the family (the ones with most "exposed nerves"). Eight of them had been single children.

Of those who show spontaneous remission, one can postulate that there had been a loss of, or no development of spirituality before the disease manifested itself and a deliberate development of spiritual discipline preceding recover. We are in this world in a learning situation and the factors that allow forgiveness, new life and freedom are available.

Perhaps, multiple sclerosis sufferers belong to a particular type of very sensitive people whose receptive system is more vulnerable that average. They feel pain more acutely, are often withdrawn and have been unable to build up resistance, either in their immune system or in the psycho-spiritual aspect of their lives. Some such patients, of course,, utilize to the full all available services but, from secret observation when they are left alone, they may be seen to do far more for themselves than when outside help is at hand.

The cause of the disease remains a mystery, but a far greater mystery is the healing that can be found through Christ.

Myalgic Encephalomyelitis

M.E., or the post-viral fatigue syndrome, is being recognized increasingly in the medical world. In the past it was commonly regarded and dismissed as hysterical, self-centered odds and ends of unrelated complaints in a lazy person. Today, so many patients present with common symptoms whose onset can be dated that the new diagnostic label is well established. (Undoubtedly, the hysteric still tries to exploit the situation.)

Initially, there is an influenza-like illness, often with a fairly high temperature, some signs of meningism – that is, meningeal irritation with headache, perhaps stiff neck and resistance to flexing the body. The patient usually recovers within a few days, but is left for months or years with aching limbs, headaches, hernial fatigue, coldness, depression or loss of concentration. Some even become suicidal. (A very full list of complaints is found in Myalgic Encephalomyelitis by Cecilia Woodey.)

Treatment should include the development of patience and healthy living from both exercise and eating whole natural foods. Eating habits should reflect vitamin consciousness; nature provides the correct balance, but this is destroyed by "fast foods."

Damage can be done by the unnecessary prescribing of antibiotics by doctors who feel obliged to pacify their patients. Oral antibiotics can sterilized the gut and destroy vitamin-B formation and absorption. Antibiotics have no effect on the virus anyway; they are simply a "cover" against superimposed bacterial infection. The differential diagnosis, however, must rest with medical expertise for many symptoms of M.E. are indicative of other illnesses – for example, anorexia nervosa and liver complaints.

A professional twenty-eight year-old man was anergic (suffered from a lack of energy), depressed, frequently cried, had aching muscles and was disinterested in his work among people. His family tree revealed that an ancestor had committed suicide. He had been an evangelical priest who would not pray for the dead and, in the other world, must have felt guilty about all the people he had failed to help and his own "escape" from this world. Resolution at the Eucharist brought the patient tremendous release from his mood swings and a new motivation. He still needed megavitamin medication and found a new companionship in learning regular spiritual discipline.

Two sisters (aged forty and twenty-nine years) of a lady with M.E. and breast cancer had died from the latter disease. The family tree showed a history of deaths from cancer in the past three generations. There was also a pattern of disobedience in marital matters, a lack of family cohesion, love and trust; also, many deaths had occurred at very young ages, plus stillbirths and abortions. At a Eucharistic service, the lady was able to apologize for the misdemeanors of her family and commit those who had died without forgiveness and repentance. She saw a wooden gate beside which stood the Lord Jesus and a flow of people coming and going through the gate. Before passing through, her father paused to give his daughter a word of thanks and appreciation.

Since that time – and after a successful operation for her breast cancer – she has undertaken a regular spiritual discipline and has been confirmed in her local church. The myalgic encephalomyelitis has almost ceased to trouble her, producing only occasional symptoms of nausea or dizziness.

Obsessional Compulsive Neurosis

Patients suffering from this condition feel forced to carry out repetitive actions, repeat words or thoughts which are quite unproductive. They commonly have to complete a numerical cycle. Differentiation is needed here from so-called "ticks," commonly facial grimaces, which may have a neurological basis but which are, more often, childhood habits or hysterical reactions. The condition may be part of a psychotic illness and may initially need medical treatment. It is essential to explore the detailed history of onset and to study the repetitive action to ascertain its content and meaning to the subconscious. Lady Macbeth constantly washing her hands to remove the guilt of her actions is a good example.

While the repetition of positive words or thoughts, for example, the Rosary, may help to drive out evil ones from a distraught person, the unproductive checking of a door lock ten times becomes destructive of both time and motivation of life. Guilt or fear seem to be the common factors in obsessional behavior. Patients are usually responsible sensitive types.

Three women each had a habit of jerking their heads to the right, twisting so the left cheek was foremost, contracting the left jaw and eye muscles. One even raised her left shoulder. They had all, in their childhood, been slapped across the face by mother's right hand and later in life, any slight criticism or opposition within their families would set these spasms in motion. In each case, forgiveness of the parents proved to be the answer.

A twenty-three year old male who was depressed with frequent crying and poor sleep, repeated over and over again that he had sinned against the Holy Spirit. After a year, he finally confessed to having taken a car full of girls to a fair, whereas he had originally promised to take them to an evangelical meeting. It took many months of living alongside him helping him to build up a new discipline of morning prayer and quiet and carrying out the thoughts which came in that time, before the cycle was broken. He took up teaching and five years later became a successful priest.

A bright, artistic young housewife had to wash or clean everything several times over. She was afraid to cook for her family. She was terrified that she would infect or poison them. Prolonged questioning revealed the story that, when she was five years old, she had hit her small brother over the head with a golf club. Her terrified mother had shouted, "You could have killed him!" this had not apparently affected her until she had a family of her own.

One day, after months of helping her to develop a habit of morning quiet times when she could pray and learn to listen to God, she was holding a towel in her hands wondering whether she should wash it over again. When the thought came, almost as though a voice had spoken aloud, saying, "It is quite all right. Go ahead and use it." The thought came with such quiet confidence that she readily accepted it. From that day, she had not further trouble.

Kleptomania can also present as an obsessional pattern. A widow of sixty always stole outsize men's overcoats and would immediately show them to the nearest policeman. She was also an arsonist, trying to burn down police stations. She lived like a tramp and the authorities had stopped sending her to prison. On research it was found that she was the granddaughter of a bandit who raided small towns and set fire to police stations. This man had died in a fight. No one had mourned him or held a funeral for him. Within twenty-four hours of this revelation, the woman was completely transformed and unrecognizable. She had a new hair do, bought a new dress and went to a dinner party which she helped prepare.

A man in prison for the fifteenth time always stole taxi cabs. He had been adopted. On discovering who his real mother was, he felt he knew where he belonged and never stole again. Did the warm taxi cab perhaps represent his unknown mother's womb?

An adopted boy, nine years old, stole sweets and money only to give them away. He never kept any for himself. He insisted on holding hands and would never sleep alone. He had been adopted to replace a stillborn boy who had not been given a funeral service. This one had received the name and birthright of the dead child. A Eucharistic service held for the dead boy stopped all the abnormal behavior in the living one.

People with sexual obsessions seldom seek advice. A religious person, who may suffer homosexual or heterosexual obsessional thoughts may ask for help as they battle against their moral judgments. For them ritual of a spiritual nature will help to blot out the other until a new freedom releases them into positive growth.

A single woman, a Jewish immigrant from Poland, aged forty-five and now living in America, had had many hospital admissions for her obsessions, which had made her life increasingly unbearable. Every action she performed had to be repeated ten times. She had received a variety of treatments. Among these was behavior therapy during which the nurses, every hour, would throw a pack of cards on the floor which she had to pick up and count in front of them. They hoped in this way to exhaust her and break the obsession. It had no effect.

It transpired that her family had been farmers on land over which the Germans and Russians were constantly fighting. She and her mother lived in a hole in the ground. The Germans took the rest of the family and other relatives who all died in the gas chambers. She was finally smuggled out of Poland and reached America via Switzerland and Israel.

Now, without any explanation of what he was going to do, her Christian psychiatrist decided to experiment. He placed some bread and a cup of grape juice on her bedside table and told her to repeat a prayer saying, "Dear Lord Jesus, I am sorry I have always ignored you. I am sorry for man's cruelty to man. I am sorry I have never prayed for members of my family who have died. I want to commit them to you that they may go on their heavenly journey." After a short Bible reading the doctor quoted St. Paul's words about the Last Supper then gave her the bread and the grape juice, finally saying the Lord's Prayer. It had taken only ten minutes. She was then tested out. A book was thrown on the floor along with her face cloth and torn up pieces of paper. She was asked to pick them up which she did calmly without repeating the process of feeling any need to do so. She left hospital the next day fully cured.

The repetitive acts of the compulsive obsessional would appear to run parallel with the visitations of those who have died unrealized. In some, these patterns of behavior are reinforced so strongly by repetitions that an actual fresh fronto-thalamic tract is established in the brain. This may have to be severed surgically, the only risk being that other normal tracts may also be damaged. Modern techniques limit this risk. To experiment with the spiritual, on the other hand, carries no risks and opens up a whole new life for the former sufferer. Patients suffering from obsessional illness have said, "It's like a living power taking over the whole," or "I've been caught in a battle between extremes of torment and possession, a lying spirit distorts my will. I must reclaim my mind." It is this which needs to be examined and healed.

Osteoarthritis

Osteoarthritis is a condition occurring in one or more joints in which there is degeneration of the cartilage and proliferation of bone resulting in a painful disorganized joint. It is equally common in men and women, but is most common in older people. By the age of sixty, 80 per cent will show evidence of it on X-ray though only a quarter of these will have symptoms. There are many known conditions in which this can occur, but in many cases there is no identifiable cause and this may need to be sought.

A thirty-eight year-old man had a bilateral hip replacement which ended years of crippling pain. The diagnosis of osteoarthritis had seemed like a comfortable blanket – he was now adequately labelled and documented. Some years later, the question arose as to why this had happened in an otherwise healthy man from a healthy family and why the bony structures has been so pressed upon that the circulation prevented development and caused pain. Investigations showed that the man's parents had been taught in their rigid religion and scrupulosity that all sex was dirty and of the devil and, as a youth, he had learned the same precept. The idea of sex was trampled on despite his being very fond of a girl.

One of his aunts had never married; another's marriage was never consummated; a third aunt had produced two children – but it was a family joke that they must have been "virgin births!" He himself was the youngest of four children, his mother's favorite. In the psychosomatic sense, his knees were always clasped together to cover the whole perineal area. In this mode, the blood could not circulate, develop or repair.

A very austere fifty-four year-old spinster suffered from arthritic hip joints. When asked whether she knew of any miscarriages in her family history, she immediately crossed her knees, pulled down her skirt, folding it over her knees and then covered the fold with both hands. She denied all knowledge of miscarriages, but later admitted that she had an adulterous relationship which fortunately had not resulted in pregnancy.

Mary was a housewife who had been married for twenty-one years. Both of her knees were extremely swollen, red, creaky and painful. She dated the onset of this condition to the first night of the honeymoon. Within her heart Mary had always kept great spiritual faith and throughout her life knelt by her bed for evening prayers. Her husband had not known about this until their honeymoon and, when he saw his wife on her knees, became very angry and forbade her to do so again.

When Mary came for an interview we devised the phrase, "the knees that will not kneel before the Lord in prayer." Deliberately, she began again to kneel for evening prayers and she apologized to the Lord. Her husband took no notice! Over the next few weeks her knees were healed and all the years of medicines and physiotherapy were ended.

In attempting to treat these conditions one has to be aware of their origins, which could be infection or poor nutrition. Study from the organ language point of view, however, is fascinating and can lead the patient to see the situation objectively and provide the key to any change in direction or decision that may be needed. When an area is chronically traumatized, we try to protect it by immobilizing or physically squeezing it and holding it in spasm. This induces stagnation of the blood circulation and the area becomes swollen, red and painful. At this time, calcium deposits and osteophyte – hard, bony outcrops – are formed in bones and joints. This is known as cervical, lumbar of cranial arthritis, depending upon the area affected.

A painful neck might result from a whiplash injury, but proud, haughty, cynical people can produce their own cervical spondylitis. Similarly, one might find that pain in the lower dorsal vertebrae of a housewife relates to family burdens, the lumbar vertebrae to the male manual worker who has been "moonlighting," and the sacral and iliac regions to whose with sexual indulgences. The shoulders in pain "speak" of the burden carried by a housewife with an ungrateful husband; if her right shoulder is affected, then she is actively resentful and wants to fight (if right-handed). Thus, arthritis in the knuckles of the right hand may represent the desire to punch or scratch and in the right index finger may indicate a critical and bitter tongue directed against others. When only the base of the thumb in painful, then the person possibly whispered behind people's backs. with a cupped hand over the mouth.

In two cases, men's right ring fingers were arthritic – they were carrying guilt over extra-marital affairs. Conversely, the left hand is the receiving hand, but in two other cases the left index fingers suffered when the men were pointing out trees that they had chosen to steal from government property. The right knee can become painful in women who want to kick a male in the groin; the right foot when they wish they could stamp in anger or "kick against the pricks"; the left foot, when the sufferer is the one who is being badly treated.

Bad memories, negative attitudes, resentments, hate and anger can each cause stagnant circulation. Spiritual transformation, which is available to all, ensures that the body systems will function normally.

Phenylketonuria (P.K.U.)

This is one of many so-called inherited multifactor disorders. Environmental elements are thought to cause additionally greater liability and it has been observed, also, that there is a higher incidence of P.K.U. among related people. Laboratory tests of the blood state will prove the situation. From birth these patients cannot metabolize or assimilate aminoacids, so they require supplementary feeding throughout their lives. They deteriorate mentally and, usually, die young, with abnormal ECG's and often having suffered epileptic attacks. The increase in people's consultation of, and dependence upon "genetic counselors" often produces advice on whether to have children at all, artificial insemination, or testing of a woman's amniotic fluid for a decision over termination of a pregnancy.

The aunt of a mentally very backward twenty year-old girl, diagnosed as a P.K.U. sufferer, drew the family tree and noted that all except one branch of the ancestors who lived four generations previously, had been born in the south of Ireland. During the potato famine in April 1845, the more active younger members of the family had fled to England and abandoned their unburied dead and their dying older relatives. These people had never been mourned, so a Requiem Mass was held and they were prayed about as an apology, a mourning and as a committal. The girl, who lived two hundred miles away, had neither been thought about nor prayed for during this Mass but her symptoms disappeared. Weeks later, it was discovered that these two events were correlated, for her mental state had become average. She had been on a strict dietary supplement for P.K.U. but now was able to eat normally. Two years later, she has an unusually capable mind, is happily married, and shows a normal Guthrie blood test.

"One swallow does not make a summer," of course, but this could show another breakthrough in that, despite our vast advances into the material analysis and understanding of biochemical data, we in the medical world are not yet addressing the fundamental cause of abnormality and of stress patterns. Perhaps, we are merely manipulating symptoms and closing our eyes to the spiritually eternal origins of disorder and revolt. Relating this theory to the Irish dependence upon the three per cent protein content of potatoes might show a fascinating association with Phenylketonuria. A responsible exploration of such an approach could be very rewarding and, even, provide the answer.

Psoriasis

Psoriasis is a skin complaint occurring in mainly circumscribed, well-defined, red and silvery scaling plaques of varying size anywhere on the body, usually appearing first on the elbows and knees. It is a chronic complaint but can have long periods of remission. The cause is unknown.

A man of forty-eight had a scaly rash, diagnosed as psoriasis, which completely encircled his trunk from the middle of the chest to the lumbar region. He was healed immediately after a Eucharist was held for his mother's two abortions and his own wife's two miscarriages. He had no other living siblings.

A twenty-eight year-old man was of the fourth generation to suffer with psoriasis. It now, unusually, involved his face. There was history of illegitimate births in the family.

A thirty-seven year-old woman had the rash on the front of both lower legs. She was very resentful towards her stepfather who wanted to kick her out of the home.

A woman of thirty had developed psoriasis after her parents' divorce of which she felt very ashamed.

Psychosis

Among themselves, psychiatrists' tension is released in private joking, for example, they say: "The hysteric talks of his fairy castle, the neurotic builds it and the psychotic lives in it!"

Psychosis is the term applied when there is a gross impairment of a patients' own insight into his condition, where all sense of reality is lost and there is no contact. Mostly, such patients are unwilling to suffer any interference because, to them, there is nothing wrong; everyone else is out of step.

First, this condition may be caused by organic disease and damage, injections, drugs, blood vessel changes, hormonal or degenerative changes – as in the senile. Today's drugs can be helpful, but not necessarily curative and such people need care.

Second, in the schizoid pattern, hereditary, environmental, organic or biochemical damage may or may not be found. This psychosis usually begins in youth and is treatable on a long-term basis. The grouping is applied to a very wide net of patients, many of whom are included by doctors who say, "This seems like it" – often an inaccurate and even cruel diagnosis, particularly when unsupported by a doctor's drawing of the family tree. Anorexics may appear in this category since, usually, they deny that anything is wrong and many complain of being influenced or possessed.

Third, manic depressives have irregular mood swings that can be unipolar (only in one direction) or bipolar (from a high, through normal, to a low). Each extreme needs care; the low state can be paranoid with a system of antagonistic or even suicidal delusions, as they return to normal and understand how they behaved; in the high state, they may have reached grandiose or even messianic heights. Today, careful control by the drug lithium carbonate has returned many such patients, usually older, to useful lives.

Schizophrenia

This diagnosis can be made too easily and used as a convenient "waste-paper basket," when a therapist has exhausted all other possible tests and drug trials. It should be used only with great care and after consulting other opinions, for it declares a lifelong condemnation of a patient. In casual conversation and in the popular press, the term "schizophrenic" is intended to be a derogatory smear upon those who, perhaps, show extensive mood swings or unusual behavior, yet live in the ordinary world. Some of these types of

people have other predominant areas of the brain showing exceptional skills and genius – for example, Van Gogh and his artistic
ability. They can be designated as mildly schizoid. Full-blown
schizophrenics, however, have no insight into their condition; at
any given moment they believe literally that their behavior is normal (like the mother watching the parade who insisted that her son
was the only one in step!).

In hospitals, temporary relief is obtained by heavily tranquillizing patients for their own and everyone else's safety. Fortunately,
chemistry nowadays is so well-researched that doctors are more
able to correct the chemical controls that have become abnormal
with years of subconscious stimulus. There is no evidence that this
is genetically determined. Some families show similar traits, but
this can be accounted for adequately by the extensions of Carl Jung's
theory. In *The Archetypes and the Collective Unconscious*, he writes
of "states of possession in which the possession is caused by something that could perhaps most fitly be described as an ancestral
soul, a striking identification with deceased persons." He does not
suggest any way of dealing with such a situation.

Popular articles such as the series on schizophrenia in *The Times*
newspaper of August 1985 are stories of doom and gloom – but
they are written from the materialistic point of view. Some practitioners see psychiatry aspiring to become scientific, whereas it is
mostly an art. The very fact that there is a multiplicity of theories
and whole books on individual aspects of the subject indicates that
medical opinion is still far from the answer.

A group of thirty-one patients, each of whom had multiple
admissions to hospitals for schizophrenia and were on follow-up
drugs, was examined with Jung's observation in mind. Until then,
therapy had been used to blot out the nuisance factor of both patients and symptoms and the new approach was welcomed by the
patients. With empathy, listening and patience, the therapist entered into the sufferer's world of unreality, asking details of all
auditory and visual hallucinations, observing behavior and mood
changes. Then, with the patient and his relatives, the therapist
matched this information to a specific dead ancestor – especially
to any who were unmourned or who had left unfinished business.
Each patient was taken through the process of Requiem healing

and all thirty-one were freed from their symptoms and taken off drugs. A four-year follow-up verified their continued recovery.

A twenty-six year-old Englishman insisted, for about fourteen years, that the BBC had broadcast a continuous message that he was to be hung on the orders of Hitler and Mussolini. He could not live outside hospital, where he was treated with drugs and ECT, as he would attack any household with a television aerial. Unknown to the patient, his father finally matched this behavior with the disappearance of his eldest aunt's German fiancee. He had been called up for army services in 1938, but both the English and German families were conscientious objects. From the day he was seen off at a Channel port, neither family had heard of him. In 1975, without the patient's knowledge, a Mass of the Resurrection was held in Church for his German uncle. Next morning, he telephoned from hospital to his father saying, "The BBC has switched off." Within eighteen months he was weaned off all medicines.

A man of forty-eight years was delighted that, after thirty years treatment, someone asked him for details of his hallucinations. He explained, "Lots of men are killing each other with swords; there is blood everywhere, a roaring sea, wind on my face, the smell of sulphur and blinding flashes." It was discovered that he was the direct descendant of pirates and naval captains since 1580. The man was released that same evening after prayers and two days later the family attended a Requiem Mass. Through this, his brother became a priest, and the former patient is now a college lecturer.

A twenty-eight year-old woman, having been committed five times to mental hospitals, finally disclosed that she "lived" with her lesbian friend who had died three years earlier. She was freed from her symptoms within two days by the ritual mourning process of the Requiem Mass. Six months later she was married and has been able to help many other people.

Healing the Family Tree expounds this approach and there is evidence from some forty-two countries that it is an adequate D.I.Y. beginner's manual. There are no dangers, overdoses or side effects involved; chemical or hormonal imbalance is secondary to the dictates of the subconscious mind. It is as though a candle is alight in the gloom, but most people have their backs to it and are manipulating and researching only the shadows that they can see. The challenge is to try to face the reality and perspective of our short training time here on earth.

Of seventy-five cases where this approach was used, a four-year follow-up showed that thirty one patients remained healed; five showed no improvement; three had committed suicide; twelve had continuing drug treatment plus Eucharistic services. There was no contact with the remaining twenty-four patients who did not answer letters.

Treatment with tranquilizers and phenothiazines, provision of sheltered accommodation and tender loving care, or Dr. Hoffa's mega-vitamin therapy with B3 nicotinamide, has restored many sufferers. The occupational therapy of regular exhausting physical work, together with being well-fed and having adequate sleep, has helped some people to reorder their lives and create an accurate brain and hormonal balance, as originally designed.

In all cases of schizophrenia, the date, mode and pattern of onset must be established. Then a counselor uncritically and with empathy is able to enter into a patient's world, then the vast dimensions of that world which is so real to him, can be observed and the patient brought to a position of insight within the spiritual realm. The advantage of these Eucharistic approach is that it cannot cause harm; and it is entirely loving.

Skin Complaints

The skin is the largest organ of the body, with wonderful protective systems, healing abilities and a continuous multiplication of cells with a huge back up of countess blood vessels, blood cells and fluids. It can expand or stretch, for example, in pregnancy or obesity, and return to normal when the excess weight is lost; in old age or starvation situations, however, it tends to lose its elasticity. If it is constantly irritated by misuse of chemicals, renewals can "over repair" to the extent of becoming cancerous – for example, after contact with tar.

Itching of the skin is, basically, the body's method of drawing attention to a fault – for instance, an insect bite – and it causes us to rub or scratch in order to increase the circulation and dilate the blood vessels. Psychic trauma will reduce the itch threshold, making it more severe and more prolonged. An antagonistic paranoid person may itch and scratch so much that eczema develops or may scale extensively as though there is a wish to "shed the skin" to change the situation! Elbows and knees often show this change in people who "elbow their way through a crowd," or kick (an action controlled by the knees). When itching occurs right around the body from back to stomach, it can represent a child who was conceived and is cared as in abortions and miscarriages. Exudations from the skin in cases of eczema can be correlated with suppressed weeping emotions.

Urticaria and "nettle rash," an allergic reaction, may follow eating certain foods, for example, strawberries or shellfish, but often correlates with suppressed resentment in irritating situations. Sufferers may have felt wronged on occasions when no retaliation was possible and they were neither able to run away nor even express hostility.

Sweating skin, controlled by the hypothalamus, can be firstly, a system of reducing body temperature via the head, trunk or back of the limbs. Secondly, sweating of the palms of the hands and soles of the feet is a primitive response to fear and represents a primeval urge to escape by hastily climbing a tree.

For all skin conditions, a general physical examination is essential, especially bearing in mind diabetes and vitamin deficiencies (for example, pellagra is common in undernourished communities) since the skin works, also, in the utilization of vitamin factors. Listening to the patient is the most important single therapeutic factor, in order to establish the stress occurrence and its time and place geographically, together with relationships and attitudes to other people. Abreactive techniques add little, for, which ever route is used, the subconscious situations must be dealt with by the patient's fully conscious decision – for example, moral decisions and apologies can be curative.

Fifty year-old Arthur had generalized psoriatic exacerbations in a band around his abdomen and on corresponding areas of his back. He had no sisters although, in drawing up the family tree, it was discovered that his mother had two abortions and his wife two miscarriages. These four babies were brought in family love to the

Eucharist, apology was made to God for having ignored them, followed by their committal to God. Within three days, all traces of Arthur's skin condition had disappeared. This may suggest then, in the context of the possession syndrome, that the children were trying to draw attention to the fact that they had existed in the abdominal region.

Jean, a married thirty-six year-old woman, suffered from scleroderma (a scaly blackness of the palms of the hands), the onset of which had been gradual. When her confession and the commitment to God of an abortion coincided with her healing, it was realized that to Jean, this had been a gross sin in an otherwise very moral and upright family.

For eighteen years, from the age of eight when she had been raped, a woman had suffered from innumerable skin "diseases" of the feet and hands, all unresponsive to ointments. It was thought that the cause was fungal but, sometimes, the symptoms would disappear overnight. Also, a dermatitis which followed flushing of her head, neck, forearms and hands, and eczema of the back of her elbows and knees, similarly switched on and off. Forgiveness of the man who had raped her as a child brought partial relief, but further understanding was needed. Her feet and hands presented to her an involvement and willingness to walk against moral laws, in spite of being an ignorant child when the rape happened. At times she felt ashamed and the skin of her head, neck and arms – that others could see – blushed with shame. She felt defiled, unclean and angry and took these feelings out on her skin. Under the cloak of the exfoliating dermatitis, she took umbrage in the shadow of a labelled illness – hiding behind the doctor's diagnosis. Exposed areas of the skin are our contact with the outside world – hence, we can be pale with fright, red with anger or blush with shame.

Stammer, Left-handedness and Aphasia

Stammering results from the indeterminate control in the frontal lobes of the impulses that go to both sides of the brain. When there is conflict, the message coming via the thalamus and central nuclei (where all body motor functions are con-ordinated) has to travel, by use and training, to one side or the other along tracks that are gradually increased in facility, according to the determined voluntary or involuntary dominant control. There is coordination with the other side via a vast branching area (the corpus callosum). In people who stammer, the message route is interrupted by indecision, emotion or physical accident, control then being thrown from side to side. The speed of the stammer is similar to a reverberating current in electricity, except that the neurological system with its ion charges and chemicals uses only 1/10,000 of a volt.

A thirty-six year-old woman had a rigid, moral upbringing. She became a sexual pervert and developed a stammer gradually as she discovered and became involved in her husband's criminal activities. She reverted to normal when she decided personally on a *volte face*, and started taking the Eucharist again as she used to do.

Sixty year-old Daisy stuttered from the age of eight, when she was sent to her father's study for him to decide upon a punishment for some long-forgotten misdemeanor. The child was ordered to stand beside his desk, at attention and in silence, for a whole hour while he continued with his work, before pronouncing judgment. Daisy began to tremble with fear and, since then, stuttered and found difficulty in initiating the first word of any sentence. This improved when she was able to forgive her elderly father and apologize for the resentment she had felt against him throughout her life; they became reconciled.

Al was a vicar who suddenly developed a stutter at fifty-three years of age. Sometimes he was speechless, following the death of his brother who had shot himself through the mouth. This had not been faced honestly; everyone pretended he had been shot by a burglar. Being a policeman, he was given a civic funeral. Years later, in a Eucharistic service, the family was able to apologize to God by proxy and commit the man properly with love and no cover-up. Al was freed from a stutter and resumed pastoral duties.

A fifty-six year-old man had tremor of his hands and halting speech with the imitation of gasping for breath. This was thought to be associated with an uncle's suicide by gas poisoning. The man's fear and depression were realeased in a Eucharistic service of apology and committal.

A woman of forty-four years had a stutter associated with spasmodic torticollis (stiff neck), as though she were indicating "no" to everything. Throughout her childhood she had suffered from her mother's unpredictable temper; punishments were always face slappings – even when she was seventeen years old she would be slapped for no reason. Working in the family shop, the girl compensated by stealing sweets. Marriage became an escape, but she had seven miscarriages and only carried one baby to term by staying in bed out of reach of her mother.

Fear is a common denominator in all of these cases. In three examples of people who adopted an enclosed religious life (one of whom was an orphan), stammering and shaking were most marked preceding confessionals. Standing before God reminded them of punishments in childhood. The Negro spiritual "Sometimes it causes me to tremble, tremble, tremble" and the hymn "These though we bring them in trembling and fearfulness" express this fear.

Neill states that there are two imperative requirements from parents: a father's love and a mother's love. This allows for a gradually increasing freedom from the total care necessary in infancy, to a controlled trial-and-error learning with rewards of love, but not material gains. A child's position in its family is important. An only child, isolated and with high parental expectations, or the second child who is neither the responsible oldest nor the favorite youngest, needs to fight for its position. Such children are vulnerable.

Most people write with the right hand, but it is still not uncommon for those who prefer to regard the left hand as the dominant one to be schooled forcibly in the use of the right hand. As a consequence, they may stammer. This condition is extremely rare in the Far East. Perhaps because any slightly abnormal fetus used to be disposed of and the maladjusted were "pushed to the wall" and absorbed into the all-embracing family life, where several generations lived under one roof.

When squint and left-handedness occur in children, often in combination, investigation of both parents is imperative. Sometimes there tends to be an oppressive strictness – perhaps, from the grandparents. This forces a child to become a rebel within its own domestic setting, when the boundaries that all children need become too restrictive. It is an attempt to "break out" by drawing attention – even involving limping with the left leg. The incidence of this is always increased by excitement.

An eight year-old girl, jealous of her new baby sister, suddenly developed a paralysed left leg. She had to sit on the end of the baby's pram, but could drag herself along, hopping on her right leg. One day, in the doctor's waiting-room when it was her turn to be seen, without her mother, she skipped into the room on both legs. She had forgotten her stress because she had the doctor's undivided attention for a few minutes and, with a little prodding, she was able to express to him that she felt she had lost her status. Having established there was nothing physically wrong, the girl and her parents came to accept that there is a purpose in all our lives, and that everyone has to help others. The child learned that even her parents were under authority and she began to help her mother look after her baby sister. On their part, her parents established a bedtime review of the child's day, finishing with prayer in which she learned to pray aloud her "sorry's and thank you's."

A stressful and insecure childhood, either at home or at school, is often the cause of the development of such difficulties. Over-strict government by parents, teachers or anyone in authority, can initiate such problems in a young child, although they may not present until later in life when further stress becomes the "straw that beaks the camel's back." In a typical western-style oral examination, a student may be timid or lacking in confidence. Stress can be exaggerated by an impatient examiner and not only does memory falter but speech can become incoherent. In seven cases of stammering, family relationships first had to be restored by apology and restitution; then healing followed. The cure is love and acceptance, with forgiveness of those originally responsible for the trauma.

Aphasia, the absence of speech – even stuttering speech – demands a full neurological examination for there may be nerve damage, vocal cord growths or inflammation. Having excluded by blood tests, forms of degeneration and weakness, psychosomatic interruptions in function should be investigated.

A father, angry that his eighteen year-old daughter's pregnancy ended when her baby died in utero at eight months, became speechless when, two months later, she herself died from cancer. A neurologist found no cause for the man's disability, so he was sent to a speech therapist, but could cope with only one session. He was very angry with God and could force speech only with enormous effort in a high-pitched husky whimper. A slow improvement was seen over many months as he learned to attend Eucharistic services for the sake of his dead daughter and grand-child.

Trigeminal Neuralgia

This may be called "da Lien syndrome" which means "hit face" in Chinese. It is pain referred along the three branches of the fifth trigeminal nerve – this nerve can be compressed by tumors, or involved in other lesions such as thrombosis or syringobulbia or herpes zoster (shingles). Sufferers may have touch trigger zones, or one particular branch of the nerve may be affected when there are eye, sinus or dental problems; therefore, full physical examinations are essential. If all tests fail to show any physical change, then other factors may be explored and clinical trials with various pain-killers may be tried. Of fourteen cases, five were central in cause (i.e. within the brain), two were herpetic and even had psychogenic and hysterical origins. All of these causes must be considered since, in some cases, the subjective pain cannot be verified clinically and is claimed to be intractable.

Following an aborted illegitimate pregnancy, a thirty year-old woman developed depressive mood swings and tempers, tiredness and fluid retention. She consulted several gynecologists whose opinions varied from, "A hereditary hormonal imbalance, you'll always have it, nothing can be done," to one who performed an estrogen implant which was helpful for a few days. Eight years later, her own doctor diagnosed "nerves" and prescribed tranquilizers after she complained of left facial pain, swollen glands, heat, virus infections, dimness of vision, diminished hearing in her left ear, left mandibular joint pain and discomfort on the left edge of her tongue and tonsils. None of these symptoms had any objective reality; they were always worse in the evening and pain covered all the branches of the fifth nerve.

The woman's marriage was threatened by her husband's drink problem (he was usually drunk by mid-afternoon) and his parents always bitterly opposed her. Her own mother always had a quick temper and from her daughter's infancy, frequently slapped the left side of her face with her right hand before confining her in a room. The patient had no relationship with her father other than his disapproval and bitter tongue; there was no attempt to soften his approach. She continually flinched and covered her face with her hands saying, "whoo" and crying. The remedy lay in objectifying the symptoms, learning to forgive others, and showing the gift of forgiveness that we have been given in the Cross of Jesus Christ. Subsequently, the woman was freed from all her symptoms.

Throughout her life, a forty year-old woman had been very afraid of her dominating mother, who controlled her by face slapping with the back of the left hand or with the palm of the right hand or with a wet cloth. Her G.P. reported that, as a child, her head turned to the right whenever she entered her parents' shop. One day, in her thirties, the patient's right sternomastoid went into spasm and she said, "My head is locked." All hospital investigations proved negative; suddenly her head became quite free but locked again on the way home. Her brother had been sent abroad by the parents and, when her elder sister became pregnant, the baby was given away by them. The patient married, but was told not to have any children because they were "encumbrances." Despite this, the woman had four miscarriages followed by a boy who lived for only thirty-six hours. Her parents forbade her to adopt any children.

Trigeminal pain of the left side of her face was unrelieved by tablets and, at one time, a "faith healer" made it far worse. She also recorded that a teacher had slapped her face and her spoilt elder sister, who was given a private education, had scratched her face. She suffered from guilt, depression, shyness and fear and was ashamed of her prominent teeth and long neck. Eventually, her muscle spasms seemed to be relieved by massive doses of vitamin B-complex tablets, but her main healing, with her husband's reassuring help, came from her forgiveness of others – especially her parents – which released the sternomastoid spasm and pain.

A woman of fifty-six, a brilliant professional musician and a successful teacher, decided to join a closed order of nuns. Her music was not appreciated in the convent. Unmarried, she had always been accustomed to considerable adulation, but now she developed trigeminal neuralgia – a psychogenic slap in the face. When she was able to objectify the whole situation, she was freed from pain.

A single forty-two year-old woman cared for her invalid parents until they died; then, her two brothers turned her out of their house. Her subsequent trigeminal neuralgia was released by her intentions at a Eucharistic service.

Two single sisters lived together. For three consecutive years, one of them went away on holiday and the other one was left behind to do all the household chores – feeling as if she had been "slapped in the face." Each time, she suffered facial neuralgia which recovered only on her sister's return.

A professional man lost his position in the social services because of his high moral principles. At the same time, two of his adult children let him down. He developed a paralysis of the facial or seventh cranial nerve which showed as an inability to control the muscles of the eyelid, cheek or mouth on one side of his face. Rest, high vitamin B-complex intake and a determination to rebuild his life gradually brought the remedy. The trigeminal nerve area is the most exposed sensory nerve in the human body, and responded to a "slap in the face."

In each of these six recorded cases, the sufferer was a morally weak, dependent type, prone to cower under any opposition or family friction and recovery was slow. When the patients began to develop an understanding and objectify their symptoms, they then had to repair relationships and apologize. Forgiveness, one of the gifts of the Holy Spirit, is not something that can be manufactured, but must be accepted with love and discipline of thought.

PART II
FEELINGS AND ATTITUDES

Anger

Some people justify their anger by saying that Jesus Christ was angry, but in Mark 11.11-15, we read that after He had seen what was happening in the Temple, He went away that night and, next morning (after cool thought) He returned and threw out all the money-changers.

Some use righteous indignation as an excuse. Anger can become pathological and cause considerable damage. Adrenalin secretion into the bloodstream raises the blood pressure and contracts the small blood vessels. This is a protective, self-preserving mechanism, but to keep on with it can cause high blood pressure and hardened arteries, and lead to brain hemorrhage – "strokes." It is the natural swings of high to low that maintain each area in tune.

To cultivate purposely an anger reaction in some becomes evil and destructive of relationships. If we suppress it, then target organs of our bodies suffer. If we express or externalize it, the others suffer. We can always decide upon a socially useful goal for these pent up feelings, such as energetic digging in the garden, logging, cleaning or polishing. In schooldays there are different sports, with swimming probably the most complete exercise – take it out on the water! Karate is good, but can carry a final fault because it ends with the victor's shout representing the final kill.

A twenty-four year-old man had violent outbursts at home, terrifying his parents and siblings, and making sudden "chops" with his fighting hand on anything or anyone in the house. He was supposed to be practicing his karate exercises, but actually it was the "kill" of his very much hated opponent in the karate class. This had to stop and he was released eventually by a church exorcism. Forgiveness was the key.

A fifty-six year-old professional woman was a descendant of a Samurai family. Sudden onsets of bitter anger and depression were helped by prayer, but she was only released in apology to God for the sins of her ancestors.

Uncontrolled temper arose in seven families where the original known pattern began after a murder. In four patients, when they learned of their own illegitimate origins, they were released from anger at the time of the Eucharistic acceptance of forgiveness. In four other patients, when they became aware of and were able to pray for assorted siblings, they found a cure. The pattern of healing follows a gaining of understanding, a personal moral decision, an awareness of evil control and exorcism, finally an apology for and committal to God of any source of anger in the deceased.

There are some IRA people who "listen to the voices of the dead" to receive instructions from them for the next atrocity. (See *Spare My Tortured People* by Robert Cielou.) There are men of Jewish extraction seeking revenge for ancestors' deaths. Twelve such people from twenty-two Jewish families were healed of this attitude when they came to the Eucharist. They then called themselves "fulfilled or baptized Jews." A forty year-old woman who suffered nightmares, depression and anger was released when, in the Eucharist, she was able to forgive the persecutors who had incinerated alive seven members of her family.

Anger should be reserved for defensive situations. Within the divine economy, fortunately, individual variation is enormous. All of us are here for a time of training, but we can make decisions and changes. We accept responsibility for generations to come but, also are in the position of being able to confess and atone for our ancestors' sins. "Be ye angry and sin not: let not the sun go down upon your wrath" (Ephesians 4.26 AV).

Unpredictable tempers have been the characteristics of some professional men in the old cotton belts of America, in these it was found that they had been slave owners in earlier generations; they even had the power of life and death for they owned the slave. The present day descendants found that they needed to change the family guilt by confession.

Three unmarried sisters were noted for their tempers, in and outside their home. Ultimately they were released when they sought God's forgiveness when they found their aunts had clubbed together and killed the grandmother.

Temper tantrums in children have gone on to the point where they simulated a fit. In two of these cases, in the child's subconscious was hidden the cause for all the verbal abuse against mother; it was that mother had killed a sibling, in both cases by abortion.

In the case of a Nigerian student who lost his temper whenever faced with examination questions, it was found that this was the result of a Nigerian uncle putting a curse on him which extended to Britain – because this boy had gained a substantial scholarship, whereas his own sons had none. The curse was broken by prayer to God.

Bitterness

Bitterness "eats the heart" of the cynical, angry person who "bottles it up." Group bitterness is very menacing and has a geometric progression, fostered by oppression, real or imagined and easily whipped up in political strife and racism. Today we are fast approaching an international world, with few insulated reserves. News is disseminated throughout the world. In England, when there is a lengthy strike by a particular work-force, then everyone loses out. The basic stresses, certainly, are often political but subversion is first on the list and, bred into the long memories of families, is the old cry, "workers against the boss." Families carried the bitterness from generation to generation, but today it is unreasonable since "the boss" often is no more the owner than the workers.

Group bitterness is especially obvious in Northern Ireland where for three hundred years, it has nurtured greed and killings and deported all opposition. At Spike Island in the south of England, captives were chained to stakes in the ground awaiting the hulks to transport them to Australia. Often these ships were emptied out in the Bay of Biscay and were known as coffin ships. No one has committed all these dead to God or apologized and, in fact, they now possess and haunt the living so that they just repeat the killings, learning from the generations of the dead how to carry out these blood sacrifices. International subversion, arms dealers and occult groups under satanic dictation all maximize the disruption. Only the truth can set them free, bringing health and wholeness to the nation. Ireland, then, could once again export its priests and scholars all over the world as satanic shadows are defeated.

Britain needs to be strong yet humble, sufficiently so to apologize to man, to confess to God, to commit the dead to Him and to make restitution. This would heal individuals. The best way to do this is in Eucharistic hospitality between all churches. It is no wonder that Jesus Christ described the bitter proud Pharisee as "whitened sepulchers, full of dead men's bones... the children of those who killed the prophets" (Matthew 23.27). They probably did not understand what He meant, but it was the literal truth then and is still true today.

In recent evolutionary development, human beings have developed moral controls which are tenuous and, in a stress situation like a prisoner-of-war camp, are clearly a mere veneer. When they are removed, the primitive caveman is exposed with all his greed and selfishness, ready to use violence for self-preservation.

A forty-two year-old priest was haunted by the fact that his father had belonged to the "Black and Tan" regiment and he felt a sense of guilt for his father's deeds. (The "Black and Tans" were a motley array of English prisoners and ex-service men from the Royal Irish Constabulary recruited in the 1920's to fight the Sinn Fein. Rape, murder and pillage were common practices.) The father, now in the next world and unable to correct his unfinished business, had visited or trespassed upon his son's subconscious. The latter, being the living representative of the family carried the responsibility and could proxy his father in confessing specific sins. This he did in apology to God and he has slept peacefully since then.

A thirty-six year-old schizophrenic had been in hospital care since she was ten years-old. Both her sisters were nuns. In their village in Ireland, the grandfather's body was discovered on the railway lines and the "Black and Tans" shot their father. Neither had a funeral. The mother abandoned their small farm and moved her three daughters to the Dublin slums. Now, twenty-six years later, a Mass of the Resurrection was held with the three sisters present. From that day the "schizophrenic" was healed and within two months, she was running a boarding-house.

Bitterness is inturned anger, resentment, frustration. We "internalize" it and take it out on ourselves. It still has a physical outlet, however, whether in ulcers, arthritis or even gall bladder disease – "the bitterness of gall."

An analysis of the origins of such an attitude can lead to apology and restitution. This engenders new life and is available to everyone. The qualities we can expect from the Holy Spirit are listed by St. Paul (Galatians 5.22).

The Deja Vu Phenomenon

Most people sometimes in their lives have experienced moments or events when they say to themselves, "I have seen all this before." Then they do some act that again they think has happened before. This can be interpreted as, "I am experienceing reincarnation." In psychiatry it is known as the "deja vu" phenomenon.

There is a very simple neurological explanation. The reception of sensory impulses usually takes place first in the conscious areas of the brain; then they are passed into the memory areas and stored. If there is a delay on these neuronal routes, perhaps from tiredness or a temporary hormonal or circulatory hold up, then the message reaches the subconscious memory areas first, so that when it reaches the consciousness we "see" it already stored and so think that the situation is being repeated. This, of course, is mistaken and no argument for reincarnation.

Depression

Depression is a mood disorder that interferes with a person's life processes; it is at the dark end of a spectrum of symptoms. Some people are more prone than others and may have several attacks.

As a diagnostic label, depression must not be confused with lethargy, apathy, drowsiness, or just feeling "lousy." Today, it is estimated that forty per cent of all depressions respond to placebo drugs (strictly inert preparations used in trials of active drugs).

Mood swings are part of the natural pattern of our experience. They cover a full range of emotions from joy and laughter to worship and humility. We learn how to avoid the unpleasant, how to enhance the pleasant. Trial and error learning is seen in some of the simplest living creatures. Pathological mood swings to uncontrollable highs and lows are known as manic depressive states. Some drugs can level these mood, notably lithium. Depression by itself we can feel subjectively, or observe in others objectively with symptoms of withdrawal, fear of darkness, crying or sadness. There are seven classifications of depression and the importance of accurate diagnosis and identification cannot be over-emphasized.

Pellagrous Depression is a vitamin B complex deficiency disease. Patients usually show cracks around the mouth, brown tongue, dry scaly brown skin patches of irregular outline mainly on exposed parts, and bowel disturbances. Their weeping bouts are quite unpredictable. Sufferers are commonly seen in prisons, prisoners-of-war camps, mental hospitals and among the old, the senile and the poor. The deficiency responds quickly to vitamin B3 intake.

Reactive Depression to a sudden, acute grief is not regarded as an illness unless unnecessarily prolonged. This usually follows the death of a loved one or a separation or divorce and needs adequate mourning. The pattern of patients' behavior is of going to bed late thinking about their own loss and crying themselves to sleep. In the morning they wake late and quite happy for they have "forgotten" their loss, although the memory and their distress gradually increases throughout the day until the night of depression.

Endogenous Depression is always evident in patients' very early wakening, crying and depressed; although restless, they do not want to get up and know no cause for this. When they rise, they can work off their feelings and by evening feel better and fall asleep easily. This is common in menopausal women and is often confused with combination of the other categories of depression. The simples proof of endogenous depression is the use of tricyclic antidepressant drugs which, with careful administration, induce sleep and thus give time to restore the chemical balance. If no relief results, other areas need to be examined. Unfortunately, being so common, it is quicker for doctors to prescribe drugs as a trial rather than spend time on investigating other causes.

Pre-menstrual Depression occurs about ten days before a woman's monthly period, in preparation for which there may be retention of liquid in the body. The ankles can become swollen and there may be confusion or tension. Most women respond to diuretics or pyrodonxine (B6) and to the discipline of abstaining from excessive drinking of liquids.

Puerperal Depression is not uncommon in the weeks following childbirth. The mother's body makes many hormonal adjustments and usually nature takes its own course. Breast feeding a baby is a natural hormonal stimulus. If this depression is prolonged, however, psychiatry and medicine can provide the remedy.

Guilt Depression is caused by the burden of people's own crimes or misbehavior. Their shoulders tend to be bowed, their heads down as though they carry the world's load and they shuffle rather than stride out, not looking up into one's face. Some criminals learn to behave in exactly the opposite pattern to cover their guilt, but they cannot hide the quick catch of breath racing their pulse and blood pressure when confronted with truth machines. The guilty may not cry, but just complain – about the food, the weather, the neighbors, even the government; endless symptoms appear. They will "take it out" on the cat or dog or even inanimate objects. Penal systems are even more frustrating for they learn nothing but discomfort when they have been found out.

Another form of guilt is induced by some religious sects. People are brainwashed or even cursed. The have not taken Jesus Christ at his word. Counseling for these people is essential, during which they learn how to cope with sin and come through to the victorious life which is God's intention for us in this world. Some people's scruples become obsessional so that they are depressed and guilty about their scrupulosity. This has occurred most frequently in religious institutions where something must be raked up for the sake of the confessional. Such people have need of a gentle re-orientation.

General Depression can show up in people who are self-centered or physically inactive or who abuse themselves by lack of exercise or self-indulgence. Drug abuse can remove our controls and defenses, perhaps with the over-prescription of tranquilizers and the over-dependence on other chemicals as a counter-balance. Strong doses of coffee containing caffeine can become addictive. Cigarette smoking also is destructive quite apart from it being a compensatory substitute for nipple sucking. Those unprotected by vitamins and prayer may have periods of depression, especially after an anaesthetic. Some hypotensive drugs and contraceptives can precipitate depression.

The sullen, depressed, duty-oriented Japanese soldiers seen in the Far East during the Second World War carried threatening bayonets. They had vengeful force within them that could not be broken through and an almost inbred inscrutable quality. This has become characteristic of their world-trade dealings and there is only a glimmer of light when an individual takes on spiritual developments.

A fifty-four year-old woman complained of sudden bouts of crying, either day or night without any precipitating factor. She was frightened of the dark and of meeting groups of people, especially in the street. Her mother had the same apprehension. Doors had to be locked at home, despite which they had to sit facing the front door. Her brother, sister and nephew also did no, but they smoked very heavily and drowned their fears in alcohol. She did not. She made no close relations and only recently had married an older man, who was an invalid. Sometimes during the crying bouts, if he came into the bedroom, she would jump out of bed screaming, "Don't do it, don't do it" and finally, "No, no, no" as she curled up on the floor sobbing.

Usually, the patient slept well, falling asleep immediately, wakening briefly at 3 am for the toilet, and then sleeping until after 7am not feeling depressed at firs. She had no illnesses of note, just slight ankle edema and anaemia caused by an iron deficiency.

She was neither a pellagrous nor a reactive depressive, had already passed through her menopause without disturbance and did not carry the regular diurnal swing of moods of the Endogenous pattern. She did not suffer from Guilt Depression – she was tall, upright and was a faithful church-goer who always delighted in her own private devotions, being aware of Satan and his tricks of sabotage as she had been through the church's form of exorcism. There was no improvement.

A search through the family tree was called for. There were no losses in her siblings or in the next generation of nieces and nephews. The patient's mother exhibited similar symptoms and study of her siblings showed that a brother had disappeared on a hunting trip, aged forty years, and no funeral had been held – but her symptoms were evident before this event. The patient's grandparents were a very rigid, uncommunicative pair. Despite the fact that the graves of her great-grandparents' siblings and church records were intact, the two great-grandparents themselves remained a mystery although their names and dates of birth were known, The great-great grandmother had disappeared when her son (the great-grandfather) was nine years old. He then became a cowhand on a farm near his home in Northern Ireland and never mentioned his parents' lives or deaths.

When the grandfather grew up, he joined the Orangemen. He and his wife always carefully locked every door in their house and would not sit with their backs to a door. The great-grandfather's names were never passed down to successive generations, although everyone else's names appeared several times.

The story emerged that their house had been broken into by a gang who forced the great-grandfather out of bed, took him away and tortured him. He bled to death in pain. Protesting descendants re-enacted this episode in sudden bursts of subjective symptoms, such as unprovoked bout of crying. This could account for the grandfather having joined the Orangemen for protection and the moving to Scotland after his marriage.

A Eucharistic service was held as a Requiem for the great-grandparents, with the family present and able to pray aloud. This brought much relief to the patient.

Psychosomatic target organs in depression are represented by a slowing of functions, glandular, digestive and muscular. Patients slump, slouch and shuffle, moan, groan and cry. Sensitivity or imagined sensitivity to pain is accentuated. They are pre-occupied, absent-minded and careless. Even their pulse is sluggish; when they have swollen ankles we say, "Their hearts are in their boots." The trouble has become subjective. The first step is to help them to objectify the situation with a self-critical faculty, so that they understand that it is not their ultimate self behaving in this way. The second step is to study their family tree.

Discipline of thoughts in mood swings is important. To seek insight and look at ourselves objectively and to note the first signs of mood disturbances is a lifetime task.

A fifty-five year-old woman had been plagued by depression all her life, with unpredictable highs and lows, and was labelled an manic depressive. She had an extremely patient husband and three grown-up tolerant children. When a priest laid hands on her, she heard the words, "I want your compassion" and she knew that God spoke to her. She gradually reduced her drug dosage and finally gave up all drugs. At any time, she knows that she can pray for a reminder, an immediate recognition of her needs and that she can use the actual words of Christ in the Aramaic language: "Be with us in temptation, remind us that you are here." She had found great release from her depression.

Depressions, then, can be precipitated in various situations – puerperal, menopausal, post-menopausal, premenstrual, post-anaesthesia, or during the disorders of the C.N.S., C.V.S., gastro-intestinal system and various forms of rheumatism. One may query whether the depressive state first caused the illness or vice versa. Single, isolated people who become introverted, especially if they were formerly gregarious, can be prone to depression; similarly with those who never receive praise and, therefore, have an innate inability to give praise. To praise and be thankful even when it hurts is essential for our earthly training.

Analysis is cathartic in itself for the very fact of expressing the problem makes it more specific. Restitution may be the outcome and the wording of the prayer becomes a positive memory that can be recalled frequently.

We learn from our mood swings and can be grateful that we are not dull, unresponsive lumps of flesh. This give and take is the warp and woof of life. What can we do about it? Our response shapes our own lives, those around us, and our ultimate destiny.

Disappearances

When drawing family trees, it is often found that there are one or more unaccounted-for ancestors whose descendants may have bouts of disorientated behavior, not in continuity, but exhibiting states of confusion or "absence" – called schizoid or obsessive.

For instance, a sixty year-old man had been completely unreliable throughout his life and never kept to a decision or to one line of conduct. Recovery followed a ritual mourning for his uncle who had disappeared and who must have died many years before. Some unaccounted-for people belong to Irish families who had no thought for the old, dying and unmourned when the younger ones escaped from Ireland to another country during the 1845 potato famine. Their "hereditary" genetic illnesses date from this time.

A theologian who had lived a rather indeterminate scatter-brained life, realized when he retired that he should have prayed for his uncle after whom he was named. This uncle had disappeared, aged sixteen years, and had not been heard of since then. Over eighty years later, presuming he was dead, we held a service to mourn his death. From that time, the theologian pulled his life together and was able to help many other people.

Examples abound from the war dead or those who were lost, missing in far-off countries, alone, abandoned and in pain. Very often we have found that patients' symptoms could be their release after ritual mourning.

Everyone has an individual identity. It seems, also, that everyone wants to be mourned by their own family. Many will need their lives unfinished business taken into account so that it is not carried on to the next generation. The living can stop this process and ensure that their children and grandchildren will not suffer.

Domination

Until recent years, Nature seemed to decree that the man of a family, the protector and provider, should take the dominant role for he held the whole perspective while the female controlled the details of nurture. In Celtic society a bride arrived at her prospective husband's house with her dowry; if it was unacceptable she was returned with her dowry intact. Women were regarded as chattels. William James in his Bible commentaries discusses the condition of Israelite women in B.C. times. The stoning of prostitutes then, for instance, was not unlike the recent public execution of disloyal Arab Muslim women in a country still living at the Old Testament level of "an eye for an eye" and where the male is totally dominant.

William Wilkie, the Australian psychiatrist, has discovered another syndrome not often met elsewhere; that is the dominant, loud, forceful tough housewife. He finds that this was common in Australia where in the vast farms and outback, the men were away from home for days at a time with their stock. The wife had to cope with all the work of the ranch and be ready for the return when the ride ended. Wilkie observed that this matriarchical pattern went down the generations even in the city dwellers.

Among siblings a natural balance always prevails. An only child, a child with a single parent or one with a homosexual partner, an illegitimate child or an adopted one when others are born subsequently into the family – all of these face difficulties. Isolated children can still succeed where there is love and they can restore their own position by praying for the sins of their unknown parents and, thus, obtain their personal freedom.

From twelve years of age, a seventy-five year-old spinster had a violent and unaccountable temper. Once a professional woman, this had caused difficulties in her work. She imitated her grandmother's tempers and paranoid behavior and frequently wrote scurrilous letters to lawyers. It was thought that in this way her grandmother's character was being re-enacted. Now, in old age, she was having up to three attacks a week, splitting her family relationships and terrifying children. Her brother, praying through the family tree in a Eucharistic service, included an apology for their grandmother's temper of which, as a child, he had great fear. From that day the woman was freed from her attacks of temper. Later, it was realized that this old lady had been one of eight siblings and had been the grandmother's favorite child. From thirty-one cases of pathological maternal dominance, seventeen were healed through the gift of forgiveness.

In many circumstances, the female must take the dominant role; to do so with full insight is acceptable but now we must recognize also the possible control from beyond the grave by the attention-seeking activity of the dead, whether male of female.

In today's world, the continuing emancipation of women under equal opportunities laws seems aimed at bringing parity to the sexes, primarily in the work place. There is a similar developing tradition and restructuring of the roles in parenthood, with unemployed husbands and working wives. The psychological effects of this reversal can be far-reaching or even damaging to the original balance of a marriage when the husband was the protector and provider.

According to the works of Professor William Barclay, when Mary the mother of Christ became pregnant, she would have been questioned and physically examined by the rabbis who would have found that she was still a virgin. This must have staggered their disbelief; it had never been heard of before. In the new situation, they had to accept the word of Joseph, an upright and good man, who was betrothed to Mary. Both were close to God and He warned them to flee to Egypt. Herod's suspicions were aroused; he knew that no king would be born in a stable but, by cruelly murdering all the "holy innocents," he attempted to thwart the possibility.

Mary broke all previous codes and values of womanhood, raising women to equality with men. Her care and understanding verified many of Christ's acts; for instance, she instructed the men at the wedding in Cana to do as the Lord said (John 2.5). As a mother she followed all that He did closely in her heart, even to being one of the faithful few who remained as her Son was tortured to death. He had restated the law and proclaimed that "God is Love."

Almost the last words of Christ were to commission Mary to be the mother of all mankind, as Roman Catholic tradition understands these words. She is "omnipresent" and offers her love to all whom she received, especially the children and the unborn, when we recognize and commit them to God. She embraces and hands them over to her Son as they cross the Jordan, for they come to the Father only through the Lord Jesus Christ. On hundreds of occasions in the Mass setting we have watched this actually happening as, through the veil, we have caught a glimpse from our finite world into the infinite.

Forgiveness

The word "forgiveness" means to let off, to remit:
  "for" – in place of, in exchange against
  "give" – a free gift, a present.
The concept must have been slow to develop in humans and we do not see it in the vegetable or animal world where there is no "give away" – it is all "take" with very temporary emotions. The lioness cuffs her cubs into some display of respect, but human feelings cannot be superimposed on animals.

How did the desire for forgiveness arise in the human psyche? Early humans found that, in fighting, as an opponent lost more and more blood so it was weakened. As the blood increased, so did the stimulus and excitement, still seen in the lion or the shark. Blood was thought to be the source of life; thus, to take a person's blood was to take away his power. When at a later date a hierarchy of power was created, then the one condemned in a fault had his blood drained. The Druids, Incas, Egyptians and Chinese of BC 2000 sacrificed humans, some to appease the gods, others to accompany their overlord into the other world. An emperor could not think of being a nobody in the next world so he "kept" his retinue. Thousands of enemy prisoners were retained in order to be sacrificed to propitiate the heavenly powers who then would grant their requests.

In each civilization, there developed the idea of sacrifices for faults or sins. If the sinner were wealthy then adequate animal sacrifices would be offered to the god to atone for the sin, the sinner only losing part of his capital. The Jews instituted a very economical method whereby the rabbi laid the "sins on a goat which was banished into the desert to die." This brought forgiveness – and the phrase "the scapegoat" is now in ordinary usage. There are few references to forgiveness in the Jewish Old Testament, but many more in the New Testament. It seems as though awareness of the need for forgiveness was gradually being realized by humankind, and that it required ritual; it could not be obtained just by trying hard. Priests then took on the authority of being the only ones with the right to forgive – at a fee, of course.

At the time of Moses civilized peoples had reached a level where laws had to be articulated for every individual; they were essential for racial survival. In Leviticus, the need to confess the sins of ones' ancestors is explained. Daniel actually confesses his sins, his father's and his city's before the altar of his God. This is an important turning point, for Daniel is immediately rewarded by seeing Gabriel. He heard that he had done the right thing and had become aware of, and part of the unseen eternal world. He was seeking the remission of sin that had caused so much disaster. Ezekiel chapter 18 introduces the principle that a person is responsible for his or her own sins, and later, in 36.22-26, indicated what God will do in forgiveness: "I shall give you a new heart and put a new spirit within you." Forgiveness is also sought in 1 Kings 8, and the mentioned two or three times in the Psalms.

Confucius (BC 500) said, "I have sinned; as yet there is no forgiveness, one day a prince will come with the gift." Isaiah 61 prophesies the coming of forgiveness, in words which Christ would quote. Psalm 40 says that God wants (and gives) receptive ears rather than sacrifice. However, sacrifice was resumed after the Exile, as soon as the Temple was rebuilt. In NT times, Christ was very critical of the Pharisees and Sadducees who had calculated this business to a fine art, so that they could continue to sin themselves. They were so incensed and challenged that they finally sacrificed Him, without realizing what they were doing to human history. This one act of Christ's – allowing the crucifixion to happen – opened a new door; it was the event that proved to be the ultimate sacrifice that never required repetition. And it teaches us how to forgive: from the heart, with restitution, apology and the taking on of others' burdens.

By praise and thanksgiving, we step through the door-there is nothing clever on our part! Vast areas open up; honest apology means with no strings attached, a genuine giving up of pride-not a technique of "confession," repeating set phrases and even inventing vague misdeeds with the aim of getting a new sense of psychological release. Some even try to project their own state: "I really do want to apologize that I've always thought you were exceedingly ugly." That is not apology, that is a subtle form of attack!

Some people maintain that they are unable to forgive themselves; this is a common delusion; it really means that they dislike what they have done, and feel bad about themselves. The cure is not trying harder to forgive themselves, but finding God's forgiveness, and a new identity in that. Forgiveness cannot be manufactured.

It could be, also, that people use the idea of having "two natures" as an excuse, and blame their "other nature" – rather like the man who steals and then blames Satan for having tempted him! (There are of course different concerns, for example kleptomania, or demon possession.)

Humans always hope to earn forgiveness and freedom from guilt and shame; but we cannot obtain this either by our own effort or by gold and silver (1 Peter 1.18-19). God, by His own design, has another permanent way, a gift only if accepted. In any case, soon after the time of Jesus the Jewish Temple was destroyed, and the sacrificial system ceased.

Universally, mental problems were long regarded as the result of people who had sinned. They were thrown into prisons until in 1791 Pinel in France first suggested that they might be ill. Swedenborg in the 1740s became aware that much madness was caused by the presence of people of the other world and he wrote *The Presence of Spirits in Madness,* but he did not learn any way to deal with them. A disciple of Confucius asked, "What is the greatest virtue?" The Master replied, "The love of mankind." His disciple continued, "What is the greatest learning?" to which Confucius answered, "To know men" (The Analects).

In life, human beings move in a world of good and evil, love and hate, a very temporary training place where we have to make choices. All that is good, positive and loving is of Heaven and is God's purpose; all that is evil seems to be darkness, the absence of light, the absence of love and the absence of goodness – a hellish state. The way to rise above purely animal tendencies has to come from love. This in turn is released when we accept the wonderful gift of forgiveness, which brings salvation, new life, freedom, enjoyment, purpose, peace and love. The way of love must be cultivated by practice, even more so than any other skill or learning. Then one can be aware, using all the senses, of the unseen world in which Jesus Christ lives through all that He accomplished.

There still exist in many countries witchcraft covens where sacrifices of animals and humans are made, thereby attempting to find "kicks," by returning to primitive ritual. Today, this is often performed under the influence of drugs. The people are not concerned with forgiveness, but only with the dragging up of satanic rites as an escape from reality. They sometimes end in mental hospitals or commit suicide having turned their backs on four thousand years of human development!

Opposite examples can be found in spiritually mature mothers who, in spite of abuse from teenagers with behavioral problems can still love and forgive. Honest apology is very salutary.

A boy, aged eight years, who was afraid of one of his school masters skipped classes and picked a bunch of flowers for his mother. She questioned him as to why he was home so early. Out came the story. Instead of any scolding, she took all the blame on to herself for not having taught her son how to deal with fear, then she went with him to apologize personally to the master.

When a teenager, always very self-conscious, shy, blushing and preferring to be alone, returned "borrowed" books to his former school library and apologized, his shyness changed immediately to an outgoing happiness.

A business manager apologized for his hardness to the Trade Union leadership during a dispute. This was accepted and a strike was settled; 16,000 people returned to work.

A foreign minister confessed to God and apologized for the discarding, by miscarriage and abortion, of his own children. Forgiven, he was then freed to witness to the truth in the International Court of Justice and a charge against another country was dropped.

After a scene in the Assam Parliament, the leader of the opposition fled into hiding, afraid he would be murdered. He discovered the concept of apology and forgiveness. After he apologized to the leader of the house for having lost his temper and created the scene, there followed reconciliation and new standards of co-operation. This led to the cessation of guerrilla war by dissidents who had been backed by a foreign power.

A bigamous man, where neither family knew of the others' existence, was able to bring them all together, apologize, made a settlement with the most recent "wife" and establish a proper home to live in with his legitimate wife. To his amazement, this new lifestyle cut his desire for alcohol which had been a regular weekend problem; he also stopped smoking.

A fifty year-old Jewish man apologized to his wife for his temper, rudeness and continual demands. She had been a devout Lutheran, but under his battering had given up spiritually and was contemplating divorce. Now she was able to ask forgiveness, also, and an entirely new shared life discipline of great joy began.

Parents worried about their estranged tramp-like son were faced with the fact that they had never loved or prayed for their miscarriage. They did so and the next day the son returned. He stepped immediately into a friend's business and made rapid strides in a professional career.

The sensation of guilt is held by the subconscious. It always has a physical outlet – commonly fear, covered up by showing anger. This must not be evident in public, so glands, joints and nuerones malfunction and then medical labelling begins. The capacity to forgive is a "further on" spiritual development requiring humility and understanding, the ability to see two sides of a problem, to be sorry, to genuinely regret a situation. If someone apologizes and is merely remorseful, he will repeat the wrong but, if he is genuinely repentant, then he will not do it again. Near the beginning of the Old Testament (Exodus 34.7) it was concluded that God did not forgive, but by the time of David it was recognised that he could and did, and that such forgiveness could transform lives. (cf Psalm 103.1-5).

Munchausen's Syndrome

This condition, named after the German doctor who first described it, classifies those people who live by falsifying symptoms to gain admission to hospital or social security benefits. It is not confined to those in financial need. Doctors always have to be alert to this possibility. The individual becomes skilled at reciting textbook lists of symptoms and will frequently change names. The proportion of these cases seen are five males to one female. It may be thought of as malingering, but probably indicates a need of deeper help.

One patient in American had carefully mastered the symptoms of schizophrenia with bizarre actions and ideas and fatuous interrupting questions, ready to get up and go at the end of his regular hour armed with a certificate and prescription which he never cashed. He was seen to walk normally away from the doctor, light a cigarette and get into his expensive sports car having made an appointment for his next interview in a month's time. In the meantime, he will have visited other doctors under other names. The doctor gets a Social Security fee.

In recent years, some of these cases have sought help in religious settings in which Satan has been blamed for the trouble and numerous exorcisms performed, the patient always coming back for more. Multiple elaborate exorcisms in any case should never be necessary. The Lord's Prayer with its "Deliver us from the Evil one," should be adequate where the need is genuine.

Pain

This aspect of body function can be seen throughout the animal kingdom. Pain is a system to warn against and avoid noxious stimuli. For humans it is not unique and enables them to register touch, heat or cold, deep pressure or a superficial pinprick. The automatic nerves use a reflex which only goes to the spinal cord and straight back to the muscles of the area to withdraw from the outside stimulus. The message then travels more centrally to where already there is a constant reverberating system recording the position of every part of the body. Next, the consciousness sends messages for defence and for directing whatever movement this part is to take, even to utilizing another limb to defend, scratch or kick. These conditioned reflexes are learned very quickly in the first months of life, even in utero. Humans reason and remember far beyond any other creature, but can change an attitude and be transformed in body, mind and spirit. If a person is brought up in an atmosphere of hate, bitterness, or unwanted as being of the "wrong sex," he will soon learn that to create an illness engenders sympathy and if it is called pain then he can begin to develop target end organs.

For example, a rather ungainly, overweight housewife with an exemplary husband had a very swollen and painful right index finger. She had moved three times seeking a better climate; no medical aid helped. When she finally apologized to her husband and God for her bitter, critical, cynical tongue she was healed overnight. The blood was free to flow again and the neuronal messages allowed movement. Within twenty-four hours there was no visible sign of swelling on her fingers. As a lady, she had been unable to point at or speak against other people openly; she always did so behind their backs with her hand cupping her mouth. Her pain had drawn considerable attention and sympathy to herself. Denigrating others raised her own self-esteem (See chapter on Arthritis). Now the whole situation was reversed and she and her husband became very happy.

Pain in cancer patients is sometimes due to the tumour pressing on nerves, but often it is increased greatly by fear of the unknown and a feeling of insecurity. They feel threatened if no one is honest with them and they often realize when there is a cover up. Their real fear is of death, marked in those who have unfinished business in the world and are not prepared to go into eternity, so they tend to cling to drugs, artificially blotting their consciousness. Other patients, who are able to praise with thanksgiving, are whole people who want to know and face the truth. When this happens, fewer drugs are needed. Many have died in great joy, looking forward in spite of their disease. There should be a policy of honesty, when the right moment comes.

Pain thresholds and the perception of pain differs in people. Tolerance may be higher in the male, but lower where there is anxiety, self-concern or depression. It is very low in the drug addict especially during a withdrawal period. We should not rush to pain killers at the slightest prompting. The body sometimes needs the stimulus of pain to exercise and improve its defense systems. Mood swings, changes in fortune or in relationships all can be turned into challenges to be overcome. Conditions involving extremes of discomfort, confined sleeping spaces, long marches without food and water, physical punishments and the loss of half the body weight were inflicted on many prisoners during the last war. Despite feeling pain, depression and anger, one learned that the mind, although sometimes brain-washed, was free to roam. The spiritual entity was under one's own control and in the long hours of inactivity, the suffering could be taken to Christ, knowing that He carried more pain than we will ever know and yet remained spiritually intact even on the Cross.

Hypochondriacal traits are often experienced by medical students as they explore disease patterns. Patients who are preoccupied with endless symptoms need reassurance, provided the physician is careful in examination and avoids pain killers. Those who are obsessional from their upbringing are the punctilious who can live only within a routine. Pain to them means disaster. Their beliefs and attitudes are rigid and they do not allow for the give and take of life. They feel secure in their narrowness and allow nothing to shatter this. Such people need concise opinions and treatments.

The "gate" theory of pain asserts that it is partly controlled from the peripheral nerve endings and partly from the brain areas. These meet in spinal cord levels and determine how much it "let through" to central consciousness – there is, therefore, a "threshold" to cross. One may question to what level hypnosis, concussion, epilepsy or drugs alter the controlling factors. The fact that relief of pain can follow release from fear would seem to show that much of the pain suffered in these conditions is, in fact, a result of fear, including the involuntary muscle spasm it produces.

Respect

Considerable medical research had been carried out on heredity and environment. Some people think that lack of respect for the fetus and for the baby in the first few months of life has resulted in early and high death rates from strokes, heart disease and bronchitis. Instances of neglect of the unborn and the psychiatric consequences have been recorded in several thousand cases. (See *The Southern Medical Journal of America,* July 1987, by Dr. K. McAll and Professor William Wilson.) Nothing is hidden from the subconscious mind of the child. If children are brought up in families that to not respect their unborn babies, they, in turn, cannot be expected to respect their parents. As they grow they will discard parental boundaries. How can they know how to honor God? Without God in their awareness they will have no respect for people or property and this can lead to mugging, violence and theft.

Orphans whose parents died when they were too young to understand, need to go through a mourning process later in life. This removes the acting out of the attention-seeking teenager or the child with a behaviour disorder. When there is no challenge or adventure in life, young people manufacture their own e.g. crowd psychology in a football stadium can whip this to a crescendo. It is apparent, however, that the language of such youths is commonly echoing the voices of aborted siblings, crying out for attention.

Prison is supposed to be a curative discipline, but it does not necessarily deter wrong-doers. Within a prison's classless society, they may learn even more about the criminal hierarchy from cell mates, patterns of behaviour and, later, seek revenge against society. (Marx propagated a classless society in Russia, but had no plan for "people-power" with the resultant disastrous economics and the politics of fear.)

Throughout history, man's cruelty to man has impeded progress but respect, appreciation, team work and care can come from individual determination. The ability of the human spirit to develop and make decisions which alter the whole course of life is available to everyone. Real respect means thinking positively about other people and then helping them to implement new life-changing decisions.

Ritual mourning in Anorexia Nervosa & Bulimia

The role of unresolved grief in *anorexia nervosa* has not been explored in medical literature. Over one hundred cases of anorexia nervosa refractory to normal medical and psychiatric treatment were examined physically and psychiatrically. They were then investigated, using a questionnaire, to determine whether there had been deaths in the family that had not been mourned. In every instance this was the case, so they were treated by ritual mourning, with a four-year follow up.

Early in our enquiries we found that a number of anorexic patients had histories of one or more abortions, miscarriages or other unmourned deaths in their immediate or extended families. They recovered rapidly when the family ritually mourned these deaths. If there were signs of unresolved grief, the patient and the family were helped to look objectively at the relevance of such grief to the symptoms. Thus, they understood that these symptoms correlated with the situation of the unmourned person – that is, lost, lonely, in darkness, depressed, unloved, nameless, unable to eat or cry out.

The family was next taken through a process of ritual mourning for the identified unmourned individual(s) in the setting of a Eucharist service, usually performed by an ordained cleric who understood and was sympathetic to the situation. Preferably, the service was private since it was determined that both patient and family needed to vocalise their requests and confessions to God and to name the lost person. When the patient responded to treatment and weight gain was considered adequate, they were instructed in the continuance of psychospiritual well-being, including cognitive restructuring and spiritual exercises.

The follow up was done by mail. A personal letter was sent to each patient and/or their family to ascertain the maintenance of weight gain and the state of their psychospiritual health. Of the 115 cases originally investigated, twelve parents and/or priests refused any co-operation and five had died. Of the remaining ninety-eight cases, eight had remained unchanged, one argued against the original diagnosis and three did not answer; eighty-six were cured. This represents a success rate of almost three-quarters.

The observation that all of the patients in this series had suffered a loss of someone important in their own or their family's life was a startling find. The fact that such a high percentage responded to treatment with a cure is unusual for any illness in psychiatry. The results are unquestionably significant since each patient was his or her own control. By June 1988, three hundred and seventy-five anorexic patients had been seen where family ritual mourning was advised and the same success rate still held. Some physicians, in fact, feel that this process can claim an even higher rate of cure.

As with anorexia nervosa cases, there is a strange lack of insight in bulimia patients. These have the added factor of secretive induced vomiting and sometimes the covert taking of laxatives. When vomiting, they try to hide, but if watched they behave as if they are following a ritual in a trance. They empty kitchen cupboards of carbohydrates, gorging themselves to capacity and then vomiting, repeating this sequence until there is no more to eat.

In the psychosomatics of vomiting and colitis, it is understood that an unpleasant situation is held in the subconscious mind which must be removed, thus, there is a subconscious voiding of this by physically vomiting it away. As food is the sustainer of life, it must be eliminated from the body. Many of these patients, not feeling in control of themselves, also talk of suicide, but they usually make sure that they receive the maximum of attention and can be quite violent in protesting.

A thirty-four year-old university lecturer wandered at midnight raiding dustbins and gorging on scraps of food like a beggar, followed by vomiting. She was frequently arrested by the police. It was discovered that her father had been responsible for abortions in several women.

Binging, vomiting and using laxatives, a girl of twenty-four years had tried suicidal gestures seven times in the previous five years. Her mother was a twin who had never mourned her dead brother. Her maternal grandmother was a violent, paranoid schizophrenic, involved in mediumship and frequent trances; the patient's symptoms began at about the time of her death.

In the case study of one hundred fifteen anorexia nervosa patients followed up over four years, eighteen were classified as bulimic. Thirteen of these had family deaths unknown to the patients- in all representing thirty-seven deaths, all unmourned. These deaths were of a completely unknown cause, such as disappearances or war deaths or unknown parents of illegitimate children. Six ancestors died by suicide, fifteen by abortion, six by miscarriage or fetal accident. Eight miscarriages known about by the patients had not been mourned. Two of the bulimics had died, but they were already dying when seen. In each case a ritual mourning process was established with the respective priests. The other sixteen patients, three of who are males, are now quite well.

In bulimia the subconscious mind is aware of a family stress. The trauma of deaths that the family is ashamed of expresses itself in the most sensitive sibling, usually a girl. The theory of the Possession Syndrome may possibly provide an adequate explanation, where the unmourned dead are demanding attention by ensuring that the "staff of life" is avoided and a close-to-death situation is maintained. Similarly, the problem of the unequal incidence of anorexia in males and females (a 1:21 proportion) is probably explained by the concept of the Possession Syndrome. The frequency in the female may be caused by their greater sensitivity, child-bearing desires and maternal instincts – they could be more trusted. Of two hundred twenty cases seen, only thirteen were males. Of these, a twenty-seven year old man had an eight year-old sister who was not affected, another had a sister who had been murdered and one had a sister two years younger who was also anorexic. A single twenty-three year-old knew his anorexia began seven years before at boarding school when his best friend had committed suicide. All the rest of the men were either single children or their siblings were male, the affected one always having been regarded as the most sensitive.

There is a theory that the anorexic patient is seeking parental attention and attempting to bring the parents themselves to a closer relationship. This may be true, but more fundamental is the parental need to recognise the unmourned ancestors who for their part, are trying to draw attention to themselves via the child. While supervised nursing and discipline is needed in the majority of cases, healing results from the Eucharistic approach have been proven and were unpredictably dramatic in forty per cent of cases. All males treated by this methodology have been cured.

It is strongly recommended that this is tried, for there is no overdose danger or harm in the process. Only good can result and the new discipline which then is established makes the patient externalise and objectify the blame and introduces the lost dead to a new life.

Ritual Mourning
in Unresolved Grief

Grieving is a natural and necessary reaction to a new, deprived situation, and mourning can be salutary. To mourn means to be sorry about a death and we need to experience this in order to be genuinely understanding in another's disaster. If the loss is our own, personal decision is required. When the tears have been shed, then we can stop and think objectively. It is unwise to try to hurry someone's healing with comments such as, "Don't cry over spilt milk" or "That's that, now you must live in the present."

The hasty fifteen-minute turnover in a modern Western crematorium service where the same words can become a monotonous repetition for the cleric on duty, encourages mourners to regard it as a non-event. Even death itself can be so regarded. A young girl was watching television when her mother interrupted to tell her that her father had died. Without looking up, the child merely remarked, "He will be back tomorrow."

Westerners might learn from the East, where the mourning process is highly organized with daily, monthly and annual rituals. This may seem to us costly and time-absorbing and many go to great lengths with paid mourners, but they also involve wise men and priests of every cult to appease their gods and furnish the dead with heavenly provisions. Originally, these were wives and slaves; later they were represented as statues and then likenesses were carved on the walls of tombs; later still, paper effigies were burned.

At first, to mourn may seem to be selfish, but we must weigh up our own loss of a loved one against our loving intention to complete their unfinished business by apologies, forgiveness and restitution, where necessary. This can be accomplished most successfully in the Eucharistic setting. Just as with contrite hearts we kneel and confess to God, so it is right to give Him thanks and praise for all good things, events, gifts and emotions that we experienced with the dead person.

The effects of inadequate mourning or no mourning at all is described elsewhere (see the sections on Anorexia, Schizophrenia, Epilepsy, Diabetes). Many soldiers who fought in recent wars carry a sense of guilt both for their comrades who died and for those they had to kill. Not having been involved in any mourning process, they feel a burden of responsibility. Confession of the evil of war, apology to God and a specific committal of the dead to God is essential for their release from guilt.

Excessive and prolonged guilt after bereavement is an expression of unresolved or unrepented wrong. This can produce symptoms of agitation, anxiety withdrawal, depression or disorientation. Some seek to release themselves and their subconscious accusation by projection – that is, seeing faults in others and criticising them. Compounded grief and guilt when unresolved becomes morbid, paranoid and pathological and may even necessitate psychiatric intervention to protect the sufferer and others. In psychiatry, it is recognised that to treat excessive grief and guilt, ritual mourning processes must be carried through, verbalised and acted out, rather than suppressed. A psychodrama technique – or behavior therapy – is used following a death, involving the sharing of feelings and memories, both good and bad, handling the deceased's clothing and belongings, looking at photographs, visiting the grave and kneeling and weeping there. Talking to an uncritical therapist or a sympathetic listener about aspects of the dead person's life is an extremely therapeutic exercise. This is mostly a self-seeking release in the how-and now for the sake of the bereaved, however, and there is some resolution if the therapist is a materialist. Far quicker and more permanent is the release achieved if, together with other family members or close friends, a mourning process facing a truthful reaction to past faults and deeds and difficulties in relationships is brought to the Eucharistic setting. This not only releases the living but, also, the dead. Additionally, future generations may be saved from being pressurised and possessed.

Sadly, as yet, psychiatry avoids the use of prayer – the one lasting technique that opens up the vast other world of eternity for us and which, ultimately, is a meeting place for them with us. "Blessed are they that mourn for they shall be comforted" (Matthew 5.4). Professor Barclay's translation of this Beatitude is, "Oh, the joy of those who are sorry for their own sins, those of their family and of their nation." This is mourning in the Christian sense where sorrow is to be rewarded by joy and freedom.

Within the churches there is provision for shared mourning and the opportunity to confess our guilt and any other unfinished business of the dead, followed by their committal to God's mercy. Such a service is a natural completion for we are aware that we came originally from eternity and will return there. The work is finished and we can rejoice, therefore, that someone is released – frequently this is celebrated with a feast for the mourners.

With confidence, faith and trust, through Jesus Christ and His Father, we are aware within our spirits that the dead whom we mourn are off on an exciting journey into heaven a little ahead of us. From over a hundred cases, we can conclude that if they continually appear or talk to us, then they have not begun their journey or have left something undone or amiss that must be put straight. The Christ-oriented decision-making pattern has been achieved for us already through Jesus Christ Himself.

Singleness (or, Being Singled)

For over forty thousand years the bonding within family life has been its strength. In the last fifty years now that women have won so much independence, they have also demanded independent living. This is also made possible by our ability to build multiple small living units. Some have opted out from marriage, others have found themselves single through separation and divorce, many have given birth to, and brought up, a single child. Thus, a new position has arisen which I call "the Single Syndrome." In a general practice where the frequency of out patient attendances was recorded, by far the greatest attendance was the singled woman.

This practice of two thousand patients over a ten-year period recorded that the male population visited the surgery for psychosomatic disorders twice as frequently as for recognisable illnesses, but the women attended in a comparable mid age period five times more frequently for psychosomatic reasons; eighty per cent of these were "singled" or one could say not integrated into stable family settings.

Professor Philip Ney of Vancouver Island's research in delinquency, crime and drug addicts lays the blame at the feet of the single parent who opted out of the early controls and setting of boundaries because they had to go out to work and were the ones who had the majority of abortions.

Stress

This concept has been known throughout human history. In the two World Wars it was recognised in the "shell-shocked" and battle-weary forces. In the 1940s a new psychiatric chance was afforded them to verbalise their stresses and, thus, to work through all the deep subconscious repressed traumas, so much of war being a reversal of moral principles in the killing of an "enemy." In ordinary life we built up a resistance to distressing situations but, if the trauma of stress becomes more than we can bear, according to our personality, culture or sensitivity, then it is termed a transmarginal stress. We break down, mentally or physically and can no longer adapt.

In medicine the classification of stress symptoms is endless, for they can vary from becoming prone to infections or accidents high or low blood-pressure, fatness or thinness, from exhaustion to hyperactivity to hyper or hypo-function of the autonomic nervous system. This is fright resulting in "freeze, flight or fight."

The hysteric shelters in attention-seeking; the neurotic in a multitude of symptoms. Defence mechanisms may include denial, rationalization, escape or blaming others, thus displacing the responsibility. Positive ways of dealing with stress include taking one hurdle at a time, learning to care and talk over problems and seeing them objectively. A regular daily routine should be developed gradually. Prayer and meditation help us to see ourselves and our family in perspective, and in the context of an eternal destiny.

A boy of eighteen years, morally sound, opposed a group in his boarding school which engaged in occult coven celebrations. Twelve of his classmates attacked him with curses, organising their antipathy over many weeks. The boy disappeared and was found eventually in a mental hospital one hundred and forty miles away, unable even to give his name. He had attempted to walk home. In his absence, his parents came to a service of exorcism and deliverance in another city; the boy was immediately restored and finished his school days elsewhere. An investigation into the school itself is recorded in Lord Longford's book *Pornography.*

A newly-qualified priest was sent to a small church on a recently built housing estate. No one was interested, no one spoke to him and his attempts at visiting met with rebuffs. Under great stress, he broke down and wept a great deal. Then he tried to re-orientate his life and developed an amazing gift for listening to sick people, diagnosing accurately and taking them right through to freedom and spiritual discipline, over several months. Finally, he was given a chaplaincy exactly suited to his skills.

A high pressure London business man was taking the last train home and fell asleep. The end of the line was a distant village stop. Turning towards the usual exit beside the car park, he realised that he must have taken the wrong train. There was no one else at the station, no houses nearby. He finally contacted his brother on the telephone many miles away and spent the rest of the night in a dark cold waiting room, becoming more and more frantic. In the morning when his brother arrived, the man was completely disorientated and had to be sedated for several days. The whole event led to a reassessment of his mode of life and to a more peaceful lowered target. He had been greedy and overstepped the bounds of the body's stamina. This is known as the "burn-out syndrome."

A stern, difficult man worked hard physically at mining for gold in Canada, the target of his life being the accumulation of this artificially valued medium of exchange. There were times of boom and times of bust. He was very angry when one of his sons died through what he thought was a doctor's negligence. Both of his other sons were wasters; they died young from heart attacks as did the man himself. At seventeen years of age, his grandson was found to have malignant hypertension. He was the only male descendant of the third generation. The youth rebelled at the idea of hard work and expected money to come easily to him. His adrenal arteries were thought to be narrowed and, therefore, the adrenal hormones were not balanced- perhaps from over-stimulation or the hereditary factor. He came to England for a scheduled renal angioplasty operation. After carrying out the mourning process for his grandfather, however, this was no longer necessary. Perhaps, the dead man had been demanding attention, having realised that his life had been wasted as he had over-worked his heart trying to amass gold.

Abuse of the body's cycles and defences, especially by indulgences of food, alcohol or tobacco or the drive for the acquisition of money as a commodity, can produce hard arteries and high blood pressure. Some area in mind or body then has to give way or "go on strike." Similar stress can be caused to an individual – in some countries police interrogation methods and prisons, for instance, where brain washing techniques continue until the suspect "confesses" to whatever is demanded. In a smaller way, this may happen to young children who have been over-punished; they shut off, cannot cry, become paralysed or cannot breathe. Thus, they attempt to remove themselves from the stress, as in the "paralysed rabbit" syndrome.

Throughout our development, spirit, mind and body co-ordination is forming the defence patterns and self-preservation system for later life. Many children try out these in daring adventure, and also test parental boundaries of rules and punishment. The adult frame calls a halt at excesses and demands periods of withdrawal and rest. It is helpful to learn this withdrawal process early in life by changing often to some form of relaxation which is a counterbalance and opposite to one's work. For example, a doctor seeing patients day after day needs to spend time alone and exercise in the open air.

Spiritual stress can result from outside relationships and from urges within our nature. We can learn from the experience of others but we have to make our own decisions. Feelings of anger, hate, greed, and indulgence produce destruction; those of caring, unselfishness and purity become creative and result in joy and freedom. Thus, we can develop an area of adventure and growth in spirituality.

Tears

Tears have a physiological functional use. They come from the lacrymal gland under the upper lid of the eye and run over the surface of the eye as a watery lubrication, then flow into a tube, the lacrymal duct, which run into the nose. Another more oily secretion from along the edge of the eyelids contributes to the lubrication of these active tissues. Foreign material, such as a smut or an irritating gas, can cause a sudden increase in flooding these areas to wash away the noxious substances. The autonomic nerves have control of this reflex. If, of course, the noxious substances reach the bronchi then they, also, will increase in their mucus production.

The range of emotions causing us to cry varies enormously from individual to individual. The tough unfeeling type of person with a more boorish level of living, or the orphan with a disturbed childhood who, of necessity, steeled himself against showing any mood reaction – these do not cry easily. At the other extreme are the feelings of the very sensitive who can show great empathy with another's troubles, or a mother's longing over her child – even a sentimental memory can produce tears from such people.

Why do we cry in sorrow? Perhaps we are trying to wipe or wash away in tears a situation that we do not want to accept. A child, after a tumble , screams to draw attention, but also cries until the mother's arms enfold it. Then the tears fade away and the child surrenders responsibility to her.

What of tears of joy? The stimulus from pleasurable emotions can produce such an external expression, but not often for public show. "Laugh and the world laughs with you, weep and you weep along" is usually the case.

Perhaps then, adult tears emanate from unsurrendered pain in a relationship that is hurt or broken. Adults seldom cry from physical pain. If we steel ourselves against crying, then other areas seem to have to express the suppression – "the sorrows with their unshed tears make other organs weep." This is the common explanation of psychosomatic bronchitis when there is no infection, or colitis where there is no identifiable organism as in the dysenteries, or choryza, sinusitis and weeping dermatitis. All of these require painstaking analysis, for there will be unmourned areas of the patients' lives, usually unshared and often unrecognised by them. Having ensured that there is no infection, ritual mourning processes should be explored (cf section on Ritual Mourning in Unresolved Grief).

An old lady, a widow of eight years, said she always cried when alone and had done so for eighteen years after her husband's death, but she did not cry in company. She reckoned that she had mourned her husband and had put right all aspects of their relationship. On direct questioning she recorded two miscarriages which she had ignored as being of least importance. She learned to love, name and commit then to God. Her bouts of weeping ceased immediately.

An elderly surgeon working as a missionary saw his family for only one month every five years. He had so steeled his unselfish devotion to others that greetings and good-byes or any deep family conversation was a trigger for tears. Finally, when he had to retire with heart trouble, his family supported and nursed him – he no longer needed to cry.

A forty year-old man found that his constant weeping over several years represented a great-grandfather, an evangelist who had committed suicide. Thinking that this could be part of the possession syndrome and speculating whether to trust this man with his "visiting," he put it to the test and prayed for him at the Eucharist. The great-grandfather's sin proved to be the reason for the uncontrolled weeping and the man was able to view the problem objectively. It was six weeks before he was fully healed.

St. Paul says, "This sadness that is used by God brings a change of heart that leads to salvation – and there is no regret in that! But sadness that is merely human causes death." (2 Corinthians 7.10) We read, also, of Paul's tears of love for the people of Corinth (2 Corinthians 2.4) but even more poignant were the tears of true repentance from the woman who washed Jesus' feet with her own tears and anointed them with ointment (Luke 7.8) These are the tears that are truly needed. "In His favour there is life. Tears may linger at nightfall, but joy comes in the morning" (Psalm 30.5)

PART III
THE ABORTION SITUATION

General Introduction

Abortion is the term used to describe any premature ending of a pregnancy. It may be accidental or deliberate. Nowadays the term "miscarriage" is more often used of an accidental abortion and it is reckoned that ten per cent of all pregnancies end in this way during the first few days or weeks. The actual pregnancy may be wanted or unwanted and this can be a significant factor in the after-effects of the miscarriage. Deliberate abortion may be carried out by law for therapeutic reasons. In Britain, the Act of 1967 permits it if the risk to the health, mental or physical, of the mother or members of her immediate family of the pregnancy continuing is thought to be greater than the risk of abortion. With the risks associated with abortion now much reduced, this clause of the Act is used as an almost universal excuse to terminate an unwanted pregnancy and is rarely questioned. "Back street" abortions still occur as there is often the desire to keep the fact of the pregnancy secret.

The excuse is often made than an embryo of a few weeks is not a human being therefore the abortion is not murder so...

When is the fetus a human being? Theories vary through the ages but it is commonly described as "when ensoulment takes place." The Church once believed that it was when the first breath was taken, but this view is no longer held by the mainstream churches. Various other opinions were: when a mother felt movements and a response to her movements, when the heart began to beat, on implantation into the womb, at conception or when the neurological system was complete at eighteen weeks (therefore, when memories were recorded).

When the comparatively recent use of abreactive "truth drugs," memories within the fetus can be traced and even a recall of the actual place, time and appearance of the parents at conception can be spoken of. Many schools of psychiatry accept this, although there is currently some dispute in America over the possibility of a therapist "implanting" such memories. If, at conception there are only two cells with no differentiated system, what can store these impressions? In Jeremiah 1.5 God says, "Before I formed you in your mother's womb I knew you," and Psalm 139.13, "You knitted me together in my mother's womb." So we conclude that from conception there exists a real being, a soul, eternal, a temporary resident in human form. All life's experiences are stored there. Some we understand clearly from our senses of sight, touch, hearing, smell and taste, but there are other factors (often called the "psi" areas) such as telepathy, love, fear, hate which are all developing. How then can we presume to dispose of or obliterate this being?

From conception this soul is aware, alert, recording attitudes and words, good and bad, and continuing after birth. Thus, the terror of its actual killing – poison, suffocation, flushed away or incinerated – can be remembered. We know this from listening to a patient's complaints, such as, "I'm cold, unloved, hungry, thirsty; I must wander and wander; I can't lie down or sleep; I don't know my name; I'm breathless, frightened; someone is poisoning me; I can never go near water or flush a lavatory; I can smell burning hair; my skin feels as if it is covered with blisters." In hundreds of cases, psychiatrists have found that the symptoms match not only the method of abortion and disposal of the fetus, but also the age group of the lost child, as though it were growing up alongside in another existence, trying to get attention from family members.

A fifty year-old woman was worried about the strange behaviour of her son. She realised that he was acting out other lives and admitted that she had two abortions of illegitimate children on either side of this youth. During the Mass, however, she was aware of a strange distention of her abdomen three times and then remembered that she had also had a miscarriage, so this child was included in the prayers.

A sixty year-old Hindu mother in an Anglican Eucharist service "saw" her two abortions and her nephew who had been electrocuted accidentally dressed in white, dance off joyfully with her angels towards a very bright light which she knew was heaven. At the same time, her schizophrenic daughter who heard voices and was in a mental hospital, was suddenly healed. Follow-up six years later found the daughter absolutely normal.

A forty-six year old atheist went into a church merely to apologise to God for her abortion as she felt the discomfort of guilt. While she prayed, she and some other people present saw a group of children around her. She realised that all of her miscarriages were there in chronological order of their ages and she knew their names. At the exact moment, in another city, her daughter was cured of anorexia nervosa.

When a mother acknowledges the existence of an aborted child and prays in apology to God, naming and committing it to God, then the other's symptoms cease, usually from the first moment of this recognition of the child. For their own sakes, mothers need the discipline of regular attendance at the Eucharist.

For centuries, the practice of abortion was covert, an attempt to cover guilt, but nowadays it is both easier and more sophisticated. A mother never forgets. Statistics quoted in B.J. Ashton's article on *The Psychological Outcome of Induced Abortions* (Obstetrics and Gynaecology, December 1980) showed that guilt was felt by 55 per cent of women. Ten per cent said it had been a mistake, 44 per cent had nervous problems, 36 per cent sleep problems, 31 per cent were worried about the effect on future pregnancies, 16 per cent felt that it had upset their marital relationship. Study of 275 articles on *The Psychiatric Sequels of Abortion* showed that up to 40 per cent of the patients had to attend psychiatrists within a year of their abortion. Among New York's prostitutes, 7 per cent had subsequent psychiatric problems. In an attempt to investigate men responsible for such pregnancies, only 16 per cent had any anxiety. These figures are very disturbing, particularly as they indicate an enormous expenditure of time and money by the professional services involved.

Post-abortion Symptoms

The following list records the presenting symptoms of patients in whose families there were closely related abortions who had not been mourned. There were sent to Dr. William Wilson, Professor of neuro-Psychiatry at Duke University, North Carolina, USA, to augment his article on Anorexia Nervosa for the American medical journal. The records were extracted from a private Consultant Psychiatric practice of two thousand nine hundred family records over a ten-year period.

Physical
Arthritis	5
Gastrointestinal	22
Epileptiform	5

Mental
Alcoholic	7
Anger	31
Anorexia Nervosa	50
Bulimia	5
Manic Depressions	5
Depression	92
Other Neuroses	14
Phobic Anxiety	13
Paranoid	6
Psychopathic	15
Schizoid	59
Sleep Disturbance	16

Haunted
Person	37
Place	5
	___
	387

Therapy (spiritual only)

Eucharist begun by	319
Prayer only	31
Course adopted unknown	37
	——
	387

Results

Quick healing	254
Slow healing	74
Antagonistic to therapy	9
Results not known	44
Died	6
	——
	387

Other interesting factors

126 cases involved close female relatives.

In 30 cases the patients were sons.

In 80 cases other male relatives were involved.

In 35 cases the patient did not attend the consultation but this did not prevent resolution.

2 mothers presented with symptoms related to their daughters' abortions.

In 387 families there were 589 abortions.

422 individuals were involved in counselling.

The overall cure rate was 84%.

Ritual mourning for Unresolved Grief after Abortion
(article by Dr. McAll and Dr. Wilson in the Southern Medical Journal of July 1987)

Abstract: There is a popular consensus in the medical profession and the laity that spontaneous and induced abortions have few psychologic sequelae. A review of the literature reveals that this is not true; the incidence of symptoms ranges from 7% to 41%. Even when symptoms occur, they are said to be negated by the positive emotional responses that occur. We have accumulated clinical experience relating these experiences to the development of severe psychopathology that we believe arises out of unresolved grief. Abortions affect not only the women but also their "significant others." We present case reports that illustrate some of the sequelae, and we offer a method of treatment using spiritual intervention to resolve the grief.

Most recent studies of the psychiatric sequelae of spontaneous and induced abortions convey the idea that psychiatric complications of these events are rare and of little consequence. This impression, however, is false and misleading for a number of reasons. Technically, many abortion studies are poorly designed; they confuse the origin of positive and negative emotional responses. Nor do they accurately reflect the reality of adverse psychologic symptoms, not only in postabortion women, but in family members and significant others.

During the past five years, we have become cognizant of the frequent psychologic sequelae of abortions. Together, we have encountered more than 400 patients with conflict-determined symptoms after spontaneous or induced abortions performed on themselves or on a close relative or friend.

In a review of a sample of studies about women's psychologic responses to elective abortions, we found the same defects cited by Doane and Quigley in their view of the psychiatric aspects of therapeutic abortion: that most studies were designed poorly, did not specify the psychologic symptoms experienced by the patients, were without control groups, and showed indecisiveness and uncritical attitudes by the writers. Most important, the statistical basis for reports of positive responses to the procedure were inadequate, and the majority of studies emphasised the positive effects of abortion and minimized the negative.

In addition, several review articles contain what we interpret to be a significant incidence of negative psychologic disturbances, some reported to persist for as long as a year. This "low" (7% to 41%) incidence of symptoms is usually contrasted with a high incidence of positive feelings that occur after the abortion. As Adler has pointed out, these positive and negative emotional responses have different origins. The positive emotions are a response to external, socially determined conflicts, while the negative emotions are a response to internal, drive-determined conflicts. Even though the negative emotions are often mild to moderate in severity, it seems probable that because of their internal origin, they may persist as repressed conflicts that can surface in later life if the person is stressed by related events.

Completely ignored until recently has been the effect of abortion on family members and other significant persons. Shostak *et al* reported a high incidence of negative emotional responses in men who participated in an abortion with their wives or consorts. A single case of a child's reactions to his mother's abortion call our attention to the possibility of pervasive effects of this procedure on significant others in the environment. Further supporting this contention is the observation that abortion service personnel are highly susceptible to adverse psychologic symptoms.

Because of our awareness of these symptoms, we have evaluated all our patients to determine whether they (or some person significant to them) have had a spontaneous or induced abortion. Wethen ascertained whether the patient or any significant family member had an observable emotional response that was temporally related to the procedure, and whether this had been repressed after the procedure. From these patients we have selected six representative cases that illustrate how the event can result in unresolved grief. All had been refractory to previous treatment, but were successfully treated using an intervention that we have chosen to call "ritual mourning." This intervention is a prayer of relinquishment followed by Holy Communion.

Case reports

Case 1. A cachectic-appearing twenty-two year-old woman was admitted to the hospital with what was presumed to be anorexia nervosa. She weighed 90 lb, though her ideal weight was 114 lb. She told us that during her childhood and adolescence she did not have a weight problem, but gained 20 lb when she went to college. After much effort she stabilised her weight at 130 lb. which she maintained until the middle of her second year, when she accompanied her closest friend while she had an abortion. Because her friend was unable to act in her plight, the patient made all the arrangements. After returning to the dormitory, she was horrified by what she had done, while her friend seemed unconcerned, a response that upset her even more. Within a few days she began to diet rigidly and to exercise excessively. She persisted in this regimen until she lost not only her excess weight, but another 24 lb. In time she graduated from college and married. Her mother-in-law, upset by the patient's appearance, and disgusted by her strange eating habits, convinced the patient's husband that she needed medical help. Reluctantly, he coerced her into consulting her family physician who referred her for hospital treatment.

The patient did not immediately tell us that her eating problem was temporally related to her friend's abortion. It was only after a detailed exploration of the history of her illness that we learned of the abortion and its emotional consequences. Because the patient had a strong religious faith we suggested that she ritually mourn the aborted fetus. As such a service was within her religious tradition, she readily agreed. After the service she began to eat normally, and two months later weighed 114 lb. After her discharge she lost some weight, but quickly regained it when outpatient psychotherapy was instructed.

Case 2. Rejection as a Bible study leader appeared to have precipitated a severe depression in a forty-seven year-old housewife. Immediately hospitalised, the patient was successfully treated with medications, but when they were discontinued six months later, she promptly relapsed. Reinstitution of medication resulted in a good remission, but because of conflicts in her religious life she was also treated psychotherapeutically. In the fourth month of therapy, she confessed with great shame that she had had an abortion one year before the onset of illness.

The patient made the decision for an abortion because of her age, the effort she was already expending in caring for her three children (one of whom was dyslexic) and a large house, and many social commitments. Her husband neither discouraged nor encouraged her decision, but did support it. She believed the child would be a boy, and had decided to name him Christopher even before she decided to have the abortion. She felt extremely guilty about the abortion and her failure to grieve over the death of her child. We told her that she could resolve the grief and relieve the guilt by ritually mourning the child's death. She assented to a service during which she experienced marked emotional release. Within a few days all residual symptoms disappeared, and she has required only minimal supportive therapy since that time.

Case 3. A twenty-seven year-old nurse with a three-year history of depression and other psychiatric problems since her teens was the only child of an alcoholic mother and a father who was absent during much of her childhood. She remembered that her mother was pregnant when she was six or seven years old and had miscarried during her fifth month of pregnancy. The patient had eagerly looked forward to having a sister, whom she had named Tammy. For years afterwards the patient played with her deceased sister Tammy and carried on long conversations with her.

At age twelve she began to date, and had here first sexual experience at age fourteen. At the same time, she began to use LSD, "doing three to four hits a day" for the next three years. At age 17 she had a religious experience only a few days before she realised she was pregnant. Because of her newly acquired religious beliefs, she refused to have an abortion and chose to bear the child. After much persuasion by the child's father and her parents, she married during the seventh month of her pregnancy, though she was unsure about the wisdom of doing so. She and her husband continued their education and during the next five years graduated from highschool and a state university. After completing her education she had a miscarriage and two more children before she began her work career. It was shortly after she went to work as an obstetric nurse that she became so depressed that she required hospitalisation.

We observed the following symptoms: (1) rapid shifts of mood from elation to depression, sometimes punctuated with outbursts of anger, periods of garrulity or near mutism; (2) hyperkinesia or grossly retarded activity; and (3) gregariousness or total withdrawal. There were no changes in thought content. Therapeutic blood levels of two antidepressants and/or a phenothiazine did not change her symptoms. Lithium carbonate rapidly stabilised her symptoms, but she remained mildly depressed and withdrawn. Near the end of her hospitalisation she remembered her mother's miscarriage, and that she (the patient) had suffered much grief after it.

We explained to her the necessity of resolving that grief, an insight that she readily accepted. Immediately thereafter she ritually mourned the loss of her sister Tammy and her own miscarried child. A profound emotional release occurred, and within two days all of her residual symptoms had disappeared. She has now been asymptomatic for seven months.

Case 4. For two years, this seven year-old girl had had increasingly frequent atypical epileptic attacks preceded by unpredictable episodes of shouting at her parents, stamping her feet and falling unconscious. She often hurt herself when she fell. A single left temporal epileptic discharge had been seen in five electroencephalograms. Many different drugs had been tried, but none of them had affected the frequency or the severity of the seizures. The family did not admit to any abortions or miscarriages. When the child was examined, the conversation was opened by asking her about the brothers and sisters. She named those that her parents had already listed, but then added the name of one more whom she said was her best friend. When the examiner and her parents corrected her, she shouted, stamped, and pointed her finger at her mother, calling her a murderer who had thrown her sister away. Her mother began to cry, saying, "Look out! She's going to have a fit." Suddenly she turned to her husband and confessed, "It's true! Once when you were ill I found that I was pregnant, and I knew that you could not face it, so I went to a doctor who gave me a very rough examination and I lost the baby."

The physician, with the child sitting in his lap, suggested that they should pray for the lost baby, but the husband demurred. The physician whispered to the girl, "Let's, you and I, pray for the child." She said, "Yes, quick, quick," so they did. The father took his child and left. Four days later the physician received a letter of gratitude from the mother, who said that the child was cured, and that her own "migraine" headaches had disappeared. Three months later the husband requested an appointment because he was having what seemed to be psychosomatic problems. He recently had been hospitalised for hypertension, which had not responded to treatment. When the time came for the appointment, he was accompanied by his personal physician, a medical school professor. In the interview that followed he admitted to great anger about the baby, as well as an unresolved anger toward his mother who had died some years before. After his confession he ritually mourned the death of his mother and baby. His blood pressure returned to normal soon thereafter, and eight years later all three family members remain well.

Case 5. A professional man conducted a long search for therapists on behalf of his daughter – the cause of much gossip, an impediment to the attainment of his goals, and the cause of violent arguments in the family. The twenty-six year-old daughter had been sexually promiscuous with men who were always thirty years older than she. Inquiry into the family history revealed that the girl's mother had become pregnant by another man and had had an abortion several years before she had married the father. The mother's life before her marriage had many parallels to her daughter's. There were no other significant events in the daughter's life to explain her unusual behaviour. Because the daughter was not available, it was decided that the aborted fetus should be ritually mourned by the parents. At the service the mother was able to mourn the loss of the child, to express her love for it, and commit it to God, but during the service the father became aware of the eidetic image of a mature male figure and prayed for him. The daughter's problems soon ceased; she had been asymptomatic for five years.

Case 6. The strange stealing behaviour of a nine year-old boy had led to his receiving much psychotherapy. He stole food only to give it away, never eating even the candy that he stole. He also would neither stay in a room by himself, nor come home from school unless he could hold someone's hand. Knowing that many therapists had failed to heal this child, it seemed desirable to make a more careful inquiry into the family history. The parents stated that the child did not have a known family history because he had been adopted shortly after their own son had been born dead. The body of the deceased child had been disposed of by the hospital and the adopted child had, in the parent's minds, "taken his place."

The boy had many siblings in his adopted family, The birth of the oldest, now a heroin addict, had been preceded by an abortion. Three others were quite normal. A fourth child, whose birth had been preceded by a miscarriage, currently weighed 220 lb at age fourteen. Since the family knew of the physician's treatment approach to problems such as theirs, they readily agreed to a service of ritual mourning for the lost children. Both parents prayed a prayer of relinquishment at a private Requiem Mass conducted by their priest. In the months that followed, the obese son returned to a normal weight, and the strange behaviour of the nine year-old ceased completely.

Rationale for treatment method

Much has been written about the resolution of grief, but only recently has anything appeared in the literature about grief in response to either spontaneous or induced abortions. We have found only two reports that recognised its significance and indicated that treatment was needed. Stack, in his discussion of spontaneous abortion, observed that the following factors give rise to unresolved grief and thus a need for treatment:

(1)   others do not know that the woman is pregnant;
(2)   the woman is embarrassed to mention that she has lost a baby;
(3)   she has frequently not resolved the ambivalence of the early narcissistic stage of pregnancy;
(4)   she has not identified the fetus as a new person but rather considered it part of herself;
(5)   she is not able to identify the lost person as someone else;
(6)   she rarely sees the baby that she has lost, and so can only fantasize about the sex, size, and personality of this person who was never to be;
(7)   there was no funeral;
(8)   there is rarely recognition by the caregivers that a significant event has occurred;
(9)   caregivers, family, and friends encourage denial and intellectualization, and rarely encourage the woman to cry, or talk about her loss, or assume the role of a bereaved person.

(10) the suddenness and unpredictability of an abortion does not allow the woman a period of anticipatory grieving and preparation for the loss;

(11) guilt is a nearly universal feeling experienced by women who have had a miscarriage, and by many who have had an induced abortion; and

(12) in spontaneous abortions a sense of helplessness occurs when the woman is bleeding and neither she nor the physician can do anything about it. We have observed that many women who feel coerced into having induced abortions have unresolved grief for same reasons.

Buckles observed that when grief is found after an induced abortion, it is necessary to bring about its resolution. She believes that women have unfinished business with the "little ghost within," described by Francke, and that the unresolved grief must be worked through. Her formula for accomplishing this, however, is only vaguely described.

The resolution of grief was adequately described by Lindemann in 1944. Because he so clearly and succinctly detailed the process, we take the liberty of quoting him rather than trying to summarise his comments.

> Religious agencies have led in dealing with the bereaved. They have provided comfort by giving the backing of dogma to the patient's continued wish for continued interaction with the deceased, have developed rituals which maintain the patient's interaction with others, and have counteracted the morbid guilt feelings of the patient by "Divine grace" and by "making up" to the deceased at a time of later reunion. While these measures have helped countless mourners, comfort alone does not provide adequate assistance in the patient's grief work. He has to review his relationship with the deceased, and has to become acquainted with the alterations in his own modes of emotional reaction. His fear of insanity, his fear of accepting the surprising changes in his feelings, especially the overflow of hostility, have to be worked through. He has to express his sorrow and sense of loss. He will have to find an acceptable formulation of his future relationship to the deceased. He will have to verbalise his feelings of guilt, and

> he will have to find persons around him who he can use as primers for the acquisition of new patterns of conduct.

Our own observations are that this same understanding is highly productive when dealing with the unresolved grief that women suffer after spontaneous and induced abortions. In Lindemann's view, faith is an asset; we also have found this to be true. We use the concept of faith to initiate and facilitate the resolution of grief in our patients, even when they do not admit to strongly held beliefs.

Treatment

If we ascertain that there have been unmourned losses of aborted or miscarried fetuses, we determine the significance of the relationship with the lost person(s). Next, we ascertain what feelings were experienced at the time of the loss and in subsequent days and weeks; this is done with an empathetic understanding of the patient's pain. When, in time, they experience emotions that they have previously denied or repressed, we then use their faith (or our faith) and try, within its limits, to help them understand the future that they will have with the lost person. To do this, the therapist must have some theologic understanding of the afterlife in order to help the patient formulate a picture of the future relationship. If the therapist lacks this understanding, he can turn to a minister or a chaplain. One cannot assume, however, that all theologically educated persons believe in an afterlife or have a knowledge of it that can give such patients the hope that they require. The person selected must be capable of communicating a hopeful biblical understanding to others.

Once a patient understands the necessity for grieving and the hope that he has for the future, there must be an act of relinquishment of the relationship and the decathexis of the person. We have found that this has greater psychologic significance to the bereaved if it can take place in a ritual that provides a symbol of hope. The Eucharist is firmly anchored by Christ in His redemptive purpose for all of those who live or have died. The Christian church has consistently taught this belief from the beginning, and has included the Eucharist in funeral and memorial services for the dead. In everyday practice, the ritual of the funeral service, even without the Eucharist, is usually sufficient to promote the release of the departed into the care of God. If, however, there has been no funeral, or no intention of release at the funeral, the Eucharistic service, after careful preparation, provides the opportunity for the release of the lost person into the care of a merciful and loving God.

It must be pointed out that the participation of the bereaved, and sometimes of the entire family of the departed, is necessary for successful resolution of the grief. It is desirable , therefore, that the order of service be amended to allow the grieving persons to vocalize their intentions during the prayer of confession. This is best done in a private rather than in a congregational celebration of the Eucharist.

The service brings about the completion of their grief work and the psychologic bonds are broken, usually irrevocably. In almost every instance in which unresolved grief has been etiologic or contributory to the patient's psychopathology, there has been a dramatic and rapid amelioration of symptoms.

Discussion

Whether one accepts the lowest or highest figures for the number of women suffering psychologic sequelae of abortions and miscarriages, there is a significant number of cases of unresolved grief giving rise to clinically significant symptoms that must be dealt with in clinical practice. These cases are quite refractory to standard psychotherapeutic interventions. It cannot be said that the loss of a love object is of no significance psychologically, for to do so would be to deny some of the fundamental teachings of psychiatry. We must, therefore, realistically accept the observation that the loss of as fetus by spontaneous or induced abortion is highly significant to some women, and must be dealt with if the patient is to be restored to mental health.

To date, the full meaning of this loss to the woman, and secondarily, to the entire family, has not been fully explored. There are a few case reports of women who have been found to have symptomatic unresolved grief due to abortions and miscarriages, and there are even fewer reports of fathers, consorts, children, and parents developing symptoms secondary to an abortion. Francke has observed that fathers, consorts, and parents are further corroborated by Shostak's report of the effects of abortion on one thousand men who accompanied their partners to an abortion clinic. Three fourths of these men reported the event as a major trauma, and long after the event felt guilt and sorrow as a sequel.

Shostak et al stated that abortion was one of the major traumas that men have to go through in today's society. There are, to our knowledge, no reports of unrelated people other than abortion service personnel who have had symptoms as a result of being intimately associated with abortions. These observations, along with our combined experience in more than four hundredcases refractory to treatment, document our contention that we cannot ignore the problem and that is must be attended to by mental health professionals.

The use of Christian ritual to bring about the resolution of grief is within the cultural context of the western world, and is acceptable to most persons in our society. We have found that with adequate preparation, a rapid and complete resolution of grief takes place and the patient's symptoms disappear or are reduced in severity. Further psychotherapeutic intervention is necessary in many cases to deal with other conflicts, but we have found that this work is facilitated when the grief has been resolved.

Conclusions

Unresolved grief is a frequent sequel to induced and spontaneous abortion. The occurrence of grief arises out of an inherent installation of the child that begins with the awareness that the woman is pregnant. Installation can occur in husbands, children, and other persons who may be involved in or responsible for the loss of the child. If the loss is not grieved, symptoms can occur as a result of the lack of resolution of the grief. They can occur immediately or years later when some other trauma arouses the repressed grief. The use of ritual mourning, as embodied in a special celebration of the Eucharist, provides almost immediate relief of the grief, and in most instances, the majority of the patient's symptoms. The Eucharist is a useful adjunctive intervention in patients with unresolved grief whose belief system allowed them to participate.

PART IV
OTHER SITUATIONS

Absence

The word "Absence" is usually pronounced in the French form. In neuro-psychiatry it indicates a temporary hiatus in consciousness. The most common form is seen in a child who is being punished, particularly in one who is sensitive, hysterical or the youngest member of the family. These children will stand still, shut their eyes and appear to be deaf – an escape mechanism from the stress of the moment. If the stress is prolonged or excessive and transmarginal that is, beyond that which they can bear, they may vomit – a psychosomatic voiding of something unpleasant – pass urine or faeces or, finally, faint. (The faint is not in the hysterical affection-seeking pattern where the victim ensures a comfortable landing.)

Some children will extend their faint or "petit mal" with a few epileptoid twitches. They can do this by intention or by producing a genuine mild fit. Investigation is necessary, especially asking the parent to map such episodes and note any precursor in order to find a common cause or time factor. If there is a gradual increase in the frequency or intensity of the disturbance, then medical consultation is essential since some tumours begin insidiously. Today, one must be wary, also, of whether someone is taking drugs.

A thirteen-year-old girl developed so-called fits after her father's suicide. Five years later, she was healed after a service where she was able to mourn and forgive her father.

A child of six years had committed extreme acts of violence on-and-off for two years, when it took three or four adults to hold his demonic strength from smashing furniture. It was discovered that his father, a priest, had become involved in the occult. This revelation in itself precipitated a violent fit. Thirty-six hours later, in despair, the priest relented and went to a fellow priest for confessions and a service. The boy was immediately freed and was moved from his special school to an ordinary one.

An illegitimate boy of fourteen years, epileptoid and dyslexic, changed in a few days when given vitamin B3 and an eighteen year-old girl, classified as suffering from narcolepsy, recovered when prescribed mega-vitamins B3 and B6. The parents of four epileptoids were involved in the occult. Three of them were cured when their parents corrected this by confession, but one parent refused to do so.

The difficulty of correct diagnoses in the variations of "absence," "petit mal," epileptoid attacks and epilepsy lies in the fact that the terms are simpley descriptive and an accurate label can be given only in retrospect. Even the electroencephalogram (EEG) can show spike and wave patterns in people who have never had a fit and, at the other extreme, a full activated series of "grand mal" attacks can occur when tracing are repeatedly normal. A full scale "grand mal" attack is one where there is an aura or warning (e.g. blackspot before the eyes) in the few moments beforehand. Some patients learn to recognise this themselves and sit or lie down immediately, but some fall and hurt themselves. They become completely unconscious, lose control of the bladder and occasionally bowels; they sleep after the attack and awaken with no memory of the occurrence. Bladder incontinence is the easiest investigation because in any hysterical imitation or as part of the possession syndrome, the patients will not willingly wet their clothes. Diagnoses can be arrived at by the response to treatment

Accident Propensity

Records from hospital casualty departments show that often the same person presents repeatedly. When a patient is only once the subject, he is usually not the one who caused the accident. There are those with emotionally preoccupied minds, those who are simply clumsy, those who are too self-centered to notice, to look or to think ahead; for instance, the determined jay walker who deliberately crosses the road in traffic because, "It's my road, that car should not be here." Some people will "dare" in order to draw attention- such as the stocky, short, macho type of man, once frequently seen in Texas where he readily wielded a gun – his ancestors took over their area by "shooting it out." The modern counterpart is the man who smashes off the whole neck when a beer bottle will not open. One such, whose mother said, "I wish I were dead," killed her by smashing her head with a radio set.

It is well-established that alcohol in low concentrations accelerates deterioration of sensory thresholds and causes a slowing of basic responses, while more complex learned skills are totally lost. To drink and then to drive, therefore, is dangerous and results in many accidents. Those who do so are extroverts, careless, aggressive, anti-authority, easily distracted and moody with marked fluctuations similar to the pattern of a criminal's life style. Such understanding is interesting, but does not necessarily help.

The great-grandfather of a thirty-two year-old man had been convicted as a criminal in London and deported for stealing a loaf of bread. The descendant had wide sloping shoulders, was overweight and swaggered about, expressing his resentment, anger and antagonism in the way that he drove. He had wrecked over a hundred cars and throughout his life caused many accidents both within and outside his home, although he himself was seldom hurt. Despite extensive social and psychological work, the situation was not resolved. The question arose, also, of the reaction and feelings of the great-grandfather's family who had been stranded in London, so it was suggested that, with existing family members, the man should attend and verbalise a confessional and committal for all their ancestors. His reaction was immediate and positive. The result was great peace for himself, his wife and parents and a new acceptance by his neighbours.

An alcoholic man had two grandparents who were killed in accidents and, of their children, the first was born dead, one died on the road and three others through accidents. In the alcoholic's generation, of the three grandchildren, two died in air disasters and the other in a road crash.

Fifteen cases of people who had multiple accidents were studied. All but one person changed their attitudes when the pattern of the possession syndrome was faced and the one who refused to confront the real problems spiritually is now in a special locked mental hospital. Among the others there had been nine murders, four abortions and two unaccounted for family members. There were four diabetics in one family.

Victims with accident-prone natures require analysis and, perhaps, behaviour therapy in order to help them to "see" themselves objectively. Uncovering the family history of past generations and finding where and when the continual "accidents" first appeared is an approach that can deal with present-day situations and bring solutions. This involves time, patience and faith and a fundamental change in the sufferer's attitude. The way out for all the successful patients included healing of their family trees.

Agoraphobia and Claustrophobia

Agoraphobia, a fear of open spaces, and claustrophobia, a fear of being in an enclosed space, are useful terms describing symptoms, but both doctors and patients too readily accept them without investigating their origin. Nature provided these fears as a safety valve, especially important in the days of cavemen. Usually, in childhood we are able to push through to confidence and freedom. If the fears extend into adulthood, then a deep analysis is necessary and time must be spent exploring the earlier life, its traumatic incidents and life-threatening situations, disasters in the environment, even parents' memories of events when the patient was a fetus.

Many phobias began when a child was locked in a cupboard for punishment or by accident or, conversely, sent out of the house. A newborn infant used to be wrapped up immediately and laid apart in soundless isolation. Until then, the baby had been accustomed to its mother's warmth and living against her aorta with the ceaseless thumping heartbeat; suddenly it was deprived of this. Today, the trend is reversed and a mother may hold her baby from the moment of its birth. (See chapter on Bonding in Part VI).

In the exploration and release of the subconscious into the conscious, verbalizing is a way of sorting and most frequently a resolution in itself. Some patients need to act out the situation. One method is to accompany them into a small, dark room and lie in silence without touching them; this gives them great confidence. Others can be blindfolded and led to a convenient field or park. There, without being spoken to or touched, and walking for gradually lengthening distances, the patient will build up his confidence, developing his senses of hearing, balance, feeling with the feet, awareness of the wind or an echo. There are those who are also resentful and they need to learn about forgiveness as an active part of their cure.

A married woman in her mid-forties could never walk along a road unless a fence or wall bounded both sides. She had been classified as schizophrenic. When her mother was pregnant, she had been driven by car to the edge of a cliff by a very angry husband. Parental apology released the patient.

A woman could not bear the sound of dripping water at night. An ancestor had disappeared during the Spanish Inquisition and it was suggested that he had died in a subterranean dungeon by water torture. The prayers said in the Eucharist for him, together with the woman's mourning ritual, released her.

Fourteen agoraphobic patients, whose sibling had been aborted in traumatic situations, were cured when they recognised their siblings as real entities to be loved, named and given to God.

These conditions can be resolved by analysis, attentive listening, verbal acting out, empathy and an entering into whatever trauma caused it. The development of the spiritual person is an ongoing voluntary discipline – for instance, with morning quiet time and church fellowship where forgiveness and apology are recognized stages.

The "coffin ships" of the 1900s were the convict ships deporting so called criminals from Britain and Ireland. Many because of pressure of numbers were thrown overboard in the Bay of Biscay and their families, of course, never heard of them again. To presume this for the need of mourning has been successful. Early immigrant ships to the Americas, especially from the Scottish clearances, lost quite one third of the travellers on the journeys, this is a common factor in drawing the family trees in the States.

Alcohol and Addiction

Most extracts, medicines and tinctures have been dissolved in alcohol in order to concentrate them, so everyone absorbs some alcohol in their lives. It is the abuse of alcohol that causes problems. Humans enjoy the stimulus of the ready sugars that the body can assimilate quickly through taking alcohol, but the brain is affected and loses its controls. This, of course, makes the person feel free from any immediate worry but, in fact, it is a blotting out or dulling of the most recently acquired skills and learning, so that he or she loses insight and reverts to more primitive behaviour. Finally, a person becomes unable to weigh up any moral standards, and so may steal, rape or murder at that moment. Regrets come after the hangover has passed; the person cannot believe that he or she was capable of such acts.

A man aged forty years had been in prison several times. On pay days, when he was working, he would buy cigarettes and join his friends in a pub; this led to drunkenness and, even, rape and a return to prison. He made a straight moral decision to be honest with his wife, take his pay packet home to her and never to smoke again. Together they began a morning prayer pattern – an area of life neither they nor their families had ever known- became extremely happy, and helped many other people;

In his mid-fifties, a man who drank more than fifteen pints of beer a day had a great sense of guilt about a secret abortion he had caused. This was put right in the Eucharistic setting when he had a vision of a teenage girl saying to him, "I thirst." His addiction had been her possessing spirit calling out to him for attention. He stopped his indulgence immediately. Of thirty-three people thus treated, twenty had been cured.

A thirty-three year-old man, in hospital as an alcoholic, nursed a deep resentment against his father and brother who had both died as alcoholics, having taught him the same way of life. He went to Mass to apologize for his resentment and their sins and to commit them to God. When he awakened next morning, he was completely healed.

A woman of thirty-nine years continuously heard her dead father's voice which could be blotted out only with alcohol. Her fiancé had died a hero at sea. Both of these men needed the full ritual mourning process of the church which freed the woman from her dependency on drugs and alcohol because those who wander in limbo thirst and cannot find the cup of forgiveness. The living must do this for them.

The spouse of an alcoholic becomes the co-dependent. He or she develops a hard shell, afraid of stepping on "eggs" and teaching the children the same evasive tactics. Finally, the defence systems may break down. A lady, after living with her alcoholic husband for thirty-six years, developed cancer of the lymphatic glands and died within two months. Some of their children then revolted against their father and abandoned him, entering other styles of stable relationships. One married a father figure who acted in exactly the same way. She escaped into alcoholism also, until disaster threatened their lives and they turned to Christ.

A thief who raids houses has resisted all therapy for twenty years, whether Alcoholics Anonymous, divine healing or innumerable prison sentences. After a burglary he would sit delicately sipping pink gin, with jewelled fingers and manicured nails, until picked up in the equivalent of a gutter. He was an orphan, but refused to pray for his aborted siblings.

The fellowship of Alcoholic Anonymous removed the loneliness that alcoholics experience. There is a separate fellowship, Al-Anon, which provides support and help for the spouses of alcoholics in their friendships and home problems.

Medical treatment by aversion therapy (including vomiting when the patient sees or smells alcohol) has only a temporary effect. Drugs such as antabuse which provide unpleasant side effects if taken before drinking alcohol can break the dependency cycle temporarily. Firstly, however, an alcoholic must be convinced that he is an addict and must not drink any alcohol again or the whole chemical dependence will be re-established immediately.

In the mid-1980's, especially in America, when morphine derivatives were first available in medicine, drug addiction spread from the wealthiest to the poorest in society. Today, drugs of addiction on the market are very expensive and the law is involved in the battle against their use. As the availability varies, so the pattern of consumption changes.

Anaesthesia

General anaesthesia, making a patient unconscious during an operation, has moved a long way from the days of Simpson with his bottle of chloroform dripped on to a gauze mask. It has now become a sophisticated science with a wide variety of drugs at its disposal. Unconsciousness is induced far more rapidly and recovery is also quicker. However, during the period of unconsciousness and particularly at the point of losing consciousness and regaining it, the patient is, apparently, vulnerable to the atmosphere surrounding him or her and to what he or she might be listening to at those moments. For instance, a formerly well-balanced woman became a very disturbed patient post-operatively – the anaesthetist had sung a pornographic song as she lost consciousness.

In a mental hospital, following the stress caused to the patients by extraneous chatter at such time, the matron and doctor decided that carefully prepared phrases should be spoken as every anaesthetic was being given. This was the positive answer to the patient's negative thinking and a marked speed in recovery was observed. Depressives who had difficult relationships or a sense of guilt were told repeatedly that, "God gave us forgiveness and peace" and they heard the same words from the nurse sitting beside them as they wakened. No other chatter was permitted.

Some three hundred patients were treated in this way and the staff felt that the method had proved its worth both in follow-up care on the same lines and in the reduction of readmissions.

A sixty year-old women who, after appendectomy at the age of sixteen was classified as schizophrenic, felt she was controlled by "voices" which dominated her life. She called them "three beasties." After a New Testament exorcism she was completely freed, but had to be re-educated in the simplest disciplines of running a house.

Six years earlier, a twenty-four year-old labelled a schizophrenic, underwent a tonsillectomy operation. Her more serious attacks occurred on the anniversary of the suicide of her grandmother for whom a Mass was held, after this she lost her schizoid symptoms.

A woman of forty years, whose mother had died during an operation for removal of the gall bladder, developed fears, depression and pain. All X-rays showed no abnormalities, so it was suggested that she might be suffering from the possession syndrome- that is, her mother had died unprepared for eternity and was very resentful for the inept surgery. The woman's symptoms cleared up when, with her co-operation, the Mass of the Resurrection was celebrated.

A man in his late twenties had become a depressive after electric shock treatment under anaesthesia. He kept repeating, "I can't forgive myself, I've committed the unforgivable sin." It was realized that this attitude came from a totally earthbound state of mind and spirit. To accept being an independent spiritual entity, to look at sin objectively and deal with it by moral decision and God's gift of forgiveness cuts through the cycle of self-accusation, and adds a new dimension to life. When he accepted forgiveness, the man entered a religious order and was very content.

A seventy-eight year-old woman wakened after an operation completely disorientated. For more than a week no member of her family could recall her from this state but, finally, her own physician came and prayed with her. She recognised him and said, "Now I know who I am."

Fear frequently accompanies a patient's contemplation of anaesthesia, for he is surrendering himself to the surgeon.

Anaesthetists should develop a real sense of care and an awareness that they are not dealing with a purely physical situation which has material boundaries.

Arsonism

Sitting beside a fire, the centre of warmth, gives a very primitive sense of security with its connotations of the family circle, cooking food and heating water. Early man dropped hot stones into hollowed logs containing water to do this. He also found it a very satisfactory defence against wild animals, who always fear fire. Fire is both awe-inspiring and beautiful, but can bring about the complete destruction of whatever is being opposed. Hence, its appeal to the arsonist, who then has the illusion of power. Children may light fires for the same reason and for the excitement of having achieved such an effect with just a match. For some, or course, this becomes an obsession.

A thirty-eight year-old man, paranoid and given to interference on other people's lives, had a very low opinion of himself. He first started fires simply for the "adrenalin high" of hearing and seeing the fire engine. Then he discovered that he could become a reserve fireman but, being on reserve, he was not called out to the first fire, so he created a second one to which he would be called. This ruse lasted for eighteen months. After being shown the prophecy concerning the Christ (Isaiah 40), with a complete *volte face* he became a Christian and, by his own decision, a Quaker, as he was drawn to the quietness of their worship.

A woman in her forties had been fascinated by fire throughout her life. Within her family tree an ancestor was found who, after praying to God for a friend's healing, had been burned as a witch so that she had only the church's curse and no funeral service. Prayers commending the dead woman to God released the living women from her fear of fire.

Fire has been employed for divination, sacrifices, destruction and defence from BC 2000. In the Middle Ages, it was a tool of punishment and today it is often a means of controlling a materialistic world. Man has accepted his ability to make a fire as his due, like the availability of air and water – not as the great gift that it is – and has exploited it, bringing fear and destruction both to people and the environment. It should be used as a symbol of Divine presence and power, as a purifier and as an instrument of Divine judgment. Each wrong act needs repentance and forgiveness, so that the living are freed from the fears of the past.

In Queensland, most houses are built well above the ground and some on stilts. There was a woman of sixty who lived as a tramp and slept commonly under police stations. She had had many periods in prison, for she frequently made bonfires of newspapers there at night. Also, as a petty thief, she shoplifted items that were no use to her and got to the police with the loot, as much as to say, "Look at me!"

Then it was found that she was the granddaughter of the notorious gangster Dwyer, who, in his attacks on towns or villages, used to begin by setting fire to police stations. He was finally shot without ceremony. This lady came to a Eucharist and read out a prepared prayer of apology and committal of the ancestor. She was transformed and within twenty-four hours was able to witness this to a large gathering of people.

Astrology

According to Sir James Jeans (former Professor of Astronomy at Cambridge University), no stars or planets had or could have any possible effects on humans. It is a nonsense to believe otherwise and, as such, can be the basis of vast patterns of superstition. Early humans, terrified by eclipses or by the tail of a comet found them easier to account for by blaming something "outside." One may wonder why modern man should turn to such a device when the right road has been opened for him, infinitely more rewarding and eternal. Astrologers, soothsayers and fortune tellers in the Far East were also the letter writers and readers, peddling their skills in markets and on the streets. Having studied human nature carefully, they could make accurate observations about their clients

Superstitions devised around the positions of the stars are based upon the same charts that were used over a thousand years ago. If the "practitioners" studied the twentieth century night sky, they would see that none of these patterns now exist, for stars move in relation to one another.

Behaviour Disorders

Neglect, whether as a fetus or in childhood, is often a common denominator in behaviour disorders. The deprivation of love is not a lack of material security. A child may collapse into diseases such as tuberculosis or avitaminosis, or escape into a unresponsive dyslectic or autistic situation. Conversely, some fight back and become part of the youth gangs, muggings and the drug scene, prey to the crowd psychology of stadium fans.

To establish their own esteem they may develop terrorist tactics, their hostility spilling into bandit-like situations. Within the home this is evinced in the battered child syndrome where at any cost the adult will establish his supremacy. In the hijacking phenomena there is the "power behind the gun" where the hostage is always made to feel at fault, whatever the excuse. Beating, isolation, questioning, threats and torture enhance the feeling of power achievement and raises the terrorist's self-importance, especially when the world is watching.

There are, also, trained subversive elements, not just dealing with an individual's worth but part of a larger plan to undermine society which uses force, drugs, pornography, witchcraft or, sometimes, even rock music. For financial gain participants or audiences are brainwashed into lowered standards of behaviour. When the manipulators' work is done, they find that they, themselves, are disposable. Many have committed suicide.

Some years ago in communist countries, so-called "Quakers" returned home, following drug-induced instructions and caused havoc in the higher echelons of their movement. They were then obliterated before they regained their own controls. This has been observed, also, in the vacillation of some pseudo "defectors" who have over-stayed the drug's limitations.

Behaviour disorders are often regarded as signs of an identity crisis in contemporary human beings. This can be observed in some of the emergent new nations where people may not have long-standing secure roots and family traditions. Similarly, they may be more easily precipitated in a new city development of isolated flat dwellers, or in a small family or single parent unit. This contrasts with the large Chinese families where all generations lived together, or the large old family farm settlement of the country-side of Europe and the United States. An only child subject to parental neglect or where both parents go out to work often seeks its own identity by drifting uncontrolled, trying out various life-styles and using its school companions as the testing ground. Making their own standards, they find it easiest to be negative, critical and destructive, assuming anger to pick fights, battle with authority, trespass, and explore immorality. Thus, they create "adrenal highs," excitement and temporary adventure for themselves.

The child who is studious, quiet and has insight, does not attract attention and usually comes out on top. He or she develops a better perspective, a spiritual awareness and does not find the need for disruptive behaviour. This is the one who is more likely to regard the Holy Bible as a textbook for life. In schools where there is no religious teaching, the vacuum may be filled by pornographic material and drug experiments. Many popular newspapers and the media concentrate on negative and salacious news, for their readers depend upon bad and provocative incidents for their vicarious satisfaction.

Our failure to act responsibly for one another allows the voices of deceased family members to pierce our consciousness. As abortion, divorce, and amorality increase and the lack of adherence to God's laws for parenthood abound, children in desperation seeking the boundaries of discipline, often indulge in even wilder behaviour far beyond the limits of acceptability.

Prof. Philip Ney of Victoria, Vancouver Island, has many articles on behaviour disorders. In 1993 he said that the majority of these youths had single parents, most of whom had had abortions.

A man of seventy-six had a very disturbed and unpredictable life; he also appeared to be anorexic; it all began at the age of sixteen; after years of hospital admissions it was seen that on his family tree an uncle had disappeared at the age of sixteen. He must by now be presumed dead, so a Requiem was held, immediately, this man that day was transformed and has helped many others since.

A County Council thought they had a perfect answer for all their cases of behaviour disorders and set up a boarding school in a distant other county for 180 boys, at the Council's expense. There developed amongst them initiation ceremonies which were finally found to be extreme homosexual tortures, with some masters and senior boys taking part. Secret investigations revealed these disturbances caused illnesses and crime. Finally, it was handed to the police who uncovered vast stores of pornography, of drugs, of arms and ammunition. Margaret Thatcher was then Education Minister and the whole was brought to her notice. This resulted in expellings, prison sentences and a large number of staff dismissals. Years later the follow-up of some of the boys found that many were criminals, one (well remembered at the investigation time because of his threats) was on a life sentence for murder. Others learnt from it and made strong moral and spiritual decisions.

In Glasgow, a teenager left her mother (a single parent) escaping to the south; the mother, who was also a prostitute and a witch, tried with her coven to follow the girl with their curses. The girl came into an evangelical group who helped cleanse her and protect and train her. She married one of the fellowship and in three years they went back to Glasgow as missionaries to the slums.

Nail biting is frequently a childhood complaint, and usually people grow out of it. To discourage the habit, children's fingers are sometimes painted with bitter quinine. Often the areas may become fungal or infected and require treatment with an appropriate ointment or tablets. When the habit is continued into adulthood, it has been noted that the person may be the middle child of a large family with sibling rivalry. Such children often opt for "dare" situations in the home or at school in order to draw attention to themselves, although they usually keep within parental boundaries for fear of punishment. They are probably conscientious perfectionists, but are frustrated by the achievers around them.

A forty-six year-old nun was always organizing – very competently but with far more zeal than necessary. She was the middle child of seven, most whom were brothers. As a child she had been a great tree climber and led in daring exploits. As a nun she was courageous and achieved much with her organizing ability, but drove herself to the point of brinkmanship. At such times she always chewed her nails "right down to the quick" and wore herself "to the bone." She was able to surrender the spiritual responsibility and claim healing at the Mass.

A medical student had been a nail biter from infancy and all the antibiotics and paints which had been tried in the past were ineffectual. When he qualified ahead of his siblings, his new-found therapeutic skills well compensated him mentally; he no longer felt the necessity to chew his nails, so the habit left him.

Blasphemy

Many patient in their depressive mood swings search their consciences for some thought or behaviour to blame. A common area is the guilt of having blasphemed and thus breaking one of the ten commandments. This, they have been brainwashed to believe, is an unforgivable sin. It may be so, but the reading of their intent lies at the root of the matter. In the New Testament many laws were changed from negative to positive ones, but not the laws against blasphemy and necromancy.

A seventy-two year-old widow uttered a string of blasphemies whenever she knelt in church to pray and had to leave each time. She revealed that her parents had quarreled continuously and sworn at each other. When she was able to apologize for their behaviour at the Eucharist, she herself was freed.

A man in his mid-twenties was constantly swearing and blaspheming. His father had died the previous year and his mother moved away to work during the week. He and his brothers had been brought up without boundaries. Drugs, sex, and the occult occupied him most of the time, but he went to church on Sundays when his mother came home. At school there had been frequent classroom battles because he was ambidextrous and he was often punished for this. His best friend had been killed in a car accident, then his brother had a cerebral haemorrhage after an accident, became an epileptic and died three years later.

At this point the patient began hearing voices, smashed up his mother's home, threatened her with a knife, and hit young children. He would cry, apologize and then do it all again, saying that his dead brother was directing him. He became the exact opposite of the very artistic youth that he had been years before. He had to be committed to a mental hospital where his brother and sister were taught to listen and show empathy. His mother was involved in this process of cure, for she had made many wrong decisions for which she was able to apologize. She then initiated exorcism using the Lord's Prayer and an on-going pattern of the Mass of the Resurrection for those who had died with unfinished business. It was revealed that there had been an abortion, a miscarriage, a born dead uncommitted baby and a murder in the previous generation. Physical and mental frustration in the son had been evident, but he was healed.

In nine cases of people who sought help over blasphemous guilt, all were released through prayer patterns and discipline. An escape mechanism from this guilt is expressed by a reversal of intention in the form of a mirror image from the left to the right half of the brain where anything good had to be made bad by swearing, blasphemy, hitting out, threatening those most loved and respected. It is as though the devil takes over – a personalized antithesis to goodness, light, joy, and love. An experimental approach for such patients would be to make them repeat regularly the Lord's Prayer in which there are many intentions that can develop in the mind. The last line, "Deliver us from the evil one," can be used as an exorcism.

Burial sites

In the exploration of disturbed patients one needs ultimately to determine when and where their symptoms began, and were there any other sufferers.

For example, in Malta when schizoid patterns appeared in several instances, it was found that the home had been built beside a burial site. Because of the scarcity of soft land on this island, every ten years cemeteries are prepared for re-use and with all the many wars over its territory there are some very crowded spots.

There are some catacombs and in one recently seventeen children disappeared on a school exploratory party. In Sicily in a village near Palmero, within a Catholic Charismatic group, some youth claimed to be visited by voices. Back in the south of England an Italian said, "Oh, I know the place, it is also the entrance to the Catacombs, a terrible place for all the mummified bodies are hung up on the walls and there is a competitive state as to who spends most on the preservations; one child's body is still so perfect and in a glass case that they think she is actually still alive after two hundred years; I think she needs a committal service," Here in England this service is carried out without telling the Sicillians. Later, we heard that at that time the voices ceased.

In a vicarage in England there was a bedroom that never was used; it was regarded as unpleasant and always had hundreds of flies with a daily pile of dead ones on the window sill. It had a window looking down into a graveyard. The next question was, there must be some restless soul with unfinished business; so they held a service for the unknown person and it was honoured and all was cleared and no more flies came into the room.

At Wounded Knee in South Dakota is the mass grave of three hundred fifty Red Indians, shot by the American Cavalry in 1890. There is a permanent guard of natives, for they do not want anyone to go and give them a proper funeral service, lest the dead should cease to haunt the white settlers.

Other stories of this nature are in the book *Healing the Haunted.*

Cousin marriages

Genetic factors in disease constitute a vast study but, in itself, are not the subject of this book. In Britain, however, the proportion of first cousin marriages is one in two hundred and research has shown that they are accompanied by a higher incidence of perinatal deaths, congenital abnormalities and mental retardation, particularly if there is a history of disorder. Deaf mutes, blindness and cystic fibrosis of the kidneys are the most common disabilities.

The Family Trees of twelve families consulted revealed two perinatal deaths, nine diabetics, five suicides, three schizophrenics, six mental hospital depressives, three people with cystic fibrosis, two with club feet and three who were blind. In the next two generations of one family, nine died in accidents leaving only one descendant. In another family, there were three succeeding generations of cousin marriages, all of whom were diabetics.

Each family was advised to adopt the Eucharistic approach and, in a follow-up, it was found that ten families had continued with this. The three cystic fibrosis cases had died welcoming heaven; the three blind were living very creative lives; six of the diabetics were under better control than before and two of the schizophrenics were free from all medicines. Two of the diabetic cousins had a vision during the Eucharist of a DNA spiral reordering itself, extending upwards and downwards through all their generations. (The nucleus of every cell contains chromosomes in which are genes composed of deoxyribonucleic acid – DNA. This consists of two polynucleotide chains; it is here that genetic information is stored. The two chains are twisted together to form a double helix and there is specific pairing between the two chains. When nuclear division occurs, it is postulated that the two strands of the DNA molecule separate and, because of the specific pairing, each chain can then build its complement. In this way, when a cell divides, genetic information is conserved and transmitted to each daughter cell).

In one family with four disturbed people- two depressive and two schizophrenics – one suicide resulted, but one member became a priest, one a schoolmaster and one a nurse. These three overcame their disabilities through Divine Grace.

Criminality

Is heredity or environment to blame for the emergence of the criminal in society? Statistics prove little – each case must be considered separately. Disraeli said, "There are lies, damned lies and statistics." An inborn wish for "more" pervades the whole animal world, including humans; goods are usually willingly shared with offspring or stored against time and season – harvesting is a very natural cycle. Self-preservation and defense forced humans to extend and strengthen their boundaries. Strength became of paramount importance, and in due course, therefore, so did arms and wealth.

Different cultures through the ages had to make laws for peoples' survival. Many were public health laws. Polygamy was essential is some lands because of high infant mortality and the short life of the average adult. Rules on sexual licence amount the South Sea islanders varied with their initiation ceremonies at puberty. Nowadays, for instance, the practices of Maoris of one particular community differ from those of another- each has its own cohesion. Throughout the civilised world, laws must be revised to take in up-to-date situations. Nakedness and homosexuality are normal in some South Seas islands until marriage after which monogamy is strictly observed. Unfaithfulness and adultery in some Arab countries are still punishable by death.

In Britain, the beginning of this century often saw a Salvation Army representative at law courts, looking for the needy and the criminal, like a police court missionary. From this, the Probation service developed – now staffed by highly trained people. The night watchman became the "Peeler" of Sir Robert Peel's inspiration and prayer. He fought for them for fifteen years and they became the basis for our present police force. There is still a need, however, for "special hospitals" where the criminally insane are kept. The inmates are in a hopeless state, rarely getting out; if they do leave, no one trusts them. The majority return to "hospital" within three months. Those who remain in society only do so by virtue of a transformed spiritual relationship with God; the efforts of such as the Matthew Trust helps to bring about their rehabilitation.

Group therapy was first designed and carried through at the Henderson Hospital at Banstead, although other institutions now use the same approach. A social worker is present at the daily sessions where not more than twelve patients learn from free speech and openness, guided by therapists, and come to understand that they are not alone since others face the same battles with life. Every session ends on the positive alternative, encouraging them to stop and think, consider the other person and observe the results. The patients are made to live together during the day so that, if anyone steals from another, there is nowhere to hide and he sees the immediate effect of his action. To play games, cook, eat and work together is enforced all day. The therapist must be a person with a mission, for this is time-consuming and there must be great empathy between him and the patients. The evening is the vital time inasmuch that almost a brain-washing technique gives them material to ponder through the night. They are persuaded to adopt a maturing process since often they are very immature in their perception of values. (They can be held compulsorily by Order 26 of the Mental Health Act and if they remain criminals after this treatment, then the ordinary courts and prisons will contain them).

Today, many people accept that much of what is known as "heredity" comes from the lessons learned by the fetus before birth – for instance, a threat to life, rejection, family quarrels, sexual abuse, smoking, alcohol and other drugs that inhibit development. After birth the same conditions may prevail, causing immaturity, hand to mouth living, greed and violence and, later, as the person grows and gains in intelligence, so more skilled ways are used in planning crime, especially as a result of group thinking.

Thousands of children enjoy the excitement of scrumping apples or showing off a "dare;" to their friends. The rush of adrenalin makes them tingle as they discover an unknown ability to climb a high wall or tree. This is referred to as "adrenalin high" and children within their peer group can work themselves up to such a state. Those who have caring, "listening families" where parents give proper time to their children, seldom reach the courts. If they do, it only happens once, for the whole family takes on the responsibility and blame. The influence of television is a faster way of learning both good and evil.

From Old Testament times, God-fearing cultures have identified crime as evil, satanic and fit for punishment, wrongdoers being imprisoned or killed for any deviation from the norm. Forgiveness was sought, but the true way was not opened up until the coming of Christ.

Stealing and killing were considered criminal, and even into the nineteenth century in England a lord of the manor had the right to hang anyone who stole from his land. Bishop Mortimer of Exeter, in the 1960s had twelve gibbets removed from the walls of the archway between his palace and the cathedral. A different rule applied in China. If one's servant stole from a neighbour for your benefit, as master you were supposed to congratulate him.

Behaviour and aversion therapy are basically crude aspects of psychiatry, involving the use of electric shocks and disgust to train the mind into breaking an undesirable cycle. Such a correction may last – it is preferable, obviously, to locking a person in prison – but it does not put anything in its place. Socially useful, compulsory labour is beneficial for those with lower IQ, especially when appreciation and attention are given. Such people gain from team work and the visual construction of end results.

For some, however, crime for self-gain is not the objective. There is often a strange lack of understandable motive – e.g. stealing useless objects or other-sex clothes, hoarding, hiding or a magpie attachment (this applies to both adults and children). Many hope for attention; they want to be found out. They are isolated, feel unloved, unrecognized, insignificant, the middle member of a large family, perhaps small and weakly, introverted, an orphan or, frequently, illegitimate. Analysis confirms these findings.

Throughout life, a criminal is running away from reality. He is most afraid of death and has a low pain threshold. Death to him is like a serpent's sting; he thinks he can avoid it by hitting out first, collecting defense mechanisms or escaping into the numbness of alcohol. Sin is a real factor – if there were no laws there would be no sin and no criminality. The animal world is not aware of sin unless, by a process of reward and punishment for instance, a dog has been trained and so carries conditioned reflexes. The dog, nevertheless, has no perception of death and it cannot make decisions for future behaviour.

Psychiatrists with a materialistic approach miss the whole point of life in that they teach the absence of "free will." Like them, Eysenck (Professor of Psychology in London, who can from Germany) thinks that man is the product of heredity and environment and conditioned reflexes; any area that is unmeasurable or cannot be reckoned statistically, does not exist. The criminal lives in sin within Eysenck's world and is, in fact, spiritually dead but, as St. Paul observes, all may come into real life by making the right choice while here on earth. Of forty-two such people dealt with in and out of prison, some refused any help and continued their pattern of destruction, but three-quarters were healed and came to understand and adopt a new discipline of life.

A fourteen year-old youth was trained as a look-out for a gang of smash-and-grab raiders. Twenty-four years later, he was their trusted driver and for several months each year they toured the world, spending the proceeds of their crimes. The agreed pattern of the gang was that anyone caught would never be contacted again by the others. Eventually, the man was convicted, on his own, of the theft of a watercolour painting and sentenced to three years imprisonment. He was friendless. The man from whom he had stolen, however, visited him regularly in prison and, on the thief's release took him into his own home. Such amazing trust won him over and gradually the old life lost its attractions. Relying on a belief in God, he was able to forgive his unknown parents. He found a simple, steady job, married and now has a child. He is no longer a criminal.

Curses

The earthbound, uncommitted dead can be vulnerable to Satan and his minions, with the angels of God's kingdom and Satan's fighting over them. In the Eucharist we show Satan's defeat not only to ourselves, but also to the lost dead and the principalities and powers, thereby delivering souls from bondage and setting them free to continue their journey towards God's kingdom. We offer them an opportunity at this time and show them that Christ made the way to Heaven open by His Ascension (the first born from the dead). Previously, man waited "in the bosom of Abraham." They can still choose not to go, however; some need more teaching and prayer than others. If the living, by witchcraft or with curses, cut off the light, then the absence of God's light is real darkness and Satan can then enter, with fear, loneliness, isolation, depression and misery. This is what the lost souls then "moan" through the haunted living member of their family or, if none is available, then through anyone who is unprotected.

The most evil curse or swear in the Chinese culture is "Ts' ao ni-di ma ma" which means "curse your mother," The Chinese are far more aware of their ancestors than other cultures and honour them greatly. Before Christ there was no other intermediary between themselves and God, therefore, to curse an enemy's ancestors was to bring evil upon him from which he had no protection. This curse is still used in other cultures where, regrettably, people are less aware of the importance of ancestors. In American and Britain it comes out as "You son of a bitch" or, in Cockney parlance, "Cowson."

As we pray and release folk we should consciously claim God's armour for them as defined in Ephesians 6. Primitive people, who do not yet understand, may need further explanations concerning these words. The apostle reminds us of the commandment "Honour your father and your mother, that it may be well with you and that you may live long upon the earth." This admonishment is followed by the exhortation to be strong in the Lord and in His power by putting on the whole armour of God so that we can stand against the devil's schemes. The Lord's statement of protection, "My grace is sufficient for you" is like a canopy, a complete covering within which we are safe.

A Nigerian student in England was terrified when he was about to sit his examinations. He declared this was because of a curse put upon him by his uncle when he had obtained a scholarship and his cousin had not. The student was released from fear when he went to a Eucharist service and there claimed protection.

An American mother, three daughters and two sons were all involved in criminal activity. Their family tree revealed that an ancestor, who had been one of the witches of Salem burned at the stake, had died cursing her family. At successive Masses new life began in the family.

There is, then, a new concept of the mechanism of spells, curses and witchcraft-deliberate evil. This is quite apart from brainwashing, auto suggestion, mass crowd psychology or hypnosis, all of which can be used for evil. Those who stay within the protection of God, whether living or dead, cannot be cursed; those who neglect to do so are vulnerable.

Death

One of the mysteries of nature is the process of death which should be far less traumatic than birth with all its attendant pressures and the awakening of organ function. The first breath is so crucial, such a struggle- and yet, joy for the mother. It is a creative moment which we have all experienced. On the one hand, there are the efforts to revive a new-born baby with oxygen tent and resuscitation techniques; on the other hand, thousands of babies are being aborted. To observe, under ultrasound, the death throes of the unborn in an abortion operation is paralleled only by the torture chambers of mediaeval times.

Throughout life humans are subject to the fear of death: it is inborn and a quite natural hurdle that we all contemplate. We have always feared the unknown, the darkness – this is part of our self-preservative animal nature. (In pre-historic times, the caveman would throw stones into his cave before entering, to be sure that no bear or wild beast was hiding in it.) In so many minds, death is associated with pain and suffering, and we do not want to anticipate the trauma surrounding it – occasioned by accident, disease or the ravages of war. These are abnormal, unnecessary and not intended by God.

Pain is a message system that tells the mind that there is something wrong. As controllers we can answer, "Right, I know, I will deal with it in time. Just let me finish this job!." Too many therapists have not come to terms with this phenomenon themselves, so are quite unable to give an honest appraisal to their patients which could enable them to face the real issues of life on earth. Sharing with the family all aspects of the situation brings, peace, joy, freedom from pain and the courage to explore eternity. In sixty years of medical practice, I have been with hundreds of terminal cases. Only once has there been an angry reaction from a patient on learning the truth – the man claimed to be an avowed atheist, needed many drugs and died in great anger, although his family were helped spiritually.

To lose all fear of death can be a great shared adventure between doctor and patient. At the end, then the mind filled with peace and joy and often with a flowing radiance, many have sat up, opened their arms and welcomed people aloud, by name, who have been former family members. Others pass quietly and peacefully "in their sleep" as if at the end of evening prayers.

Death should come when we are old and tired, all our work completed, our training here concluded with no left-over or unfinished business. The body's various organ systems should close down slowly, the whole pace of life giving longer time for rest and sleep. Our task is to be ready when our time comes.

Deceptions in Healing Movements

Whenever "healings" occur and people display such events, others take advantage of it for their own profit. In the Eucharistic setting and with the Lord's Prayer this cannot be abused, for it is available only in the Lord's living presence.

Some "healers" use crowd brainwashing techniques, others perform in smaller groups; people are too easily diagnosed and condemned, followed by a sudden pronouncement of freedom from Satan. William Sargent's book *Battle for the Mind* is eighty per cent accurate, but his gross inaccuracy was the criticism of John Wesley. Sargent asserted that Wesley preached damnation and sudden release whereas, in truth, Wesley preached 40,000 times on the love of God and only once on Satan.

On must be wary of public "healing" meetings especially when mediums are employed. There is no examination of the patients and frequently the apparent "healing" is merely a shifting of symptoms so that another area of the body is more disturbed afterwards. Although at the time the "lame walk," in public, within a few days they may be dead from a totally different diagnosis. This has been a frequent deception.

Harry Edwards performed in public with seemingly miraculous releases on the stage. A small British Medical Association committee, following up these cures, found that actually there had been only a shift of symptoms – for example, a woman's backache disappeared, but she died of cancer of the breast, and a youth in a wheelchair walked free, but died within a week of heart failure.

Staff working in a mental hospital visited some so-called healers whose patients were landing on their doorstep. One of these "healers" advertised herself in the telephone directory as a psychologist. We discovered that she was a crystal gazer, an arthritic, who did not know the Lord's Prayer. She asked for help for herself but, on our second visit, she refused to admit us. The local vicar came to assist. Another "healer" was a village plumber, in trouble with the police, who had been abusing female clients. One used the pendulum, a colleague used the black box – for which they both charged fees. At a home of "healing" in Northern Ireland they hit people on their heads with a large Bible, shouting "out, out." This was supposed to be exorcism.

The inventor of radionics, De La Warr, showed me the interior of a black box and laughingly spoke of the gullible non-scientific people who fell for the "cure." For a black box to send out frequencies for healing is quite impossible but, by suggestion, those who want to be influenced can think themselves into any situation. He made up a list of imaginary illnesses – for instance, "the liver is not in tune with the spleen." Genuine symptoms change, however, and the body exhibits other outlets for the basic problem which then is called by the name of a different illness. Psychosomatic expressions abound in target areas, known as "organ language."

A fifty-two year-old woman went to a "healing service" where people handled her and decided that she was possessed by a spirit of fear. They spent thirty-five minutes "exorcising" this but, afterwards, she really was full of overwhelming fear. She had never known fear throughout her adult life, so she came to psychiatry for help. Release was achieved through prayer, not exorcism. It is perfect love that casts out fear. We have found three similar cases resulting from this suggestive ritual.

A more recent public example was the Bawani and his California Valley community. Apparently, he was originally a most gifted philosopher and, in South India, even missionaries respected him. He was offered land, money and power and then indulged in free sex. A controlling woman with him amassed an enormous fortune and made herself his private armed guard. Things went wrong and his former adherents tried to leave. Those who did so had no money or possessions, as everything had been handed over on joining. He is now a fugitive from the law and has ruined the lives of many people.

There is no hiding place, all will be revealed and every sin will be found out, so sin is counterproductive in the end. Francis Thompson's poem *The Hound of Heaven* illustrates this:

> Halts by me that footfall:
> Is my gloom, after all
> Shade of His hand, outstretched caressingly?
> "Ah, fondest, blindest, weakest!
> I am He whom thou seekest!
> Thou dravest love from thee, who dravest me."

Thus, we would do well to make our peace now in our full consciousness and enjoy the freedom and joy of the present time. Only then can we realize that God has always provided for our every need.

Dreams

The rhythm of rest and refreshment throughout nature has wide variations yet the most common concern light and darkness. Some creatures hibernate, plants are seasonal, but man and animals all have a need to sleep. In our body systems there are many interdependent rhythms.

Our usual pattern produces a physiological need for the seventh day of rest. Chinese villagers, until western penetration in the 1980s, used to have a break every five days for market day. There they worked throughout daylight. The hours of darkness in the west do not determine people's sleep-some claim to require six hours, others average eight hours. Older people often find that a ten minute to an hour's afternoon nap is very rewarding. During internment by the Japanese, from weakness some prisoners would sleep for fourteen hours.

There are many books on dreams, such as those by Carl Jung, but it is necessary to understand the psychology. In 1960, Bailey (senior psychiatric lecturer at Edinburgh University) and some colleagues conducted experiments with volunteer students who were willing to allow EEG records to be made while they slept. It was observed that during sleep there is movement every ninety minutes when the alert or waking centre sends out signals in the medulla – there is a slight limb movement, eyes move in their sockets, eyelids flicker and there may be a change of lying position. At these times (every ninety minutes), the student was wakened and asked about his dream. He could write down a complete incident made up from conscious experiences, usually quite reasonable and perhaps covering a full foolscap sheet of paper. Each time he stirred in sleep, the amount of movement and alertness was more pronounced. Finally, he was fully awake, but his recall of all his dreams was a confused skim of the tip of each dream, neither consecutive nor reasonable, and he was unable to write much about them.

This could be a necessary part of our subconscious sorting process of memories. Some people claim that they do not dream, but their EEG's record the same rising tempo of alertness. It is probably more likely that they cannot recall.

The substance of dreams are memories, unfulfilled desires, other people's adverse intentions or even occult rubbish (especially in children brainwashed by the media or by other children's imaginations). Some dreams step backwards in time, some forwards, but our conception of the vast dimensions of time and space around us is limited by our present brain which only occasionally has moments of insight. "For now we see through a glass, darkly; but then face to face" (2 Corinthians 13.12). We walk as though blinkered. Why do we need to spend about one third of our lives in sleep? Perhaps it places us more readily in a learning position in the temporary training ground we entered at conception.

"We are such stuff as dreams are made of, and our little life is rounded with a sleep" says Prospero (*The Tempest: Shakespeare*). In *Much Ado About Nothing*, Leonardo says, "We will hold it as a dream till it appear itself," being willing to wait until it becomes reality. The soothsayer, asked in *Cymbeline,* "What have you dreamed of late of this war's purpose?" replied, "Last night the very gods showed me a vision," thus anticipating a successful outcome. (In his plays, Shakespeare mentions dreams about two hundred and forty times and sleep nearly twice as frequently).

William James, the American psychiatrist, in *The Varieties of Religious Experience,* states that "If there is another world, then they can only communicate with us when we are not asleep and not awake." Psychiatrist call this twilight state, as we fall asleep or as we awaken, the hypogogic and hypnopompic moments of our existence. They are extremely important for, if paper and pen are always beside the bed and these first thoughts are recorded, they become evidences of reality in the day to come, instructions for direction and inspirations for guidance. Testing this, one finds that a sorting out takes place so that the positive surfaces, although they may seem dreamlike, result in the same thoughts that are meaningful, creative and outgoing. Working on this theory, we have discovered areas that in ourselves, by ourselves, we would never have known. We might speculate, therefore, that there is then a superior being who wants to talk to us and, realizing that we are receptive, trusts us with responsibilities far exceeding any expectations.

The saint rises in the silence of early morning. Confucius in the *Four Books* says, "Where the good and evil of the past day is neutralized in sleep, this is the time when I get up and think." In the same book there is an amusing quote from his conversation with the philosopher Chuang Tze, who said, "Last night I dreamt I was a butterfly going up and down the river amongst the lilies." Confucius replied, "How do you know you're not a butterfly dreaming that you're a man? He also said, "Man is heaven and earth in miniature."

Every child has the right to draw "the sweet infant breath of gentle sleep" (*Richard II:* Shakespeare). It is essential that children go to sleep, secure, comforted and forgiven. This should come from the parents who, even before birth should talk to the baby. Then, quietly at bedtime, they should give a child time to listen and to absorb peace. When children are old enough to understand, they should be taught to listen to an inner voice and to list all the "sorrys" and "thank yous" of the day. In prayer they can be handed over to God so that His intentions are fulfilled and the angels watch over them. As adults, a new discipline is to go to bed with thoughts of gratitude, ready for an early working out in the spirit before the world wakens and interrupts, and to be able, at those waking moments, to catch the content of a dream and write it down.

The psychosomatics of dreams lie in the physical state of the dreamer; these are often compensatory for any deficits or even for adopting an awkward position in sleep.

A therapist, in a dream, saw a skyscraper. From the top, a radio mast, emitted, in written words across the sky, the word "help" repeatedly. Three days later in another city he saw an identical building which he entered. The elevator attendant opened one of the many lift doors, took him up without any instructions and, when the lift stopped said, "third door on the right." The therapist knocked on that door, a weak voice from within bade him enter and a lady said, "I have waited for you for three days, I'm alone, will you pray with me?." He did so and she passed on into Eternity.

A former prisoner-of-war of the Japanese who had witnessed much killing and punishment for many years had nightmares in which he was being executed. He always wakened crying and afraid, much to the annoyance of his wife who had to listen to this repeated pattern. Finally, he decided to try prayer and asked that the Lord Jesus would enter his dream. The next time the nightmare came, Jesus Christ was in the cart with him; a mixture of a French

Revolution scene with the guillotine ahead, and Japanese crowds cheering. The man knew that no one else could see Jesus Christ who said, "I will hold your hand and take you with me as soon as your head comes off." All fear left the man and he started to laugh so loudly that it wakened him and his wife who, rather crossly, said, "Now what?" The dream never recurred.

A physician dreamed that he saw an old lady leaning out of a window; he knew her name, but had no idea where she lived. Later that day, as he drove through another town, he saw her waving to him from a window. She had been trying to find the doctor in the telephone book, but had failed. Now he went up to her and they were able to pray over and find a solution to a family problem. She was only visiting that house for the day.

A group of people intended to visit a haunted site but were influenced to a more complete work when the leader was told in a dream at 2 a.m., "Go and preach to the departed." Next day, they discovered that it was a disaster site where many children had died who had never heard of God or his Kingdom.

A successful evangelist, rather full of his own ego, dreamed that he was standing before the "pearly gates" of heaven. At first the gates seemed rather small; nothing was happening and he heard nothing. Then he began to shrink, became a minute speck, far smaller than an ant in proportion, and crept right down into a dark shadow beside one of the pillars. All the warm golden glow was now by-passing him. Feeling bereft, ashamed and insignificant, he waited. Finally, he heard, "That's right, you wait there until I choose to speak." He knew then that it was God he needed.

The name "Donald Edwards" came to me in the middle of a night and the words, "He needs to take the more difficult decision." This was written down. Next morning the name was sought in telephone directories. When the correct telephone was answered, the message was given. The man said, "That's exactly what I needed to hear. Who are you, how did you know?" He was told that, "It came to me in a dream from God; never mind who I am.

Drugs

From early ages human beings have experimented with natural sources of minerals and plants for healing. Instinctively, a wounded animal will lie down in a bed of sphagnum moss, used in World War I for dressings when wool was very short. In prisoner of war camps, baked mud was used for dysenteries and grass was chewed for its high vitamin C content. Patient research has extracted the active principles from folklore. For example, crofters in the Scottish highlands knew that the flowering foxglove plant was good for heart conditions more than a century ago; it was a folk remedy used by herbalists and became the origin of the medicine digitalis, refined and synthesised, which is a vital heart remedy. From the Chinese herb Ma Huang comes ephedrine with its adrenalin-like property so helpful to asthmatics. The vitamin B complex was analysed and now B12 is made for the treatment of pernicious anaemia and B3 for the pellagrous skin condition and mental derangement. Nicotinamide, the chemically active absorbable B3, has other imitations; the tricyclic antidepressant tablet is virtually the same as B3 and is very effective in the treatment of endogenous depression of the menopausal type.

Drug variations are endless. Firms compete with one another in multi-million pound research, seeking to be "first" in a discover, and their salesmen try to convince doctors with free samples and reminders. There have been law suits between firms involving stolen patent rights, smuggling, black market, customs evasion and even international subversion.

At a recent conference of one hundred twenty psychiatrists on the over-prescribing of tranquillizers, the conclusions were that we were pleased to be able to "label" a patient, leaving him neatly filed on a shelf or safely shut up in a mental hospital – perhaps, so heavily doped that he could neither complain nor demand attention. Off our backs, as it were, and out of our hair! Thus, we were not treating or curing the illness, merely containing the condition whose origin we never knew. Certainly, laboratory analysis can demonstrate changes in human diseases and trace the effect of drugs, but this provides no ultimate answer. Insulin for the diabetic, an amazing discovery by Banting and Best and, later, Barger's discovery of the actual formula leading to its manufacture, saved lives, but did not cure. (See chapter on Diabetes).

Many drugs have a resultant dependency, such as the smoker's addiction to nicotine, and some can be destructive and cancerous. Many can remove an individual's ability to make decisions, or lower morale. Some addicts even become satanic. The most successful centres for their "drying out" are Christian ones where the service of Exorcism is available. Other addicts may have been acting out a mother dependency with deprivation, put into their minds by an unborn sibling. This calls for the church's pattern of the Eucharist.

The alcoholic's adverse development can be broken only by his dependence upon God, the twelfth step of Alcoholics Anonymous. In the alcoholic "bouter" who suddenly loses control, one may safely investigate "who" took him over at the moment and what urge within him was the trigger mechanism that prompted the escape into unreality. Who was saying in his subconscious, "I thirst"? It is observed that this "thirst" is insatiable and whatever liquid is to hand will suffice. Waterlogging ultimately can produce confusion, but an alcoholic content brings a quicker blotting out of stress in the subconscious and, therefore, is sought. It is often found that the distressed one is an ancestor wandering the "waste howling wilderness" where, of course, it is dry.

A twenty-one year-old Jewish heroin addict who had built up gradually from his school days with soft drugs was now completely dependent and hospitalised. His mother lived on an income from fortune telling, totally against the laws of her religion. The youth telephoned his mother and made her renounce her way of life. He had discovered the Lord's Prayer in a book he had never read before – he thought its title was Gideon! When he said the prayer, and used the line "deliver us from evil" he felt immensely happy. Next morning, he knew that he was healed, without withdrawal symptoms.

An eighteen year-old heroin addict who lived at home became intrigued with the possibility that he could be possessed by a lost and ignored ancestor. He drew up his family tree as far as he knew and, being an Anglican, he rounded up ten of his relative for a service of the nature of a Requiem with two vicars. During the service they became aware of the presence of other entities who were not on the tree the youth had drawn up. One was recognizable by his name and uniform and, when the family was questioned about this apparition, it was admitted that the man had existed but was a family secret as he had disappeared. The heroin addict, unknown to the family, had been given the name of this man. Three days later he had a job and had no need for heroin.

Another eighteen year-old heroin addict was picked up by police in the railway arches of London. She had escaped from her home in Glasgow where her mother was a medium in a spiritualist set-up. The latter was very angry when approached and asked to change her style of life. She organised witchcraft-like curses upon anybody helping her daughter. There was some temporary disruption in the hostel where the girl was taken and the mother telephoned to enquire how the curses were working. Immediately, Exorcism and Deliverance was prayed and the patient was freed from this psychic trauma and any bondage with her mother. She learned to stand on her own feet within a month, free from drugs, but needed considerable long-term care for she was almost illiterate. A small private college accepted her for training and five years later she was married and doing social work.

Although it is easy to record patients with a dramatic transformation, many of them are of the vulnerable, inadequate or immature personality type and it is necessary for them to live in sheltered and controlled situations where there are creative occupations and group therapy. From a group of eighteen male and fifteen female hard drug addicts who sought help, eighteen cases needed such supervision before returning to the world of work and family acceptance. Only four did not improve on the pattern shown of immediate release.

Many medications have side effects, some of which can be put to good use, for example, the trycyclic antidepressants in small doses are excellent in the control of juvenile enuresis. The whole subject of tranquillizing drugs raises the question of whether they break into an individual's voluntary control of his or her spiritual development. Some claim to have become more aware of occult forces while taking drugs. When the mood swings and symptoms can be traced to a familial pattern, then the spiritual approach should be tried. A married lady in her fifties was very disturbed and depressed, with early wakening and nightmares. On taking tricyclic antidepressants she slept longer, but the nightmares greatly increased. She felt unable to pray and finally gave up all drugs and through the Eucharist she committed her ancestors to God. All her symptoms disappeared and she felt fully in control of her new life.

Modern medicine has a vast array of extremely helpful drugs that control and relieve symptoms. Some have a curative effect and allow the patient to adjust, help to produce antibodies and expedite convalescence. An attitude of gratitude is not without its own healing atmosphere. People develop compensatory escape occupations apart from their usual daily work and most, by deliberate choice, wish to remain intact and in control by choosing something creative, for instance, improving the home or gardening. Some need to be alone – the opposite of their surroundings in working hours. There are, however, aids to others who have not thought about the issue and find escape in habits that ultimately produce problems. The single chief cause of disease is addiction to tobacco, the second to alcohol and the third drug abuse. Under these influences, the human spirit becomes possessed by others who are lost, but the sick addict does not understand this.

Frigidity

This is a term frequently used to denote an unwilling participant in the relationship of intercourse. It has ruined many marriage partnerships. Often the male is too keen, too fast or too rough, exhibiting an animal nature. Equally often, the female is afraid, slow to react and shuts off without any climax. Each needs to study the other's moods and learn to accommodate. There are, however, other aspects of the situation.

A beautiful woman who had been rejected by her parents as an infant and handed over to an aunt and uncle to be brought up as an only child in a rigid Victorian setting, never really trusted men. This continued throughout a stormy marriage but, later, she found her own siblings and was able to be far more amenable as a wife.

A women of thirty-two years, feeling that her marriage was breaking down because of her frigid stance, sought advice. When the family tree was drawn up, she revealed her own abortion, her mother's two miscarriages and that her grandmother's twin had been still born. For these four a mourning and naming service was held. The woman wept during the ceremony and said, "They have been telling me not to get pregnant, for if you do, we only get thrown away." After this, she entered into family life with great joy.

The mother and mother-in-law of a fifty-one year-old woman had always "put me down." One was angry because her husband died very young. The other's husband was completely obsessed by the stock market and was apparently very successful in the business world, putting on a good show, but at home his pretence failed. He had not time for their only child who became a homosexual, always looking for father figures. The wife herself had been conceived out of wedlock and brought up in foster homes. She became nervous and frigid. Her healing came from the pathway of prayer, by discussing the memories of all the little girl stages of rejection in her life and then the realization of being loved by the Eternal God.

Incest in families can lead to frigidity and a knock-on effect for future generations. Married men who feel guilty about their frigidity may blame themselves, thinking they must be homosexual. In fact, it may be the result of the parents' sexual abnormalities during or around pregnancy that have been stored in the memory. Sometimes it stems from the sports and team games of school days; then, in marriage, the female relationship does not stimulate.

Abuse of sex is the strongest tool of subversion and has destroyed whole empires. There is a Chinese story concerning a woman known as "Beauty of Beauties" who had been trained for many years in the extremes of sexual warmth and frigidity. She was given as a gift to the Emperor and, being able to condition the Emperor to her demands, gradually took over. Within sixteen years, this Empress had given the whole empire to her own country from which she had come.

Maturity is an awareness of development and of the temporary nature of life, with an understanding that the sexual urges are a gift for us to learn to control, instead of allowing them to rule our lives.

Gambling

Humans have always gambled – they have to take chances and learn from trial and error experiences. This has led some people along devious paths where they have gained or lost purely transient worldly things and, often for "the kicks," have gambled what they have won only to lose everything. In the world today, the objective of obtaining "something for nothing" extends from a game to a habit, then becomes an obsession and, finally a means of entry for many other evils. Satan takes over, relationships are ruined and lives are ruled by anger and rebellion.

In one family, a fifty-six year-old ancestor took a chance, failed and shot himself. His son and then his three grandsons all became gamblers. In the fourth generation, a descendant did the same while his wife, a heavy smoker, died from lung cancer. Their daughter, despite knowing the danger, continues to smoke – in effect, gambling with her own life. She knew that she had not been breast fed and now longs to be cuddled, although her aura of smoke keeps many people at a distance. Members of each generation have suffered from stomach problems – a feeling of being, "punched in the epigastrium."

One woman, distressed by the lifestyles of her several children (one daughter, for instance, would do anything to obtain money for drugs), sought help. Her prayers changed the situation and when these teenagers (the sixth generation) heard of a possible escape route from the family's hereditary problems, they all willingly began attending Mass and became involved in the Franciscan Community. The girl on drugs was healed very quickly, much impressing those who knew her.

A man of thirty-nine years, whose grandfather had invested all his money in a hospital scheme which failed, emigrated with his family and became an import/export trader. His son gambled on the money market; his daughter-in-law gambled with cards. She broke up the family. Two of their sons are manic depressives, the third attempted suicide wanting to know about the next world. He lived, was converted and now has gambled his life on the belief that God is real. His broken marriage is healed and he has united his children in a stable home.

A Jewish man, destined for the priesthood, decided that there was no money to be made in that calling so he took up hairdressing. His work was constantly interrupted by telephone calls involving financial calculations and his clients complained. At the same time, there was much conflict with his wife about the money he was losing on this gambling. They were challenged to listen to God together and take a chance that He had a plan for the man. This worked, for it was discovered that the hairdresser was a brilliant mathematician so, aged thirty-six years, he went to college and gained a degree in mathematics. Then he joined a large Swiss firm as an accountant and his home life became happy and outgoing. He and his wife always kept up their morning quiet time to listen to God.

A doctor was the third generation in a family of physicians who were also alcoholics and gamblers – in poker, golf wagers, and with patients' lives. They had been protected by their status in the hospital service. He wanted to stop the rot for he realized that this situation could continue into his children's lives. Firstly, he found his own freedom in the Eucharistic service when he apologized for his medical relations and, also, for the several wives who had died young in the three generations.

Gambling may be a part of human development, but the real winners in this life are those who gamble on the existence of God and His desire to create beings with whom He can communicate.

Hypnosis

The frontal lobes of the brain seem to be the area from which we initiate impulses that set off actions by the rest of the brain, but what causes the first spark, or where it comes from, we do not know. It is a mystery – perhaps, the basic source of life, the spirit. This factor we can make objective, standing as it were outside ourselves and measuring our thoughts and actions.

Under hypnosis this critical faculty is surrendered; in fact, hypnosis can be performed only on willing subjects. It is easier if they are of limited intelligence so that they are not mentally resistant to the procedure; sometimes they need training and considerable patience before the therapist can reach deeper memories. The aim is to tap early memories that could explain present behaviour patterns. (This is an untrustworthy method in hysterics for they can fabricate nonsense.) It is not therapeutic in itself; the after-care, explanation and release into a new life will lead to healing.

A nurse who had never been able to flush a toilet repeated details of her birth. She had begun to breathe when cold water from the lavatory pan was used – it was the only water available. When this incident surfaced from her subconscious, she was freed.

A diplomate in his thirties suffered from an intractable pain and weight on his left shoulder. Under hypnotic therapy he recalled the date and the scene when he had to deputize for the ambassador of a tropical island. The natives were to regard him as the ambassador and he had to stand in the heat wearing full uniform with extremely heavy epaulettes. Objectifying the dishonesty of the situation brought release from his pain.

Fortunately, time can be saved by the doctor's use of a small amount of the anaesthetic either. On this verge of consciousness questions can be answered without going through a patient's consort, and far earlier memories reached. A forty year-old nurse, concerned about her lesbian tendencies, was able to go back to intrauterine life and told of the eight men with whom her mother had intercourse at that time. She said, "I will never trust men again in my life." But within six months of this discovery she was engaged!

By using a very small dose of pentothal (an intravenous anaesthetic), slowly administered over a period of more than two hours, the doctor can hold a conversation of which the patient has no recall. It is essential, therefore, to make a tape recording so that he will recognize his own voice and the truth. The patient cannot fabricate under pentothal. For instance, a homosexual man in his fifties was able to listen to all his mother had said and done to him from conception to eighteen months old, including an attempted abortion. This was the reason for his decision that women were not to be trusted.

Under hypnosis it is impossible to cross patients' moral boundaries – it wakens them immediately. (This is, of course, a contradiction of what happens in popular fiction.)

The psychiatrist, Dr. Arthur Girdham, now retired, used hypnosis and published *The Bloxham Tapes* which he believed established proof for a theory of reincarnation. Ian Wilson author of *The Shroud of Turin*, researched his theory and decided that not one of the stories revealed under hypnosis held together. In a difficult "case" it was found that the patient had been a librarian who had unwittingly absorbed her story from a book. She recounted the date of which the heroine had died and, when Wilson checked, he noted that she had repeated accurately all the dates given in the book. He visited the grave of this actual character and discovered that there was a different date on the tombstone. It was established, therefore, that both librarian and book were wrong. In another case cited in *The Bloxham Tapes*, when I met the patient on a television interview, he told a reasonable story but, to me, he seemed to be imitating an ancestor who had drowned at sea. I suggested that he was bemoaning his lost state and needed to be prayed for. The man responded, "What a good idea, I will do that." These cases, then, seemed to have resulted from the possession syndrome where former inhabitants of the earth trusted sensitive patients and were actually seeking help to escape from their troubled state.

Hysteria

As a diagnostic label, hysteria is under constant discussion in medical circles for it is neither measurable nor does it depend upon any material body change, and no "treatment" alters the patient's performance. They are called "patients" simply from the effect of their involvement as nuisances in the physician's sphere, that is, they have behaved hysterically. The majority of such cases are women. They seem not to be fully conscious at these moments, their volition is impaired. There is out-of-the-norm misdirection, beyond the control of their wills. They seek some imagined gain – attention, sympathy – yet cannot express what they need. Wrist-slashing, diving through a glass door, or an epileptoid type of fit exasperates those around them.

A psychologist, Piaget, wrote in 1960 about hysterics, "They say, 'I cannot'; it looks like 'I will not,' but it is 'I cannot will.'"

Their gestures must have an intention like an actor's – trying to put across a message; "Pity me, love me, comfort me, I'm nobody, I'm lost, I'm depressed." The sudden speed with which a hysteric can "switch on" is alarming, and an entity that is violent and regardless is then present. They would deny that this is premeditated. Mental hospitals cope with such incidents continually; punishment does not alter the behaviour and drugs only dull the thinking.

The hysteric is easily suggestible, usually with a medium to low IQ range, enjoying attention and, therefore, easily hypnotizable (see section on Hypnosis), thus losing excessive carbon dioxide which is essential to the normal stimulus of breathing. Then follows cramp-like effects as the muscles go into spasm, first in the extremities, then in the muscles of the abdomen, the limbs and finally, the throat where the effects stick. Even at this stage the hysteric can suddenly switch off all the symptoms. (Are there memories of supposed deprivation?) Ultimately, he needs to reach the point of prayer, for example: "I accept forgiveness for my ancestors and also forgive them for any bad effects on my life; may they too forgive, and thank the Lord for removing any such effects on my memories, my emotions or my life."

Crowd hysteria, battle hysteria and tribal hysterical rituals result more from a brainwashing origin and are followed by a great "let down."

Other hysterical manifestations have descriptive terms for easy labelling – for example, hysterical fugues, wherein the person loses his memory and, if travelling, has no idea of identity or place. This is commonly a mind-dictated escape mechanism when stress becomes unendurable – known as transmarginal stress. It occurs often in war-time as "shell shock." Sympathetic listening is needed, sometimes with the patient under mild anesthesia. (The drowsy period after a midday meal is an excellent time to relax and unravel.)

In hysterical paralysis, anaesthetic areas and pain areas should be examined carefully. False anatomical pathways, showing that the patient is lying, are easily spotted by a trained physician. The "glove and stocking" variety with false nerve distribution is common; hysterics do not realise that there are no nerves that function within these circular limits. Hysterical motivation is always for attention-seeking. Women presenting with hysterical pseudocyesis (false pregnancy), frequently imagine that they will produce a new Christ and consider themselves madonnas! Mary Baker Eddy, in 1866, was a famous instance. A fifty-three year-old woman, suffering from false pregnancy, was the child of cousins who married; she herself was a very disappointed spinster and needed care for twenty years before she was able to live an independent life.

A woman of thirty-six years became a nuisance in her neighbourhood with hysterical outbursts in the front row of the church and telephoning for immediate help from social workers. Tranquillizers, although quietening her, were no solution. Investigation showed that she had had a miscarriage of her own and that there had been two unrecognized siblings. When she understood that these could have been trying to attract attention, which she had by copying, she was able to commit them to God and then herself became peaceful.

If hysterics cry "wolf, wolf" too often, physicians might miss the true diagnosis one day, so it is always safest to treat the symptoms seriously and conduct a therapeutic trial. It is possible, however, that the whole concept of the possession syndrome could be the ultimate approach; certainly no harm can result from teaching a person to pray in the right context – for some, it is an instant cure. Hysterics are those who, throughout their lives, are still seeking the protection of the parent figure, without which they have no boundaries. They may develop psychiatric problems which, in turn, may lead to physical problems.

Incest

Sexual intercourse between members of the same family has been condemned among the human race for over four thousand years. An inbred species ultimately destroys itself as the genes carry the weakest traits. If parents indulge in this with their children then the latter come to regard it as the "done thing" and later become promiscuous. As adults, if they have a marriage partner, reproduction is secondary to intercourse; they do not trust each other and are often frigid. Broken marriages frequently result and succeeding generations do not value marriage.

In a family of six children, the three eldest girls were prostitutes, like their mother. Two of the boys were constantly in trouble with the police. When the mother became a Christian, she put things right with her children by honest apology and open discussion but it was revealed that their father had regularly sexually assaulted every child from infancy, teaching them that this was their duty. He now disappeared. The grandfather had been murdered and the grandmother had become an alcoholic before she died. In their ancestry, a witch had been burned at the stake and the family felt that a curse had been laid upon them from that time. Now the youngest child, thirteen years-old, became anorexic, chain smoking, too weak to attend school, but wandering around for much of the night.

The whole family tree was drawn up. There had been three suicides in one generation and, although the total number of miscarriages and abortions were unknown, those that could be identified were named and the mother and her daughters committed them to God in the Eucharist. The first night that they confessed in prayer and confided in God, the youngest child went to bed early. She wakened to demand breakfast, followed by large meals all day. She fell asleep in the evening and wakened late the next morning – again hungry. This pattern continued and she was restored to a real health and a rejoicing family. The next stage was to look for their father.

A married woman of thirty-six years, afraid of the impending breakdown of her marriage, regarded herself as frigid. This was traced to a lifetime fear of her frequently drunk father. Even today she shrinks when she hears the squeal of tires on a road. Throughout her childhood this heralded his drunk, late arrival home, when he used her for oral intercourse. Realization, prayer, conscious discussion and a new honesty with her husband saved the situation. Then she found that real love involves patience, kindness, temperance, tenderness and joy.

A diabetic mother was concerned for her son who was in his twenties. He lied and stole indiscriminately, none of the goods being of any use to him or his family. He lived in a permanent daydream and dressed himself in various military or police uniforms, always fabricating the relevant badges and passes. His mother had had both abortions and miscarriages – marriage to her had been cheap. His grandfather had attempted to drown one of his sons in a rage and poisoned another. Each of his daughters had been put in convents to escape from him as he had taught them that their duty in life was to satisfy his sexual passion. The man was an army deserter and eventually fled abroad where he led a dissolute life and died an alcoholic. The young man was acting out the guilt patterns of this grandfather, whom he had never met. Psychiatric treatment brought the conclusion that he was "possessed." The mother, who had originally sought help about her own experiences of sexual abuse as a child, now learned how, in the Eucharist, all these other facets including her son's lying and stealing began to clear.

A man of fifty years who lost a fortune through gambling, alcohol and prostitution, indulged in oral sex with his three children, all of whom were under ten years old. They taught other children and the youngest developed epileptoid fits. When this was discovered, the children were sent abroad to their mother and taught how to pray the Lord's Prayer for protection. They refused to see their father again. He was a damned person (Matthew 18).

In eighteen families, each involving between one and eight young victims, it was the mothers and children who were helped and saved. Their memories cleared and, with open discussion on the subject, they were able to forgive and find a healing, spiritual discipline leading to maturity and wholeness.

In two cases where an older brother was the cause, there was some resolution for them and stable marriages. In no case was the father, the instigator, released from his guilt and each turned to prostitutes.

A father, under threat of insecurity in his home life or from financial loss, may find his wife is the stronger parent figure. Frustrated, he secretly vents his inadequacies on the children. (This is seen commonly among displaced persons.) Incest becomes a covert sexual stimulus, with little forethought being taken for those of the next generation who can be destroyed by diseases such as AIDS and who stay immature, withdrawn and frigid. Change can only come spiritually.

Memory

Memory is one of the most amazing gifts with which man is endowed and plays a significant role in everyone's life. We have the ability to learn, retain, recall and forget, each an active dimension. We can filter facts and experiences and send them on from the short term memory to be stored for later recall. The physiological understanding is a complexity we cannot grasp. Creating conscious memory can stimulate mood, speech and movement. The original sensory impulses have to be learned and sorted from sight, hearing, touch, smell and taste, self, family and spatial awareness, and then collected into memory areas, many being active at the same time. These are layered down as engrams or holograms, forming the mental records which are the basis of memory. We know that the most recently acquired experiences of learning are the most tenuous and most easily lost as, for example, in old age when childhood memories are the last to be forgotten. In the alcoholic or drug addict, the more civilised behaviour patterns are dulled at first, continuing to the point of only having the reactions of primitive man.

There is another controlling memory pattern before any brain cells are formed which can be illustrated by the use of pentothal abreaction (or "truth drug") where the patient reveals his "awareness" that "before conception he was in some safe, peaceful, warm hands." This is a different memory process which can be engendered voluntarily by spiritual discipline, or destroyed by indiscipline. There is no area of the brain substance where this can be located; it is a facet of the eternal part of an individual's makeup – the soul. After conception, growth and development in this life, with its additional memories, it is prepared for another life of which we can become aware only by practice.

Carl Jung describes seven layers of consciousness including family consciousness, collective subconsciousness and organic unconsciousness, all of which contribute to our memories and influence our attitudes to life, race and creed. An area that we cannot pinpoint is family consciousness or a sense of belonging. The family with its personal memories, alive in this world, is intrinsically part of a vast area of ancestral memories in the family subconscious. Thus, the ancestors who are already exploring eternity and whose experiences echo in the corridors of memory, can exert a unifying and creative influence on future generations.

Families that listen to each other stay together loyally and, at reunions, recount and express gratitude for the accomplishments of their forebears. The younger members who listen are thus encouraged to emulate these positive patterns. Such trust and faith within the family does not come through human wisdom; those who experience it know that it is only by the creative power of God that it can be achieved.

Racial memories are buried deep. Many generations of evolving patterns differentiate families and nations, much depending upon climate, colour and philosophy. It is claimed that we store everything we have heard or see, including pre-birth phenomena. The problem for most people is the inability to recall this data at will. For example, in the emotional trauma of an oral examination, one's mind may go blank but when the emotional overlay is under control, then the mind centres on the required area and all the connection neurones of recall work in unity to supply every detail – of smell, sight, sound, touch and taste.

Today's breakdown of family – the one-parent situation, more abortions, smaller family units – with the inevitable incomplete boundaries and controls, results in the loss both of community within which a family functions and of firm roots in a specific family tree. This, in turn, can produce "lost" people with immature behaviour disorders.

Abnormal recall, where one of the connections to a particular sensory area is disturbed, may cause one thought to dominate to the exclusion of others, or its absence may allow other areas to predominate. Some message systems are preoccupied or disrupted by weariness so that sensory phenomena reach the subconscious before reaching consciousness, producing the "deja vu" syndrome (see section on Deja Vu). Drugs and alcohol alter incoming and outgoing signals and co-ordination, as does the scar tissue in multiple sclerosis and Parkinson's disease. In some, there is a purposive attempt to suppress recall, commonly used by some old and lonely people or by hysterics. Chemical, metabolic or vitamin deficiency can produce schizoid patterns of behaviour where the conscious is disturbed. The patient may suffer depression or insomnia, hear voices or see things – real enough to him. The paranoid developes a whole system of "remembered" antagonisms by other people where no actual facts are presented. The obsessional has the same abnormal demands emanating from the subconscious.

Humans have an amazing inborn urge to create, repair and restore; their cell metabolism is a positive force, integrated and coordinated. Thus, memory areas with past unpleasant connotations can be eliminated. For example, remorse usually is a system that repeats the same faults, whereas repentance and forgiveness is the way in which the slate is wiped clean and the fault is forgotten. This positive on-going healing process is the experience of the majority. Those who dwell on and cultivate the negative can become introverted, depressed and paranoid. They often drag others down with them and drugs only temporarily dampen and drown their nuisance factor.

Healing of memories is healing in retrospect, time being just another dimension. To most people, the past is past and has been dealt with, while the present is the only time that exists and that we can attempt to control. Our Lord Jesus Christ, however, heals our hurtful memories at their source as He is active in all time. We can develop the art of listening and making occasional guiding suggestions to help a person relive and unburden areas which can then become objective and be sorted into acceptable patterns. The whole technique of the analytical approach depends upon being relaxed, and learning to talk through a situation. Sometimes, acting out the actual event as in a pscychodrama is also necessary. Psychologist Andrew Salter in *The Case Against Psychoanalysis* questions the value of many sessions with an analyst, holding that, following Freudian theories, some patients were not suffering from neuroses at the beginning of their treatments, but developed a real disturbance, increasing in proportion to the number of sessions which, therefore, was definitely harmful. Healing of memories depends upon differing levels of expectation, and complicated adult feelings can be shown to have stemmed from simple situations.

A thirty-six year-old single woman, the eldest child of five, had never experienced any meaningful relationships, hated men and was worried that she seemed different from others. She was very intelligent with an IQ in the region of 140 and had held many responsible positions. Despite having been given much advice she now contemplated suicide. Seeking help from convents, the key was found in her childhood memories: she had been conceived out of wedlock and had precipitated her parents' unhappy marriage. Being unwelcome and always blamed for the marriage, she had been made the household drudge. In the Eucharistic setting she discovered a new-found ability to forgive her dead parents. This was the answer for her.

A so-called schizophrenic aged twenty-eight years, was healed when she heard her own recorded voice, under pentothal abreaction, recounting the arguments of her parents about her birth when she was three months in utero.

An asthmatic of twenty-eight years, whose attacks only oc-curred at two o'clock in the morning when he was staying in cities, found that his mother could recount an incident when he was eigh-teen months old, of burglars attacking their house at exactly that time. Through prayer, he understood this memory and when he realized that there was nothing to fear, his attacks ended.

A recurring memory of cuddling her yellow doll when she was two years old, puzzled a forty-five year-old woman. She sought advice from her church and was told that "the Lord wants to do something for you." In this prayerful situation she was given a review of her birth and early life when her father had demanded that his wife should produce a son. Both mother and baby were terrified at the birth of a girl and the father walked out without speaking. The scene with the doll followed two years later when the emotion of loneliness was paramount – the much wanted boy had been born and all attention was given to him. During an air raid, the mother held her baby son in her arms while her daughter was left to sit alone and unloved on a three-legged stool as the bombing went on. The little girl was very frightened and clutched her doll, but was used to not being held since her brother had been born. This incident had never been recalled in conscious memory and its importance in the formation of her attitudes had not been known until the Holy Spirit revealed it. Each evetn was then delib-erately recalled but now the woman was aware of another figure. It was the Lord Jesus Christ standing by her mother's bed at her birth saying, "What a beautiful little girl, she is lovely." Similarly, during the air raid she saw Him standing behind her stool as she huddled under the stairs, with His hands on her shoulders dispelling her fear. The result of this "assisted recall" was that her memory was changed. Knowing that the Lord had been present at those times healed the hurtful part of these memories and so she was able to develop a loving attitude to her parents for the very first time.

As an adult, however, her brother also came for help because he could not relate to his wife, children or friends in a meaningful way. He said, "There's something black inside me and nobody is going to touch it." The ferocity of his statement showed that this was the key to his problem. He felt that he was hated and despised by his sister who had been jealous of the love and attention he received. His sister realized this, apologized to him and asked his permission to pray to the Lord to heal him of these hurtful memories. He agreed and knew that the Lord had touched him, although he would not admit that he had any faith, and kept saying, "Look at me, I'm smiling." The black "something" inside him, which he had so completely shut away to avoid the teasing and taunting, was his own emotions.

A priest complained of a recurring nightmare in which he had to go into a mortuary filled with refrigerated dismembered human bodies. Around the walls on shelves were large bottles containing heads which snapped at him as he passed. The attendant was his dead father who had been a mercenary during his life. When the priest asked what he could do, the answer came, "Re-member them." This we did in the Eucharistic setting and saw the bodies remade and washed clean of the blood and mud which had discoloured them. Then, with the priest's apology to God and to them for his father's actions, they were able to continue to their rest. The nightmare has not recurred.

A patient in her fifties had a great fear of death which had cut her off from travelling or even joining in the community life. I asked whose death she had witnessed. "It was my little sister. I was only three years old when my father lifted me up to kiss her dead body. I can still feel his arms under mine." We then prayed for forgiveness for the anger and fear that she had felt throughout her life. She was free and later heard that her twin sister, who had the same symptoms, was released on the same day although she lived at a considerable distance. Now, eight years later, the lady spends much of her life helping others face disastrous memory patterns – one patient, a leukaemia sufferer, has been healed for four years, while a man awaiting spinal fusion was healed in twenty minutes.

Occult

Occult means hidden but the word is now associated with forbidden aspects of knowledge, that is, seeking a hidden way of knowing against the laws laid down in the Bible. Activities that are abominable to God are listed in Deuteronomy 18 as primitive testing by fire, divination, witchcraft, wizardry, necromancy, enchantment or charming, consulting fortune tellers. In the thousands of years BC the Israelites had learned by trial and error that such pursuits brought disasters, so these words were pronounced almost as public health and survival laws. By the time of Josiah (BC 641) many occult practices – and prostitution – had been introduced, but the destruction of life was so great that, although he was a priest, Josiah conveniently uncovered a book of laws which saved the nation.

In our world today, we still have not learned these lessons and we have ouija boards, pendulums, horoscopes, mediums, clairvoyants and astrologers. These areas of the occult are not harmless games – they can become an uncontrolled indulgence, the thin edge of an occult wedge, that finally leads to complete destruction of family members' freedom and prosperity. Those involved in any of the "black arts" invariably end in mental hospitals with various diagnostic labels or meet traumatic deaths. Some identify such practices as Satanic, that is, a force that is entirely negative, earth-bound and exactly opposite to God, in fact a reversion to a more primitive state in human evolution.

The occult is the antithesis of religion. It kills any spiritual sensitivity and lowers the individual to the level of an animal. Drugs are used to dull the censor and enhance lust. Perverted sex often follows and may end with animal or human sacrifices. When children are sacrificed, the practitioners are damned (Matthew 18.6).

The repeal by the British Parliament of the Witchcraft Act and then the Abortion Act within the past twenty years has precipitated wide-ranging increases in greed, license and national peril from within. We seem unable to learn from the decline of ancient Greece where homosexuality, pornography, worship of the human body and intense investment in "sport" concentrated the people's minds on superficial targets.

There are earth-bound beings who have not started on their journey into God's kingdom; they cannot find their way although the are able to "see" what happens on earth. They are lost and unhappy and cannot make decisions for themselves – this is peculiar to the living. Thus, contacting them from earth (via mediums) is firstly, selfish and secondly, cruel to the lost for they want to go on and not stay tied down by being called upon. They can "possess" the living in their attempts to gain attention. Those they "visit" may hear voices, become depressed, refuse to eat, suffer insomnia or throw epileptoid fits. Such patients then are given psychiatric labels and physicians attempt to dampen and control the symptoms. The so-called illnesses displayed are poor mimics of the lost state of the earth-bound spirits. The subconscious picks up their pressure and patients act out specifically their main complaints. St. Paul said in 60 AD, "We are not dealing with flesh and blood but with the principalities and powers of the outer world of darkness." Medicine needs to understand in order to tackle the fundamental cause of diseases without being side-tracked by materialism.

A woman of twenty-three years, schizophrenic and unresponsive to medicines, had become ill four years before, when she and her mother were playing with a ouija board. The hospital sent for exorcism and she recovered.

An eighteen year-old man wished to leave the coven where the practices now disgusted him. He had been elected secretary and, therefore, was the only person who knew members' identity for contact – they had killed his predecessor. This man's only escape was suicide. Unfortunately, he did not seek a sanctuary, but merely discussed the dangers.

A man in his thirties was in hospital labelled schizophrenic. He had accepted this in order to escape from a coven. He then left the hospital with a new identity and moved to a distant city. An alcoholic woman in her mid-forties was cured when her mother's curse on her was broken. A forty-year old woman from a family of mediums and covens also involved a voodoo priest who cursed all the families involved. Then followed alcoholism, one suicide, diabetes, epileptoid attacks, gall bladder inflammation, colitis, depressions, insomnia and the foretelling of certain deaths. Only one person in this family has remained "straight."

In fifty-five recorded family trees, living people were ill following dabblings in the occult. A sensitive, suggestible member of a family can be indoctrinated very easily into fear of an illness, and loyalty maintained on the basis of that fear, especially if the person knows no alternative or protective prayer which is, of course, the supreme power of God.

Orphans and the Illegitimate

Many who have been adopted have lived wonderful lives for which their adoptive parents must take credit. They have been loving and honest throughout and provided a male and a female, father and mother figure, keeping within the boundaries and always being good listeners.

On the other hand, some find themselves in an anomalous position, appreciating the present, but with vague memories of another couple who were their real blood parents. Many unanswered questions hover in their subconscious – who are they, royalty or servant? Where did they come from? Were they legitimate yet unwanted, or a disgrace smuggled away? Did they escape from the threat of abortion? Were there other siblings? Does security depend on a house, or money, or belonging, or on family love?

When seeing and listening to patients' symptoms of anxiety, depression, guilt and other disturbed behaviour, it is possible sometimes to match these to a situation of interuterine insecurity and threats that the fetal mind picked up. After birth, then the separation, not being breast fed, an inability to trust changes of authority, figures or places of residence, pile stress upon stress.

At the other extreme is the experience of a baby girl born just before Japanese internment. There followed endless moves from prison to prison, deprived of all material comfort, food, warmth, shelter, witnessing punishment and torture, yet this child knew her mother all the way. Her arms and lap were "home" throughout the four years that it lasted. In the final weeks before release they would cling together during the bombing raids. This child today is a devout fifty-year old woman, a most loving mother with a beautiful character. Home was security and love, centered on watching her mother's face in captivity in her childhood.

The only security known by a thirty-six year-old man is to sit in a single prison cell, chain smoking. He is aware of exactly how far to go with the police and how to be given solitary confinement by threatening a warden. Thus, he is sure of a good Christmas dinner in a centrally heated cell. He prefers to be free in the summer, living on unemployment benefit. He ensures that any work he obtains is soon terminated. He has lived in excellent homes, but always steals from them in the end, then drinking and smoking all the money away. This is an attention-seeking position. The man was adopted at the age of three and his adoptive parents kept a public house. His craving for alcohol, therefore, began as an infant. His mother, a prostitute, had had several children so there are, therefore, real blood parents and siblings. Some of these may be aborted, crying out for attention, but the man refuses all care or attempts to help him. Even Alcoholics Anonymous has given up.

A single twenty-four year-old girl was the eldest of five children. The father was completely unconcerned with any of the children and the mother regarded them always as her burdens. The eldest girl was expected to do all the rough work in the house. At her interview in a distressed, non-stop, child-like voice she listed all the "awful" things done to her, none of which seemed traumatic at all, but were endless nonsense. She complained of having been terrible assaulted, so she intended to send a complaint to the Bishop. After several attempts to discover the truth, finally she said that when a priest gave her the wafer at the Eucharist, his finger had touched her.

In drawing up the family tree, it was found that her mother had been adopted. Then the girl's grandmother had taken over her life as compensation for having no children of her own. This situation had been kept secret, but on the grandmother's death, the girl was using every means to obtain attention. This is hysteria, although the answer lay not in the diagnostic label, but in the necessity for the grandmother's tie to be broken in prayer so that she could continue with her journey in the next life.

A schoolgirl of fourteen who had been adopted at three years old was sent away to boarding school because of her behaviour disorders. She was classified as hysterical, sometimes schizophrenic but was healed of these symptoms when she learned to attend the Eucharist and pray for forgiveness on behalf of her real parents. She also requested healing for the hurt memories of her infancy which had produced such violent reactions.

A married fifty-five year-old dominant woman with three children was very depressed, although acting out a grandiose role. The artificiality of the dinner parties that she gave had become painful to her family and apparent to the guests. Finally, on seeking advice for depression and sleep disturbance, it was found that she, her mother and grandmother were all illegitimate. She was able to apologize for this and for her antecedents by praying in the Eucharist. Therefore, she continued with this spiritual intention and was herself healed but realized, also, that she had ended the spiral which would now not continue with her children and grandchildren.

In two cases, disturbed adopted individuals, in the Eucharist setting, said that they had seen in their visual imagery their real parents who were, therefore, now dead; they had been able, in prayer to release them so that they met each other and could begin their journey to heaven.

In forty-three cases, twenty-eight were released from their symptoms. Two were complete failures, still complaining; one who had actually known both parents eventually committed suicide; nine had illegitimate parents and grandparents; three had an illegitimate great-grandparent. The symptomatic complex was included in all their depressive mood swings – that is, unspecific guilt, sense of rejection, negative reactions to love, unpredictable outbursts of temper, sometimes sleeplessness, loneliness, an unloved feeling and, in more than half, smoking and stealing. The psychosomatic expression of their insecurity from interuterine days arises in memory traces, threats to life, lack of trust in those nearest to them, an unwarranted sense of guilt and shame passed on from parental figures, anger and frustration. Such symptoms are carried by proxy from those who, having died, are seeking attention because there is no time pattern in the other world.

Sleep

"Sleep, that knits up the ravell'd sleeve of care" (*Macbeth:* Shakespeare.)

The diurnal rhythm of day and night is a physiologically established necessity. The world record for doing without sleep is eleven days. Many people exaggerate when they complain of sleeplessness, but there is enormous individual variation. In tropical climates, most need a nap after midday. Rapid eye movements in sleep comes roughly every ninety minutes. The EEG tracing at this time shows some wakening but not to consciousness. In sleep other hormones are released that renew tissues, especially in children.

Lack of sleep for people in many professions, for instance a physician on call, a shift worker or a student who studies best late at night, is not an issue but a neurotic or self-centred person will consult a doctor. Failure to fall asleep initially is the commonest complaint and the pattern of this should be investigated. There may be specific worries or lost relationships; over-indulgence with too heavy or too stimulating meals or drinks; watching terrifying television or having bitter arguments. Evening should be a time of unwinding and freedom, when any activity should contrast completely with the cares and duties of the day. Beds should be used for sleep, not for reading. Perhaps the advent of the bed headlight correlates with the modern demand for sleeping tablets.

Early wakening depends upon each person's measure of time. Some people find this to be the most productive period of thought and it is necessary then to write, at the time, all one is contemplating so that the mind can move on and progress to completion. It is useful to rise and drink some water before returning to bed and falling asleep again until a more acceptable hour. Dreams should be noted on paper so that they can be studied later.

In physical disorders, real anxieties or depressions, a physician may need to intervene. Pre-sleep training can be instigated, that it, thinking through the relaxation of every part of the body, beginning with the limbs, ready for contemplation. Here the spiritually developed individual has an advantage for the scriptures give food for thought and a discipline of thanks and praise, enumerating all good things and thus, engendering positive objective thinking. A simple pattern is to choose the names of ancestors or living family and thank God for all their good qualities. Such people find that they have to kneel or sit up to pray for they know that the moment the head touches the pillow they are asleep – sometimes even forgetting to put out the light! Counting sheep is a pointless exercise when one can count blessings – there is always something to be grateful for. At this time, too, we can broaden our horizons and expect new thinking to emerge as we waken for a new day.

Physical exercise and the full use of every limb during the day is essential. The old and senile who lie in bed decalcify their bones which then break easily whereas the child's intense activity, dancing and jumping, stimulates bone quality. This is immensely important in mental hospital patients where some are so drugged that they sit half asleep all day and require even more drugs at night. Such was the pattern of some schizophrenics, so it was decided to do the opposite and observe results. The patients were sent as farm labourers and, although slow and in need of supervision, gradually their drug dosage was reduced. Some of them returned to the outside world, maintaining their improvement with some daily physical labour. Physical exhaustion enabled them to sleep well without any drugs.

A thirty-two year-old lawyer became schizophrenic in the early 1960s; drugs affected his brain. He began to improve only when he agreed to do outdoor labouring. After six months he was spending half the day labouring and half at his office. A year later, he was working full time but kept his evenings for hard physical work.

A senior churchman and his wife endured very disturbed sleep for over forty years, wasting much energy. They had been treated by psychiatrists and had attended many therapy sessions. During a Eucharistic service, they heard families praying for their unborn and aborted babies. Never having regarded their own early miscarriage as of any significance, they suddenly realized that this was causing their sleeplessness, so they decided to take the baby in prayer to the intent that they would pray for it in such a service where they recognized, loved and named it. The mother dissolved into tears. She said she could "see" a grown-up daughter and "hear" her name. From that time the situation was resolved and their sleep was unbroken, without the help of pills. They stated categorically that their daughter had been trying to gain attention for years, but they had never understood.

Before sleep, children need to unburden the day's conflicts and enumerate all the good happenings, surrendering themselves as infants to parental care, then later learning to do this in prayer to God, so that they will sleep loved and secure. One youth could only sleep on his right side with his back to the wall, preferably in a corner. He overcame this phobia when it was realized that he had been conceived and brought up during the war when his mother literally always had her "back to the wall."

In the mid-brain is a "sleep center" which, therefore, is also an awake or alert centre. Sleep is a process whereby the central systems of neurone to cell synapses actually withdraw and distance themselves so that impulses do not find the electrically stimulated hormones to carry a message. The initiating areas of the frontal lobe cease to create, messages do not go to motor areas. Sensory areas cease their input to the cortex, not unlike a vast railway system where gradually all the lights go out and the trains come to a stop. Only the autonomic system, carrying the heart and breathing, digestion and absorption, continues. The alerting system will come into play only if the stimuli from sensory areas are threatening. There is an increasing intensity of the whole alert system every ninety minutes, until the final wave – the morning awakening.

A very few people have hypersomnia; they are escaping reality. There is also the hysterical escape of those trying to draw attention. The child in whom pain or terror is so great it can stimulate an "absence" (see section on Absence) or whose fever forces unconsciousness, would be classified as somatopsychic.

"Unless the Lord builds the house, its builders labour in vain. Unless the Lord watches over the city, the watchmen stand guard in vain. In vain you rise early and stay up late, toiling for food to eat, for He grants sleep to those he loves." (Psalm 127)

Sport

The wonderful exhilaration of youthful pursuit of the freedom of the elements – to run, to ride and swim for hours, in wind, air and sea, stretching every limb almost to exhaustion and then to rest, wash, eat and sleep – it is a great joy and can be continued throughout life. Unfortunately, many people have damaged themselves in competitive violence and the resultant torn tendons and muscles or twisted and over-compressed vertebral discs, have crippled them in a particular area for the rest of their lives. The whole body then has to stagnate because a knee or a disc is prone to pain. Is this done for glory or for personal publicity? We learn team work at school but this should make others great, while we learn to give and be humble.

In Greece, the wonderful Olympiads became a worship of the human body that opened the flood-gates to homosexuality, promiscuity, false gods and finally, to the decline and destruction of that civilisation. One of the programmes outlined in the *Atheist's Agenda* by Dillon McCartney in 1948 includes all sports: "Get the western nations fully involved in competitive sport- their money and time, their TV and radio – then they will become morally soft and an easy target in which communism will flourish and an easy take over in their soft belly of unguarded indulgence." Not only must we avoid these physical disasters, but spiritually we must break the cycle of obsessions.

A forty year-old man with a brilliant brain was obsessed with cricket. He failed his university course, became a cabbage and entirely self-centred. He came to the point where with new spiritual freedom he could have taken Holy Orders, but instead he chose to watch cricket so would not have time to study. The result was disaster for his family as he drifted from one job to another, never allowing his capacity to develop.

A depressed woman in her late thirties made many suicidal gestures in dreamy trance-like states, sometimes three a week, despite having an excellent husband and her own children. She herself, an illegitimate child, had been adopted at three years of age, to replace a brilliant teenage athlete who had so many medals and trophies but who had died suddenly from peritonitis. His parents always talked of his successes and the adopted child was constantly punished because she did not emulate him. She stole some of his relics thus bringing more punishment on herself although, in reality, she was trying to gain attention for the lost son. In his earthbound state he was lonely and angry with the child who had replaced him. He was quite unprepared for death and both he and his parents were angry with God. He demanded attention for his own troubles and was unaware that he was part of another world. Both the son and the adopted daughter were released in the Mass of the Resurrection.

A forty year-old woman was extremely restricted in her activities because of repeated strains in the lumbo-sacral and cervical areas of her spine. As a teenager she had so thrown herself into sports, representing her country at hockey, netball, cricket, athletics and swimming that there had been little time for anything else. The continuous pain in her back and legs made her very tired and irritable. The results of throwing the discus and javelin, where she had gained a place in the Olympic athletes squad, were chronic spasms in the neck muscles with an accompanying headache which rarely eased. After returning to her church and apologising to God for the misuse of her body in youth, her lower spine was released and then strengthened and her neck condition began to improve. Two years later, she could move her head freely in all directions.

We can learn from the life of Eric Liddell of *Chariots of Fire* fame. Even in his school days, he always kept his eyes on God. He was a brilliant rugby player as well as a champion sprinter but his disciplined approach to sport, as in other areas of his life, meant that nothing was done to excess. Despite being the fastest short distance sprinter in the world, he refused to break God's law and compete in the Olympic heats on the Sabbath. He then ran in a race four times his normal distance and, through this step in faith, God sustained him to an amazing victory and a new world record.

Suicide and Para Suicide

A personal and collective feeling of guilt is built into the human system which, for most people, forces them to seek an explanation for this act. In Britain, suicide used to be a criminal offence (it also affected the laws of inheritance) and someone who attempted suicide was regarded as a felon and taken to the magistrates' court. In the 1930s, junior hospital doctors frequently were called to court to give evidence about their patients' circumstances and whether or not they would have succeeded in killing themselves but for the hospital's intervention; the behaviour of the spouse was discussed openly. (Such appearances for attempted suicide ended in the 1940s.) The inevitable publicity always brought shame to the family, for the person was exhibiting an inability to cope with life's problems. The church added to the trauma by refusing to bury such a "criminal" in consecrated ground, merely holding a perfunctory committal service elsewhere. Suicide is regarded as a violation of God's design in love and is the antitihesis of the command "love and obey."

Our natural inbuilt duty is self-preservation, but there are three main classifications of potential suicides – those without any sense of responsibility, those with a partially diminished sense of responsibility, and those who are purposive suicides. There are also accidental suicides. The first group comprises those who are unable to see themselves objectively – for instance, the pathological mental sufferer or the schizophrenic in his fantasy world. They are often made doubly irresponsible by massive drug doses.

At Knowle Mental Hospital in Hampshire, the railway passed through the grounds in a cutting, its road bridge forming part of the main entrance to the hospital. This became a frequent site of suicides. The endogenous depressive and the manic depressive patient has such moments of thoughtlessness.

In a catatonic stupor (where a person in a fit holds himself rigid), mental illness or high fever there is a total lack of awareness. For example, some patients in a hospital situated at the top of a cliff above the sea, simply walked into the sea to die. Two senile women escaped one evening clad only in their nightdresses. Missing for fourteen hours in the middle of winter, they were presumed dead but, next morning at around eight o'clock, they were found standing in a pond with icy water above their waists. They had wanted to see the beautiful stars in the night sky! Neither of them suffered any after-effects, not even heavy colds – they had probably never heard of pneumonia. This is the passive state in which, in cases of shock or thoughtlessness, people have taken their own lives.

The second group includes those with partially diminished responsibility as seen in the hysteric who will try any tactics to gain attention. There is usually a flight of ideas wherein they do not weigh consequences. After repeated suicide attempts, occasionally they have died when, possibly, they did not intend to. They usually write notes or expect to be "discovered" by a regular visitor just in time.

An eight year-old girl in a mental hospital ran down the cliff and swam a long way out to sea, screaming all the way, thus ensuring much attention. A boat was launched, but every time the rescuers tried to grab her she dived underneath and surfaced on the other side. Finally she was dragged back to shore.

Manic depressives, whose moods fluctuate in irregular swings over days or months, always have danger points which occur when they are coming out of a depression into a neutral point. They are then able to review their behaviour and sometimes commit suicide. As soon as the manic phase begins, they forget the past. Those who live with them become aware of these moments and can plot the up-and-down curves. Controlling medicines such as lithium are best administered by the person who monitors the swings and, therefore, can adjust the dose. The depressive who is able to vocalise his anxieties is in a better position than the one who tries to cover them by blaming sleep patterns, headaches or gastro-intestinal symptoms. The therapist should always be aware that these could be obscuring an underlying death wish.

Purposive suicides are the third classification. In cultural or brain-washed circumstances such as can be seen in the Japanese military class, the Samurai, there is a reversion to a primitive state which has nothing to do with the development of spirituality and, indeed, is a negation of the facts of eternity. Men choose to enter into a pact with mindlessness rather than life and are indoctrinated with the wish to kill, to be killed and so invite death in wartime.

They are considered to be "heroes, for the defence of the empire" or "dying in a noble cause." In some situations, however, people consciously risk or sacrifice their lives for others. It is a very natural instinct between parents and children, firemen, lifeboat crews or sometimes, by accident, scientists. For instance, Marie Curie, the dedicated discoverer of radium, did not realize that her X-ray experiments which greatly advanced the frontiers of medical knowledge, were to be the cause of her death.

Threatened and attempted suicides should always be taken seriously. Time must be spent listening to the people concerned and ascertaining the background and cause of their troubles. Often it is unexpressed failures that they are taking out on themselves. Careful listening will reveal other pressures not in the patient's consciousness – perhaps, the voices of the lost, the earth-bound.

The psychosomatic evidence in self-destruction can be verified only by using this reasoning in a provisional or estimated diagnosis and by trying the appropriate therapy. The possession syndrome may explain a large proportion of symptoms. When a President of the Royal College of Physicians was asked, "I believe that you consider sixty per cent of all illnesses are of psychosomatic origin?" he replied, "No. It is over ninety per cent." The neurotic, anxious type of adult results from infancy, so family and environment are significant factors. Later in life, when stressed through isolation or any other reason, patients may convert their moods into somatic targets, headache being the most frequent, followed by insomnia, indigestion and heart symptoms. If no therapy relieves them, then mental illness may be the next step.

Patients from seventy-seven families attending therapy sessions for depressive neuroses were investigated. Sixty-four had threatened to commit suicide; three finally did so. In each family, at least one ancestor had committed suicide – even up to six people. Nine of the dead had been involved in the occult. Fifty-two of the patients were diagnosed as suffering from the possession syndrome and were released after the subsequent Eucharist service.

In a study of 247 anorexics, suicide had been talked about by fourteen per cent and nineteen per cent had attempted it. There is a theory that anorexics in their own minds have determined upon an acceptable slow suicide without involving family guilt.

Statistics show that women are more prone to suicide than men and urban dwellers more than rural. The average age is between twenty-five and thirty-five years. The more intelligent will turn to psycho-religious alternatives. People who have never developed a higher layer of their personality will take out the guilt and despair on themselves when they are under stress. They finally negate the purpose of their intended time of training on this earth. The effective, positive relationship of a therapist who is willing and able to listen, can help them to see themselves objectively and target a higher personality development, thus preventing suicide. (Some tricyclic drugs are helpful temporarily.) The possession syndrome should always be considered as a possible cause in the differential diagnosis.

Para Suicide

This is a term applied to people who make suicidal gestures at some point in their lives. They are commonly very sensitive teenagers who claim to be lonely, useless and unloved, or hysterics seeking attention. Unfortunately, they are an annoyance to others and are given short shrift when they present at a hospital's Accident & Emergency Department with slashed wrists or to have stomach washouts for their "overdoses." In general practice, a doctor who is alert to this type of person will give such a patient more attention and prescribe mild tranquillizers or antidepressants only in small packets of the "push through" method of packaging. This delays the impulsive swallowing of a bottle full of pills. There is a need to question the patient's sleep pattern and the precipitating cause at the moment of tension and also to listen patiently to each proffered excuse. Every symptom must be followed up to ease the current situation, bearing in mind that, occasionally, the suicidal gesture might be fatal if there is no one near at the time. A chemical imbalance results in those who starve, vomit or purge themselves for they also remove the vitamin B complex from absorption into their bodies.

An eighteen year-old bulimic girl had made twelve attempts at suicide in six months. She said, "I'm lonely; a black cloud comes over me; I like the hospital to wash our my stomach contents." She cut her wrists because she felt that she was the rotten fruit on the branch of the family tree, for her sisters were all successful with their own businesses and houses. In fact, she was much loved and constantly attended by her parents, but failed to acknowledge this. The black cloud, the visiting voice, the loneliness were traced to an early induced miscarriage of her mother's the year before the girl was born. When this was explained, floods of tears appeared and she said, "Why did you never tell me? I always thought I had an older brother." She was then able to pray for him.

Sometimes a potential suicide says that they think there is some-one lonely on the other side who wants that person to join them. It is important, therefore, when examining the patient's family, to question whether possible anyone had died unmourned and could be searching for attention.

Healing the Family Tree

PART V
THE BODY

Face

Wonderfully designed as the most prominently positioned part of our anatomy, the face is the area for receiving and emitting signals and also for exposing our vulnerability. From infancy we learn to observe others' expressions, showing mood and attitude and, in turn, we expose our reactions in eyes, lips and cheek colour. Some people try to hide behind dark glasses, with hair styles obscuring the face or with beards, moustaches and cosmetics – adornments to distract another's gaze. Many try to cover up by acting other roles and hiding what is wrong – putting on a brave face, saving face, looking askance or having a hang-dog look. We face a situation, look face to face or set our face against something. We hide our face in shame, blush with embarrassment, turn pale with fear. In analysis, a psychiatrist must look as well as listen – the face is the key factor. This can bring understanding, but not necessarily cure.

Healing of facial ailments obviously depends upon diagnosis. Many children's skin troubles are caused by infectious diseases. If seborrhoeic complaints persist in adults then their lifestyle, diet, exercise and hygiene require to be reviewed. Dermatitis and its further stage of exfoliation may represent the extreme of blushing.

A thirty year-old single woman always looked downward with head bowed, no face being visible. She said little at first in the interview, but within three hours revealed that two of her siblings had been born dead and incinerated. Beaten as an infant, she ran away from home, was raped twice, had an abortion and now lived in a haunted house. She heard voices telling her to kill herself, which she had tried seven times. With many compulsory hospital admissions, there had been the usual diagnoses with the corresponding gamut of ECT and drug treatment. She responded, however, to the fact of being extremely sensitive to people in the eternal world. She felt that they knew she could help them one day through the Eucharist and they trusted her. At the end of the day's interview, the woman was happy, able to look one in the face and delighting in the objectifying of all her "symptoms"; she could pray aloud, at last.

A thirty-two year-old woman, convinced that she had a crooked nose, wanted to hide herself away and demanded plastic surgery. After two operations she became very depressed and violent, continuing her demand. She spent eight years in mental hospitals, two in a padded cell, and then complained about an ancestor who had been a witch and who controlled her life. Exorcism and subsequent deliverance released her. She changed so suddenly that her family was shaken. She became a fashion shop buyer and, after eight years follow-up, she maintained her new lifestyle.

A married woman of forty years always covered the left side of her face with her hand and pulled out hair on that side. Throughout her childhood her father sat on her left at meals. He frequently hit her; she neither loved nor trusted him. She was able, in prayer, to forgive her father.

A secretary in her sixties frequently covered the left side of her face with her hand until she was helped to the realization that she was fending off the shame of the lifestyle of her criminal brother.

A professional man's career was threatened by his intense blushing in public. Exploring the family tree, it was revealed that he was actually the son of his favourite aunt. When this was acknowledged, it brought great joy and release to all concerned.

A divorced and remarried woman in her late thirties always kept her left cheek covered by her hand. She talked about her domineering grandmother, mother and first husband – but she did not want to discuss a previous abortion by another man. Finally, she was able to pray for the baby.

A single forty-five year-old man developed tinnitus (a high-pitched buzz) in his left ear. He was an unwelcome baby, always ignored by his father. The pain radiated from his ear to the left temple. Although he had never been assaulted by his father, this area equated with having his ears boxed. When his father died, the symptoms became so severe that he sought medical advice. A high vitamin B complex improved the situation but the real curative therapy was to pray for and forgive his father.

In presentating ourselves to others, the skin of the face is the first surface of defence – deeper lie the muscles, and there is nerve involvement. The slightest variations in features distinguish one individual from another. Some are endearing, beautiful, inspiring or fascinating; others are intimidating, ugly or even repulsive. Every aspect reflects the person behind the face. (To cover with a mask usually hides ugliness.) We react to what we see, an open honest face is healthy and depends upon the spiritual, curative gifts of love, forgiveness and peace. "We with open face, behold the glory of the Lord and are changed into his likeness" (2 Corinthians 3.18).

Hands

"I have written your names upon the palms of my hands" (Isaiah 49.16).

In nature, humans possess the most highly developed limbs that are capable of grasping. Not only do they work as sensitive extensions of our bodies, but they act out and emphasize our emotions. We are not concerned with their use or appearance, but with some of the psychosomatic expressions that indicate the problems being faced. Much can be deduced from a handshake. The very fact of the open hand, for instance, shows that there is no hidden weapon and no threat between the people meeting. A wet, perspiring hand indicates a state of fear; a strong, dry grip suggests confidence while weak, limp fingers show no actual intention of welcome.

The difference between right and left is important in diagnosis. The right, the dominant side, is active, creative and outgoing; the left represent what is done by others – this is received by the subconscious as anger, resentment or hatred. In Britain, the wedding ring is placed on the left hand and in some churches the bread at the Eucharist is placed in the palm of the left hand and then put into the mouth with the right hand. Both hands are affected by the wringing hands of a miser or the cringing beggar who holds out his cupped hand and cannot keep it flat. Dupuytren's contraction is often seen in gamblers – in one family it occurred in three successive generations.

The wife of a gambler had arthritis of both thumbs. She had been on the brink of disaster for years and, literally, sat on both her hands fearfully wondering what he would lose next.

The palms of both hands of a woman developed "elephant skin." For many years her husband had not allowed her to touch him. When she confessed to having procured her own abortion and was able to commit the child to God, she was healed.

Individual fingers have their own "language" – for instance, the diagnosis of the rheumatic thumb joints of a sixty year-old man was that he was a busybody, always interfering in other people's affairs. A woman's osteoarthritis of her right index finger represented her gossiping about other people. She did not point consciously, but whispered behind her cupped hands. With an apology to God for her behaviour, she was healed.

A married forty-five year-old man had a constant recurring exfoliative dermatitis of his right ring finger which ointments had never helped. When it was explained that this represented the other women in his life, he was able to correct the situation.

A man of sixty years suffered from Dupuytren-like contraction of the little finger of his left hand, but he also had cramp pains. Release came when he was able to forgive his father who had constantly slapped him with the back of his left hand as a child. Throughout her life, a woman of forty-eight years had claw-like hands. Many attempts at diagnosis failed. Eventually, she understood that, in utero, she must have registered the knowledge that her father was consorting with prostitutes, without his wife's knowledge. He had never been an open-handed man. With this realization, the woman's hands were healed.

A Franciscan priest always performed his duties admirably, but when he was to receive the wafer at the Eucharist on his own hand, he would tremble unaccountably. Finally, he acknowledged the association with the frequent canings on his hands meted out by his father, which he had deeply resented; this he had to forgive before the situation was resolved.

Kidneys

These are hidden organs lying at the back of the abdomen, well-covered by the rib cage, but still exposed at their lower poles under "floating ribs.' They are vulnerable, therefore, to external trauma and may be damaged by a hard blow from the front. Above the kidneys lie two small adrenal glands supplied by the kidney arteries, which secrete adrenaline.

The asthmatic, in panic, does not produce sufficient adrenaline, whereas an angry, over-indulgent person may produce too much. The cortex or surface of the adrenal glands houses a separate ⸓et of cells which manufacture the hormone cortisone. This controls the rate of metabolism, the repair system of the body. Cortisone is made from cholesterol and vitamin C. In the Western world, most people have an excessive intake of cholesterol from fatty foods, but require a daily supply of vitamin C as this cannot be stored. The kidneys purify the blood, acting as a constant filter for the body's chemicals. They usually carry two-thirds of their tube surfaces in reserve and excrete waste products drop by drop into the bladder.

Children who suffer from enuresis (incontinence) are often subconsciously seeking their mother's attention. They respond well to small doses of tricyclic antidepressants and most of them grow out of the habit as they mature – some rather late than others.

The kidneys are very resilient but can become "waterlogged." A patient who drank fifteen pints a day looked obese but, in fact, was not fat; his limbs could be pitted by pressure with a finger. Such people can become mentally confused and some have to be hospitalized because of retention of liquid. Isolation and control of their liquid intake usually effects a cure.

A seventy year-old man had a cancerous kidney removed. Two years later, a secondary growth in the pleural cavity was excised. He remained breathless, giddy and very depressed. During a psychiatric consultation it emerged that he had never mourned his dead companions from the 2nd World War nor, indeed, the enemy dead for whom he was responsible. When this was faced, he readily agreed to a ritual mourning process through his church. Weeping and praying, he then admitted that once he had been a Methodist

191

lay preacher and he quoted, "Remember Him before the silver cord is loosed, or the golden bowl is broken, or the pitcher is broken at the spring, or the wheel broken at the well, and the dust returns to the earth it came from, and the spirit returns to God who gave it" (Ecclesiastes 12.6). Within two days, he was fit enough to tend his garden. Now rejoicing, he agreed that "the sorrows with their unshed tears make other organs weep."

We learn from ancient literature that the kidneys or "reins" were thought to be the seat of deep emotion – such as seething rage, reaction to aggression or unswerving loyalty. Here the truth was determined. Therefore, when going into battle men tightened the belts which, for defense, were broad protective belts holding their weapons with a large buckle in front to protect the solar plexus. "Take up the amour of God... Fasten on the belt of truth; for a breastplate put on integrity" (Ephesians 6.13-14). The kidneys were considered to be the source of feelings and thus the key to actions, so women would tie girdles round their waists to let them work unhampered by their skirts. This represented "facing the truth."

Thyroid Gland

There are eight ductless glands, of which the thyroid is the only one visible. If there is a failure of team work between the other seven gland systems, the thyroid may over or under-react. It is controlled by the pituitary gland; its function is metabolic and products from it enter the blood-stream. It depends upon the body's iodine intake – if this is low, the gland becomes goiterous; it can become hyper or hypo-thyroid.

The thyroid gland can swell to become visible as a subconscious protest reaction. For instance, in a family quarrel, a patient held out against the other members over emigration. When she finally agreed to go with them, her swollen thyroid gland returned to normal within three weeks. One may wonder which comes first – the glandular change or the patient's attitude.

The prevalence of thyroid disturbance in women is caused partly by their regular fluctuation physiology related to menstruation and partly by their role within the family. They are more anxious about nutrition and the general care for future generations. Some writers maintain that this is a regression into an infantile level of maternal dependence with ravenous appetites and interpersonal maladjustments. These, and geographical factors, may make the disturbance appear to have genetic recessive factors.

Surgical intervention is rarely justified because this is materialistic thinking, without sufficient time being given to consideration of a patient's stresses. Drugs are useful temporary adjuncts and thyroid substitutes are now very effective, but the analytical approach, although time-consuming, eventually faces the basic causes. These should point to phylogenetically orientated goals – which are, of course, spiritual and should prove that the patient's spiritual life is the ultimate controller – for apology, acceptance, forgiveness and humility; then healing results.

Healing the Family Tree

PART VI
THE SPIRIT

Authority to Pray For the Dead

Where an individual, at the time of his death, has not committed himself to God and prayed for his soul -even by proxy- then his is "lost." The intermediate state he enters is known as "limbo" or "not yet having crossed the Jordan." People who die with unfinished business in their lives also are held up at this point in their journey – it may be because a living person is selfishly holding them back or, perhaps, a case of "where your treasure is, there will your heart be also" (Matthew 6.21). Do the living have the authority to pray for their onward progress?

St. Paul seems to imply that they do – "that now through the Church (prayer, preaching, the Eucharist) the wisdom of God in its infinite variety might be made known to the rulers and authorities in the heavenly realms" (Ephesians 3.10). Paul gives a clear message about the transition from "limbo." "He ascended into the heights..." Now the word "ascended" implies that he also descended into the lowest regions of the earth (Ephesians 4.8-9). King David said, "Thou has ascended on high, thou has led captivity captive; thou hast received gifts for men, even for the rebellious, that the Lord God might dwell among them" (Psalm 68.18 AV).

There are many instances in the Bible of the dead being prayed for – by Elijah, Aaron, Daniel, Paul and Jesus Christ; in the Hebrew Scriptures by Jacob Maccabees and Baruch. Surely the living cannot harm anyone by praying to God for those who have died, since He is God of both the living and the dead. The new covenant of God explains that Christ died for our sins once, hence we die to sin once; Christ has abolished death (Hebrews 9). This is reiterated by the apostle Peter, "For Christ died once for our sins, the just for the unjust... being put to death in the flesh, but made alive by the Spirit" (1 Peter 3.18). He also affirms that "(the dead) shall give account to Him who is ready to judge the living and the dead. For this is the reason the gospel was preached even to those who are dead" (1 Peter 4.5-6). Christ evangelized the dead – that is, took the gospel to them – indicating , surely , that even after death there can be change, repentance and growth in faith. For example, Abel, Enoch, Noah, Abraham and Sara all died in faith before receiving any of the things that had been promised (Hebrews 11.39 and 12.1). William Neil's commentary on these passages from Peter says, "Those who die before or after the day of Christ, dying without knowledge of the gospel, are not beyond God's mercy. Every man, then, can accept or reject this rescue."

At the Eucharist, we show forth the Lord's death till He come" (1 Corinthians 11.26) – to whom? Not only to those on earth but to the whole company of heaven. "If it were not true, what do people hope to gain by being baptized for the dead? If the dead will never be raised, why be baptized on their behalf?" (1 Corinthians 15.29) At his daily Eucharist, John Wesley the evangelist recognized that, "We stand here with all those who have gone before." Archbishop William Temple, quoting the writer Samuel Johnson said, "Their prayers for the dead indicate a continuum of this life." We pray for them both here and there. Some divines delete the dead from all their prayers – one wonders why they attend funerals? We enter eternity now.

The Prebendary of Westminster, Herbert Thorndike, commenting in 1672 upon the Protestants' rejection of all the Roman Catholic corrupt "indulgences" said, "This parting from Catholic law and the removal of prayers for the dead has further and further fragmented the churches, not only paring abuses but cutting the nails to the quick."

J. B. Phillips, the writer of commentaries on Scripture, acknowledged that "The Eucharist is a unique moment when we use our imagination, for here God breaks through and touches our human lives." Not only must we pronounce Satan's defeat on earth but, equally, we must ask that God's angels know of it so that they may guide the lost souls in their charge. It is never too late for those who have died, as many can witness to their acceptance of Christ and the shedding of their problems before they complete their final journey.

Myself when young did eagerly frequent
Doctor and Saint, and heard great Argument
About it and about; but evermore
Came out by the same door as in I went. *(Omar Khayyam)*

Bonding

The fetus lies in a warm, secure environment taking part in all its mother's emotional responses, feeling her movements and hearing her steady heartbeat. Around the fourth month, the baby's own heart imitates the same rhythm, although much faster. During the struggle of actual birth, both hearts beat faster, then the cold world outside the womb forces the first gasps of breath from the infant.

At one time it was a common – and ill thought-out – practice to wrap up a new-born baby immediately and lay it alone in a separate room. The kinder and more natural method is to place it on its mother's abdomen, after the mutual exertion of the birth, before beginning the cleaning-up process. In this way, the already long-established bond between mother and child is maintained. As soon as is reasonable, the baby should be allowed to try to suckle, for then it lies right against the mother's heart and hears familiar sounds. (This immediate reciprocal attentiveness is observed in cats, rats, dogs, sheep, monkeys, goats and many other mammals.) In humans, the emotional bonding of mother and child usually continues until the teenage years when the assertion of independence heralds the beginning of dissociation.

In the early months of life, dependency is established, also, upon the father who is known before birth by the sound of his voice and physical presence. The relationship between parents and the fetus at this time is already influencing the baby's personality and establishing the pattern of response to future joys and struggles. Indeed, many problems have their roots in the early period of life – the formative years of the personality – or in inherited family endowments.

Failure to bond can result from incompatibility or traumatic emotions in either parent during pregnancy, birth or infancy. Possible consequences associated with lack of good bonding are asthma, allergies, "absences," epileptoid conditions, immaturity, fears, depression and homosexuality of the primary type, while psychosomatic target organ disturbances stem from emotions such as anger, hatred or a continually defensive attitude. Counselling such problems involves helping people to gain some insight into these origins through prayer. For instance, orphans can become aware of their unknown natural parents and see them with their adoptive parents – a loving group united by Jesus Christ. This can lead to the establishment of family relationships and thence to an alignment of neuronal, hormonal and cellular systems. Thus, the orphan may receive healing physically, mentally and spiritually and may be able to begin a more positive development in which the feeling of isolation is replaced by a sense of belonging to a family.

The Family

The family embodies unity and integrity. Parents are brought together initially by common interests, their attributes and differences in skills and sensitivity being complementary. The family unit was once the base where both younger and older members could play a useful part and had all their responsibilities.

In the countryside, harvesting and fruit gathering involved everyone and teamwork was essential. Simple celebrations by whole villages were the culmination of their labours. Gradually, this pattern of life was eroded by the lure of the cities with the prospect of easier money turnover, greater sophistication and the necessity of being "with it" and "keeping up with the Jones's."

The smaller city family, and indeed, the single-parent family has produced children who no longer know the pleasure of being part of a large or extended family. When they are regarded as disposable objects for abortion, succeeding siblings sometimes become the target of parental exasperation, resulting in the battered baby situation. During pregnancy, parents who quarrel about whether to abort of not are storing such words and emotions in the soul of the fetus and this will influence its future life. (See the section on Bonding.)

As in utero, the subconscious mind makes decisions, so in infancy it can express an escape mechanism and assume responsibility for the parents" relationships. A six year-old girl overheard that her parents were about to separate. On arrival at school that day, the normally happy, attentive child behaved wildly, screaming, "Cut off my hands." At the end of the day she screamed, "Cut off my feet!" and "Cut me off at the roots, they're rotten!" It appeared that she was trying to say, "I am the rotten fruit at the end of the branch. You only married because of me, so if I am the cause, cut me off" After several disturbed days, the parents quietly explained the situation to the child and her behaviour modified from the initial panic pattern. They were still determined to separate, however, and the little girl became very depressed.

Family life can be held together by resolution and firm intentions when the strength that God gives through His Son is sought. His gift of forgiveness and reconciliation can resolve many difficult situations. Families that spend time together, listen to one another, pray and give thanks for each other, lay the foundations for the unity of the family in future generations.

The Intentions of Prayer and the Power of Praise

When our prayerful intentions are honest and unselfish, much can be accomplished. Children's prayers are especially straightforward. An encouragement to pray, we are told, "Ask, and it shall be given you; seek, and you shall find; knock, and it shall be opened unto you" (Matthew 7.7). In his booklet *Delight in the Lord*, Father Considine (Society of Jesus) says, "Sometimes kneel before our Lord in silence: this kind of prayer will transform you."

A widow in her late seventies attended a communion service to lay her family tree upon the altar – there were no problems anywhere. Her intention was simply to thank God and praise Him for her wonderful family of nine excellent children. For over sixty years, she had a shrivelled and paralysed left leg, a result of polio, and used crutches or a wheel chair. At church , she had not prayed or even thought about her leg but, the same night, she lay awake as feeling began to return to it. In the morning, she could walk. Within a fortnight, her doctor reported that she had developed normal leg muscles and was healed. A complete reversal of medical understanding!

If God knows our requests then, by our long performances and repetitions in prayer, we may gain some personal discipline but in no way can we influence Him. He asks for the compassion of our hearts and our conscious decision to love and show forth His love. This can enable those who have died to observe all that Christ achieved. Our intentions should be expressed aloud in the simplest language and should come from our hearts.

There is power in praise. A teacher who encourages pupils by finding something positive to comment upon, for instance, creates a warm relationship in which children can blossom. It is easy to complain about negative situations, but it needs a conscious decision to adopt a positive attitude and to praise. The latter is a phylogenetic development that is available to man. A petrol bomb caused destruction in Ireland; that was news. On the same day, half-a-million people attended Mass in an Ecumenical gathering; this was not considered newsworthy. To search out the positive answer to a problem or situation requires considerable time to be spent in thought, weighing up the "pros and cons," before a correct solution can be found.

In America, there is an annual Thanksgiving celebration when the first harvest gathered in by the Pilgrim Fathers, who were the first settlers in the New World, is commemorated. Whole families come together from all over the States and, invariably, a feast is held, preceded by prayers of thanksgiving. To learn to praise extends enjoyment and can be therapeutic both for others and ourselves. A ready discipline is to give thanks and count one's blessings, thus engendering further blessings. It is our right to give God thanks and praise; it is our duty and our joy.

A Name – an Identity

Wandering through a garden, one may ask "What plant is that?" On being told its name, even an abstruse Latin one, the questioner is satisfied, but the name may be forgotten a few moments later. If the answer is "I don't know," then one is puzzled and vaguely disturbed. A child's query may be dismissed with a fictitious name, but an adult seeks accuracy although, "A rose by any other name would smell as sweet" (Romeo and Juliet: Shakespeare).

Over forty thousand new terms have entered the English language via medicine, especially psychiatry. Symptom complexes are combined and a diagnosis is arrived at. The labelling of an illness usually brings some relief both to patient and family, for responsibility thus is passed to the doctor with the assumption that, as the doctor "knows what it is," all will be well. Of course, a definite label enables another colleague to understand the reasoning behind any prescribed treatment already given. Psychiatry claims no cures, just a holding or containing programme; symptoms may be relieved and the original diagnosis or name of the illness changed, although another therapist may use an entirely different label. Juggling labels cannot affect the disease, but can help to pin-point its identity. In other branches of medicine, naming and labelling are more specific. To date, however, medical research has been unable to account for the cause and incidence of much disease and there is still an element of mystery in many cures.

There can be magic in a name. Primitive tribes claimed that to know another's name gave one power over them and often they had their own secret names within a group. Earliest humans, when giving sounds a pattern of speech, began to name objects by colour and shape and people acquired names because of their characteristics or skills. Individuals and families came to be identified by their specific natures or associated with the place where they lived and these were given names. As human beings learned to write, names became more defined and, gradually, were passed on through succeeding generations. Nowadays, some people are called by emotions or descriptive words such as Peace, Faith, Merry, Hope, Happy, Joy or Charity.

A name gives authority, whether it is of the law, the crown or of Jesus Christ. ("Jesus" alone is inadequate since it was a common boy's name in Palestine.) It is right to give Him the title "Son of Man" or "Son of God" for the intention behind this use is what matters. We can affirm that "Jesus Christ is Lord," and this title has far-reaching implications. Humans were not allowed to know God's name, so He was called "Yahweh," meaning the maker of all things.

The necessity for a name to be given to a discarded fetus, in prayers, has been proven and recorded in thousands of families from forty-three countries. Neurotic and psychotic disorders among the living often were not resolved until family members, in open confession, faced the truth and did so. "Rejoice because your names are written in heaven" (Luke 10.20).

In several families where everyone has agreed to attend a service for all their miscarriages, abortions and still-births, usually there has been no relief for any ill members until the prayer pattern is specific, the numbers correct and the parents have apologized to God and to the dead children for ignoring them, sending their love and finally (and of necessity) giving them names – for "He calls His own sheep by name" (John 10.3).

A twenty-six year-old heroin addict had been given the same name as his mother's first lover without her husband's knowledge. Although the son also knew nothing of this, he actually lived near the place where this man had crashed to his death in a fighter plane. Together with the mother, a ritual mourning Eucharist was held for him and the son as released from his addiction. Then, the secret of his name was shared with the family. "A good name is rather to be chosen that great riches" (Proverbs 22.1).

A house was haunted for many years by a man dressed in an airforce uniform and smelling of tobacco. He would knock on doors, open them and not appear. There was often a smell of burning in the house and, once, a white paper dart flew across a room and disappeared. Frequently, the man was observed standing admiring the son's car. The family dog saw, smelled and followed the visitations. Many times when food had been prepared, one member of the family would call out, "Bob, the meal is ready" before checking themselves – they did not know a person called "Bob!"

No one in the area had been able to identify the man and, eventually, it was decided that "Bob" must have been an orphan who probably became a fighter pilot and was shot down in his burning plane over the nearby sea. Therefore, having no burial and no one to mourn him, he had wakened in the other world completely unprepared. A kindly man, he had come to haunt this caring family in an effort to call attention to his lost, wandering state. A service and a committal to God ended "Bob's" visitations.

The Possession Syndrome (and Sin)

Carl Jung in *Analects and the Collective Unconscious* first mooted this idea when he states, "I am reluctant to admit that some of my patients seem to be controlled by another entity: these are states of possession which are caused by something that most fitly could be described as an ancestral soul." In 1961, the psychiatrist S.M. Yap labelled this the Possession Syndrome and, as such, it has been much discussed in psychiatric and theological literature. Ten years after this classification, the condition was called demonological but, since then, it has been suggested that there is a broader range of causes. They syndrome continues to be a very interesting area of research.

"Possession" suggests a state which, as with an infectious disease, continues until resolution or antibodies terminate it. In long-lasting cases of illnesses, this period may seem endless, but biochemical factors can be involved (for instance, in schizophrenia). Being "badgered" or "worried" aptly describes the entities identified by Jung but "visited" is probably the most accurate. Extraneous, unwelcome, subconscious "visitations" demand a physical outlet: they must have a target end organ and, as such, are regarded as symptoms by a patient who then can express these centrally recorded complaints to a doctor. They are then correlated and given a diagnostic label. The doctor's role, thus, is to resolve the various "diseases" into something that can be called by a specifically named "disease." Sometimes, of course, the patient may regard the "label" as a life sentence!

Humans, initially endowed with vast potential, can develop positively in certain areas, despite any defects inherited from parental fruits or genetic variations. Healing and forgiveness of sins are available always to everyone and, if these gifts are consciously accepted, a person becomes an eternal creature while still on earth, for he or she is essentially an eternal spirit. As death becomes of less significance, therefore, when we leave our earthly body we will have begun already the journey into a realm that is safe, loving, secure and fulfilled – Heaven. If we do not cultivate the spiritual part of our being, and align ourselves entirely with earthly targets, we ignore the purpose of life here and create our own hell. When we are disobedient to God's laws (which were made to protect us) we are led into sin – and the consequent punishment. Unresolved sin and guilt create barriers against God; then sin is fearful and its hold is strong so that we become afraid of death but, through Jesus Christ, we can be freed and saved. "O death, where is your sting? O grave, where is your victory? The sting of death is sin, and sin gains its strength from the law. But thanks be to God! He gives us victory through our Lord Jesus Christ." (1 Corinthians 15.55-57)

We, the penitent, need to confess specifically our own sins, those of our ancestors and our country. In love, we should visualise everyone involved, with apology to God, and commit each one to Him. By the sacrifice of Jesus Christ, and our prayers in His name, the interference of Satan and his minions is cut so that the angels of the Lord are not impeded; they have full authority to guide the dead on their journey heavenwards and to lead them to where we are showing forth all that was accomplished on the Cross. The efficacy of our prayers and actions depends upon the specific confession of, and apology for sins so, at the Requiem Mass and within the canopy of God's grace, we should put into words those sins for which we need forgiveness. Sin is anything that separates us from God and, sometimes, from family and friends – it is always negative and devisive. "Therefore, since we are surrounded by such a great cloud of witnesses, let us throw off everything that hinders and sin that so easily entangles, and let us run with perseverance the race marked out for us." (Hebrews 12.1)

Generational sin is best dealt with in the Eucharist where each person offers his whole family to the Lord with, especially, any unfinished business. "I, the Lord your God am a jealous God, visiting the iniquity of the fathers upon the children unto the third and fourth generation of those who hate me, and showing mercy to thousands of those who love me and keep my commandments." (Exodus 20.5-6 AV)

Bearing in mind the concept of "visiting" – a fluctuating, off-and-on condition – the first category of the Possession Syndrome may be where living people control each other's lives. This is a proper and natural state between, for instance a mother and child but, after a maturing process, the child's independence becomes of paramount importance. A mother or grandmother, however, for their own compensatory selfishness, can smother a child's development, thus affecting its whole life. (Homosexuals or lesbians may have a similar pattern of behaviour; if one partner dies, the other can continue to exert a controlling influence from the "limbo" world.) Some widows and widowers, also, continue with this domination, being unwilling for their spouses to proceed to God.

The feeling behind the assertions, "I cannot go on without you" or "If you died, I will kill myself," may stem either from selfish love or equally strong hate. Continually reliving vivid memories of someone who has died equals holding on emotionally and preventing their progression to heaven. Often there is deep regret for words unspoken – an apology never made, forgiveness neither sought not accepted or a gesture of love withheld. If any unfinished business remains from a person's time on earth, especially if it were a sudden death, there is a temptation for the living to wish them back – indeed, to hold them back and in bondage to ourselves as we seek to ease the burden of guilt for whatever we omitted to say or do. It is very serious to try to hold on to or "possess" another soul – even that of a loved one.

The dead who have not been released into God's heavenly eternal world, are still earth-bound. In his commentary on 1 Peter, Peake suggests that the sinners have left their bodies, but still live in the flesh (with all its lusts, unresolved business and unfulfilled desires). This is not intrinsically a paradoxical concept, but seems strange because it is unfamiliar.

These lost, disembodied or discarnate spirits who have not yet turned to Jesus Christ wander, looking for rest, and manifest themselves by interfering with the living, either malevolently or seeking help. They want to appeal to those who are sensitive, prayerful and sympathetic – preferably a descendant or a trusted family member. If they cannot find such a person, to whom they can attach themselves and express their discontent into that person's subconscious mind, they will haunt the places where they died, since they no longer can help themselves. Such souls are lost because, in life, they failed to deal with their sins through the forgiveness and new life brought to mankind by Jesus Christ on the Cross. Equally, those who are still alive – and with absolute free will to pray – have failed to do so on their behalf. These spirits either may not have had the opportunity to make decisions in life or, even, may have ignored the ultimate issues. At death, neither they nor the living were able to put right their unfinished business and they were not adequately or honestly presented to God at their funerals -which is the main purpose for relatives and friends attendance at funerals.

It is evident that in the Possession Syndrome those in an earth-bound state can influence the living and be influenced by them; they can forgive and be forgiven; they can choose to stay or to proceed upon their journey. Those who live, however, can show them a positive alternative to being earth-bound – freedom in Christ – but, if they are communicated with through the "black arts," they are held back and this is equally destructive to the living. Areas of our lives which are doubtful, secret, shady or tangential – perhaps, associated with transcendental meditation, witchcraft, psychic phenomena, horoscopes, mediums or spiritualists (who can contact only earth-bond spirits) or blood sacrifices – are a reversion to the attitudes of primitive man (BC). We are warned against such practices: "All who do these things are an abomination to the Lord" (Deuteronomy 18.12). If communication is achieved through the Eucharist, however, the earth-bound are set free to complete their journey. "But now is Christ risen from the dead and become the first fruits of them that slept." (1 Corinthians 15.20)

In the second category of the Possession Syndrome are the "disaster areas" throughout the word: sites of deliberate slaughter or incidents where many people have died. These are haunted places in which wandering spirits, having no descendants, remain where they died and "visit" those who pass through or settle there. Sometimes, in a haunted place, one can pick up the depressed moan of the uncommitted dead. They might be unknown people from an earlier age who lived even as long ago as cavemen. On the other hand, and nearer to oneself, they could be relatives who were lost in war or at sea – disappeared or drowned – friends who committed suicide, or those who never had a funeral or known grave. Nowadays, they could be the miscarried, aborted, still-born or the disposed-of result of an ectopic pregnancy. These are all real people of consequence and they need a name, confession, recognition and committal back to God.

We do not belong to ourselves but to God, so we must return to Him when we die. It is essential, therefore, to hold a service of committal for the dead -not of the body to the earth, but because the soul, thereby, is committed into God's care.

Those who died in war – sometimes wounded and alone in distant lands or at sea – may have had no funeral or prayers said for their lives, so that their angels cannot take them on towards heaven. The unmourned dead, those who died in anger, fear, bitterness or pain, many unrecognised and some, despite having had funerals, being buried in anger and surrounded by guns and oaths of revenge – all these have never been freed from their earthly ties. They wander, lost and haunting, possessing the minds of the living who act out the implanted subconscious thoughts that are "visited" or "trespassed" upon them. (The term "trespass" is used in the Lord's Prayer.) Guided by the echoing voices of the dead, such people continue to kill each other. Two thousand years ago, the Lord''s sacrifice – sufficient for all mankind – ended the necessity for this vicious circle. In the re-membering, re-assemling of His body in the Bread and acceptance of His forgiveness in the Cup at the Eucharist, the gates of Heaven are opened. All Christian churches celebrate the Eucharist; other believers are welcome always at these services, for Jesus Christ invited everyone.

Some unrepentant spirits try to continue their sinful behaviour through a living person who then may claim, "I can't help myself; I don't know what comes over my; I don't want to do it!" Others act malevolently out of jealousy or hatred because, for example, living members of their family have happy marriages or are blessed with children when they were not.

"I keep six honest serving men, they taught me all I know; their names are What and Why and When and How and Where and

– Who! Who is "visiting?" The answer can explain a sufferer's intermittent attacks or "visits," apparent in the schizophrenic's "voices," the depressive's mood swings, the diabetic's fluctuations, the epileptoid, insomniac, kleptomaniac, drug addict or arsonist – all of whom vary in the intensity of their problems.

When counselling troubled or disturbed patients, one finds strange variations in their notion of the dimension of time. The narrowness of their breadth of target and perspective often seems pitiable, compared with the freedom and vast dimensions available – for example, the paranoid patient clinging to old suspicions and gearing every aspect of life to personal and unnecessary defenses.

The third category of the Possession Syndrome includes people who are controlled by Satan and his minions. They may have cold, antagonistic attitudes and be able to "mimic" illness. Some have become involved in the occult either by voluntary indulgence or, even involuntarily where other people have used situations to break them down. The church's ministry of deliverance is the only way to help them. The Apostles' Creed declares that "God the Father Almighty, (is) maker of heaven and earth," enriching and enlarging our lives.

A woman had undergone three official church exorcisms during her twenty years of personal difficulties. Each time her condition was eased temporarily, but the more serious pressures always returned to disrupt her family life. During our prayers she was able to "see" her dead grandmother and great-aunt, neither of whom had approved of her as a child. The evil "contamination" that affected her was with these dead relatives who, after each exorcism, invited "it" to attach itself again to their descendant, and thus, exacerbate the temptations to suicide which tormented her.

There being no time or space in Eternity, as we understand the concepts with our limited human vision, a lost spirit can be talking, for example, into the subconscious of someone in an American mental hospital and to an ill person in England at one and the same time. When a wandering spirit is prayed for, then a patient in an entirely different location may be "healed" at the same moment. Confucius said, "We are heaven and earth in miniature."

Human beings have developed their own sense of time quite distinct from the seasonal variations of animals' behaviour – even that of "man's best friend" the dog, whose reflex systems register feeding times or memories of a kind owner when sniffing a familiar scent! Awareness of the passage of time develops quickly in childhood – days seemed endless then, but looking back from sixty or seventy years on, one can realise how short were those years and how much time was wasted, with all the "ifs" and "buts" and the pointless targets. We cannot comprehend why about one-third of our lives is spent in sleep, during which we have no sense of time but seem to depend solely upon rhythms and the alteration of daylight and darkness. To the fulfilled, there is never enough time; moments of happiness are fleeting.

The more we listen in silence to the "inner voice" – that is, God – the better our decisions and actions. We save time and it becomes our servant, not our master. Humankind has a long way to go; as yet, we are unable to even grasp the meaning or the mystery of Christ's words, "Before Abraham was, I am." (John 8.58)

Summary of the Possession Syndrome

I   LIVING TO LIVING:
Within the family e.g. mother to child, wife to husband.
Outside the family e.g. homosexual, lesbian.

II DEAD TO LIVING:
Within the family e.g. lost siblings, spouse to spouse, troubled ancestors.
Outside the family e.g. war dead, the lost or unaccounted for, suicides, the unborn, abortions, still-births, miscarriages, ectopic pregnancies, lost twins or haunting spirits.

III EVIL FORCES TO THE LIVING:
Voluntary or involuntary.

"Father in heaven, send your Holy Spirit to show us any areas of bondage that we have caused, or that have been passed down to us from previous generations. Bring back to our minds any relative or friend who has been held back by our sins or our lack of love for them, particularly any who were taken suddenly and for whom there was no time to complete their business on earth – especially those who died in wars when there was no family mourning and committal."

THEOLOGICAL POSTSCRIPT
by the editor

Is there any guide to the theology of Family Tree Healing?

Dr. McAll's work, inevitably, has had mixed reactions from the Christian Church. Like many enterprises in Church history, it rests at this point in time on three "legs":

(1) The accumulated body of evidence that family tree healing works. Some of this evidence is anecdotal, but much of it, as this book reports, is put forward as solid research. Insofar as it links the "spiritual" with the "medical," it is perhaps becoming more accessible today as modern medicine learns to take the spiritual more seriously.

(2) The tradition within the Churches that people survive death, and that (in a way which has been much argued about) what we do now influences the nature of that survival, not only for ourselves but for others. This tradition goes back as far as the New Testament Church, but the verses of Scripture referring to it are few (principally, 1 Corinthians 15.29 and 1 Peter 3.19), and moreover they do not explain how it operates – hence the controversy over such things as prayer for the dead.

(3) The claim of Dr. McAll and others that the Holy Spirit has been guiding them in this form of healing, and that it bears good fruit which can and should be tested over time.

Three difficulties in turn are generally raised by Family Tree Healing. The first is felt mainly by those brought up to think that the material, what we can touch and see, is all that matters. The whole idea that lack of a proper burial in the past could actually make a difference to a descendant may seem weird. Or again, the idea that doing something in a church service could have any effect "out there," as opposed to a psychological effect on those taking part.

The second difficulty arises because in the Old Testament, humans are described simply as "living beings," and because the New Testament speaks clearly of the resurrection of the body; the idea of a separate "soul" seems to come from Plato and Greek thought rather than the Bible.

The third difficulty is felt more by those who believe firmly in God, but emphasize that he has done all that is necessary to save us from our sins, so that any idea that we have to "add" something (especially many generations later!) is an offence to the once-and-for-all work that God has done in sending his Son to die and rise again for us.

The first difficulty is very much part of the general agreement raised by an atheist or an agnostic against any faith in a God who acts in the world, and much has been said and written about it. Such a person is perhaps more likely to be convinced by experience of healing than by anything I might write – although the contemporary "post-modern" age is becoming much more open to the spiritual.

The second has left many people uneasy. Anyone who has heard Dr. McAll and looked dispassionately at the evidence he brings, is likely to say, "Well, there must be something in it." But what exactly, it if seems to raise awkward questions about our faith? If it is true, does it mean that God is playing games with us... or that we have wasted our lives because we never bothered to spend time releasing "imprisoned" spirits? Or could it be that all this is demonic deception?

Before the Reformation took place, many monks and nuns earned income for their religious houses by praying for the souls of the dead. In reaction, Protestants argued that "as the tree falls, so must it lie"; there is no second chance in the afterlife. Indeed, John Calvin wrote a little tract called *Psychopannucia*, arguing vigorously against "soul-sleep": rather, he maintained, we go straight to glory after death.

Is there a way through this controversy? And what, indeed, is the right explanation behind what happens in the stories recounted in this and other books?

One approach is just to say, "We do not have to explain it, just do it, and rejoice in the results!" And it is true that when we stand at the gate of heaven, no one is likely to come up and ask us, "Now before we let you in, tell us your exact views on the afterlife!" Kenneth McAll as an orthodox believing Christian, is perfectly clear, along with the tradition of all the Churches, that we enter heaven because Jesus Christ himself is the way for us after death, as he is the way before death. We are saved by God's love in Christ, not by our precise theological views.

Yet the command to love God with our minds, and indeed the command to love others who have questions about the topic of this book, encourages us to try to say a little more. I want, then, to suggest a "third way," an approach which tries to do justice to the facts and to Christian theology. I do not believe it is necessary to choose between scepticism on the one hand, and a kind of Eastern mysticism on the other. (This essay was actually prompted by the shocked reaction of one reader who said, "But this is just Buddhism!")

When you reflect that God made time as well as everything else, you recognize that God sees all things (past, present, and future), yet without doing violence to the cause and effect processes within time. Another way of looking at this is to learn from modern physics, that God has not simply made order out of chaos at the start of things, but that He actually uses chaos all the time to produce order. We rightly say the "wind," for example, is chaotic, *and* that it is ordered – or in other words, that it is free, yet that you could still get a job as a weather forecaster!

From God's point of view, heaven is open to anyone who "repents and believes the gospel." His love is free, it embraces anyone who is willing to leave his or her sin behind, in this life or the next. C.S. Lewis dealt with this subject in a fascinating way in his book *The Great Divorce*. Yet from our point of view, the person is gone after death, we cannot see where.

What then of "intimations from the other side" – spirit appearances? Here again come the two common interpretations:

(a) *The sceptical or "Western" view.* It is hallucination, or fraud. Or (moderate scepticism) the evidence is just not good enough.

(b) *The mystical or "Eastern" view.* We are all spirits, moving from one existence to another: So a bit of overlap here, and a delay there, is to be expected, and the more spiritual you are, the more you are aware of it.

I want to suggest two lines of thought, which converge, although I do not claim to have the right language to synthesise them. Indeed, as they operate on different levels, it may be necessary to work with them both... it is perhaps just a modern conceit that everything must fit into two, or even three dimensions.

The first line is the idea of the "imprint": that every experience leaves its mark or imprint – not only on the individual concerned (the psychological effect) but on our space-time track (we do not yet have an accepted word for the kind of effect that is, although in the context of this book it is especially a track down and across the generations).

The second is the idea of providence: that all things work together for good (Romans 8.28)... and that we are created to do the good things that God has already planned for us (Ephesians 2.10). Healing is in principle one of those good things, and if things are not healed within one generation, then they must be healed in the next.

Heaven itself must be a place of healing. Clearly God can heal in heaven what has been wounded on earth. But what if there remains that wound in the space-time track leading into our generation, that imprint of what has gone before which really does hurt people? Then what is happening in Family Tree Healing is two-fold:

(a) People now (present) are being healed and freed, often dramatically.

(b) People then (past) are being set free, and we are granted sight of what in our time has been long delayed, but in God's time has now been able to follow naturally upon death.

Understood this way, praying for the dead is not a threat to the finished work of Christ, but a response to it. No attempt is made to bypass the cross – indeed all Christian prayer is through the cross. But it is video theology, rather than slide theology. Seen as two static pictures, past and present, there is a conflict between traditional Reformed theology and Dr. McAll's views; but in video, separate pictures are run together so that one leads into the other.

It is not surprising that communion is a natural context for healing prayer, as heaven and earth are specially open to each other in the sacraments. In communion we celebrate the one final imprint of our humanity which continually bears fruit and awaits reunion with the risen Saviour at the end of all things. Likewise, in communion body and soul are healed together with what an early Church Father called "the medicine of immortality."

In any writing about God's time and ours, we find it impossible to use past, present and future tenses consistently. All time is present to God. There is a "double vision" here, similar to the double vision which we accept easily in other contexts, such as, "Pray as if everything depended on God, work as if everything depended on you."

My words about this great subject are tentative, and if they lead others to improve upon them I shall be well content.

– Jock Stein

SUMMARY OF TERMS AND CONDITIONS

(An index specific to this book, including additional causes of disease based on case histories from the Family Tree Ministry)

A

Abscess	E.g. on right foot of ex-footballer wanting to kick his manager. Priest with "chip on his left shoulder"
Accident Prone	May be inattention or fear on the part of over-protective parent
Addictions	From peer pressures or "voices"
Addison's disease	Underactive adrenal glands usually autoimmune in origin occurred in an illegitimate child all of whose grandparents were unknown
Advocacy	Pleading on behalf of unquiet dead
Alcoholic	Work worries, shutting out memories or voices, uncommitted war dead, unrecognised babies aborted or miscarried
Allergies (incl. Total Allergy Syndrome)	Did not want to be born, living on Indian Reservation land in USA with violation of land rights. Traumatic infantile memories
Amnesia	Loss of memory, after head injury, fugue states, "absence" or hysterical convenience
Anger-excessive bursts	Abortion, curse, murder, secrets in family occult involvement
Anorexia nervosa	Abortion, miscarriage, revenge on parents, unwanted child, trying to draw separated parents together, suicide in family, grandmother evil, father in POW camp
Antisocial behavior	Adoption, uncommitted lost child, war dead; anxiety abnormal living, neurosis
Aphasia (speech disorders)	Abortion, adoption, child abuse, unwanted child, left-handed made to use right hand, suicide by gas, ancestor killed by firing squad, brother who shot himself through mouth

Aphonia (loss of voice)	Disease of larynx or vocal cords, hysteria
Arthritis	Shame, envy, jealousy, anger, abortion; bitterness lack of forgiveness, inability to face truth
Asthma	Fear – need to find origin e.g. burglars, cats etc.; ancestor suffocated in mud
Arson	Revenge for ancestral wrongs
Astrology	Ancient method of hunting for omens. Today a money-making nonsense but still popular
Atheist	Too lazy or selfish to consider God's existence
Automatic writing	Rapid writing, often hard to decipher, written, apparently, under influence of deceased relative

B

Back	Lack of support
Behaviour disorder	Battered child, deprived, identity crisis, immature, lack of parental training, heavy rock music, unrecognised unborn siblings
Bitterness	Abortion, murder, secrets in the family, generational anger, result of a curse, Satanic involvement
Black "abyss of eternity"	War death on submarine of father when patient aged 2
Black sheep	Family members who had disappeared or ran away, causing depression or schizoid patterns in descendants
Blindness	Psychosomatic – shut eyes to truth of wrong relationship
Blasphemy	Fear of condemnation, guilt is usually specific
Blood pressure (high)	Anger, general indulgence, genetic patterns
Blood sugar	See Diabetes
Bulimia	Eating disorder of gorging and vomiting, ancestral guilt

C

Cancer	Abused or over-stimulated cells out of control break away and invade other areas, "the cancer in your souls"
Catacombs	Burial places. Haunted, inadequate burials, local residents disturbed

Caveman behaviour	Regression to primitive behaviour when under stress, in prison or internment or under the influence of alcohol or drugs; resentment
Child abuse	Generational and Satanic with knock-on effect
Choking	Ancestor murdered, hung, suffocated, drowned, beheaded
Cigarette smoking	Narcissistic nipple-sucking
Claustrophobia	Fear of enclosed space, see also agoraphobia in text. Ancestral war experiences
Clearances	In Scotland – landlords expelled tenants, killing and burning
Colitis	Inflammation of large bowel, often appears to have emotional origins. Psychosomatic voiding of subconscious unwelcome family secrets. Crohn's Disease – orphan, unmourned unborn child, "bowels that yearn"
Concussion	Temporary "absence" following head injury or ECT, vulnerable time for the soul
Confused	Disorientated state of "limbo" – lost souls
Constipation	Unwilling to have the world intrude into life, escape, unfinished work, "constipated outlook." Positive change – trust – open up.
Conversion syndrome	Mental conflicts expressed in physical outlets, frequently associated with specific disturbed ancestors
Cousin marriages	Family genetic faults easily inherited
Covens	Meeting of witches; may include animal or human sacrifice
"Crossing the Jordan'	Souls going on can be envisaged at the Requiem Mass
Crying	Normal reaction in mourning situation; pellagrous in Vit. B3 deficiency, endogenous depression, hysteria
Crystal gazing	Clairvoyance, astrology, ouija board, tarot cards fortune telling, witchcraft – all use "mind" power to influence people, forbidden in Deut 18. Can often be traced through families resulting in depression, suicide, fatal accidents in family members. Family name of "Warlock" -son affected

Cursed	Mother a clairvoyant; mother a medium; palmistry, fortune-telling, cousin of witch, nephew or niece of witch; grandmother a witch
Curses	Occult, causing anger, bondage, epilepsy, alchoholism, see Derek Prince: *From Curse to Blessing*
Cushing syndrome	Pituitary gland disease
Cutting/slashing oneself	Ancestor hung, drawn and quartered. Uncle an air pilot died when thrown through broken cockpit canopy

D

Deafness	Psychosomatic – unwilling to hear, self defense
Death	God's greatest and last gift to the living
Deja Vu	Sensation of having previously experienced an event due to slowing of neural pathways
Deliverance	Out of evil into God's keeping
Depression	1. Endogenous due to chemical imbalance, including premenstrual and puerperal depression, phase of manic-depression
	2. Reactive – normal reaction to life events, e.g. bereavement, unemployment, upset relationship etc.
	3. Vit. B3 deficiency (Nicotinamine)
	4. Possession syndrome – by living or dead
	5. Occult involvement, self-induced or induced by others
	6. Disobedience and guilt
	7. Loneliness, rejection
	8. Unmourned dead, e.g. war dead where no known funeral
Dermatitis	See eczema
Dermobrazia	Self-inflicted skin damage, psychosomatic, shame of ancestral behaviour, living on haunted sites or former brutality
Dermoid cysts	Consist of feotal material, may occur anywhere in body needs to be recognized as possible undeveloped twin
Diabetes	"A punch in the stomach," sudden shock or hurt

Diptheria — Three cases of symptoms of suffocation where ancestors had died of diptheria and buried without proper funerals

Disaster —
1. Bermuda Triangle – slaves thrown overboard
2. Aborigines – almost wiped out by whites
3. Coffin ships
4. Opium wars
5. Slaves of Texas
6. Pirates
7. Vikings
8. Smugglers' tunnels
9. Polish Jewish refugees
10. Minors, miners
11. Isle of Jersey and POW slaves

Discarnate spirits — Seek attention from the sensitive living

Disappearances — Unaccounted for deaths of ancestors

Dislocation — Awareness and orientation disturbance in shock, war, prison etc.

Distant healing — Healing occurring in time and place distant from actual site of Divine Healing service

Divorce — Lack of forgiveness results in dilemma of divided loyalties in children and rejection

Dreams — May be God's way of speaking to us. Often helpful in uncovering underlying problem

Drop attacks — Faulty blood supply to brain, epilepsy, hysterical

Drowning — Of ancestor may lead to dreams of suffocation, hydrophobia

Duodenal ulcer — Some psychosomatic in origin, stress after meals

Dyslexia — Difficulty with word spelling and reading, improved on large dose of Vitamin B3

Dysthymia — Characteristics of the neurotic and introverted including anxiety, depression and compulsive behavior

E

Eating disorders — see Anorexia Nervosa and Bulimia

Ectopic pregnancy — Embryo develops outside the uterus, usually in the fallopian tube. Can go to full term but usually dies

Eczema	Skin disease – shame, abortion, suicide, repressed irritability
Emigrants	Need to mourn ancestors left behind e.g. from Scottish clearances, Irish potato famine, sufferers from persecution – Huguenots, Calvinists
Emphysema	Distention of the lungs, a common cause of death in descendants of French settlers from Nova Scotia sent south by British, any of whom were thrown overboard en route to penal colony
Enuresis	Bed-wetting, children's protest, insecurity
Ensoulment	Point at which individual becomes a living soul – Biblically at conception
Eucharist	Means "thanksgiving" (otherwise Holy Communion, the Mass, the Lord's Supper) – celebrating of Christ's life, death and resurrection in taking bread and wine
Execution	Five cases acting out subconscious fears of recorded family executions
Exorcism	Driving out evil, only to be done in name of Christ

F

Fallopian tube	See Ectopic pregnancy
Family dissension	Masonic curse, Jehovah Witness, Fundamentalists
Fear	Inadequate self-image, subconscious memories of ancestral deaths
Fits	Simulating epilepsy, aborted sibling, sibling dropped dead
Fingers	Right index finger – accusing, thumb -interfering
Folie a deux	Hysterical imitation of each other's symptoms
Follow-up	Keeping in touch following treatment essential
Funerals	Haunting from the unburied e.g. war dead, inadequate funeral, buried in hate, should be time for family confession, visual imagery, rejoicing

G

Gall Bladder disease	"The bitterness of gall." Patient often cynical or critical

Gastric ulcer	See also duodenal ulcer, stress at time of digestion, usually interpersonal
Gastrointestinal dysfunction	Abortion, occult guilt precipitating voiding reactions, vomiting or diarrhoea
Ghosts	Over-active imaginations, Bermuda Triangle type of crime, graveyard, plague pits, etc. House of prostitution, murder or suicide site, occult activity, covens sites underground accidents
Gilli de la Tourette's syndrome	Nervous tics, echoing other's words, filthy language. Ancestral obsession as, suppressed anger compensated by ritual repetitions
Glaucoma	Increased tension in eye, indulgent, hypertensive
Globus Hystericus	"Lump" in throat making swallowing difficult – ancestor drowned, abortion, family violence

H

Hair	Torn out in anguish. Scalp picking, puzzled or guilty
Hallucination	Chemical imbalance or fever. Involvement with spiritualism; grandmother involved in occult
Hands	Excessive washing in guilt
Hare lip	Incomplete development, unwanted child
Haunting	Of place or person, needs to be treated with respect and compassion, abortion, Bermuda Triangle type crime, murder, accident, suicide, bitter battles with immediate family. Ex-Christian turned to the occult
Headache	Cervical nerve pressure, referred pain from eye, ear or stiff neck. Stress, anxiety, pride. If sudden or persistent should be referred for medical opinion
Homosexuality	Two recognisable types, both treatable: 1. Primary: fetal memory or parental adultery during pregnancy, stillbirth of twin 2. Secondary: learned at puberty, needs moral and spiritual decision

Huguenot	French Protestant refugees, many killed. Left old and dying behind, no adequate mourning
Hydatidiform mole	Faulty development of embryonic cells which should have been the placenta. May grow to large size suggesting pregnancy. No fetus present
Hydrophobia	Fear of water. Unmourned ancestral drownings including war disasters
Hypnosis	The power of one mind over another, can reveal useful subconscious areas, but mind can fabricate nonsense. Method superseded by the use of "truth" drug
Hysteria	Mimicking of disease, attention seeking, abortion

I

Irritation of body areas	Alert reaction to draw attention to a physical need. "The get under my skin." Unresolved conflict needing honesty
Iatrogenic	Doctor-induced illness due to incorrect use of drugs or wrong diagnosis
Incest	Secret sexual indulgences within the immediate family, often ending in extreme disasters of murder or suicide
Incongruity of effect	Inappropriate behaviour or reaction, commonly in schizoid personalities
Ignomania	Exaggerated antagonistic opposite to the truth when the guilty one is exposed

K

Kicking	Desire to kick leading to disease in the instep in footballers, toes in rugger players, knees in women
Kidneys	"The reins," the loins vulnerable to attack, "Gird up the loins of your mind." Position of glands producing adrenaline necessary for fighting
Klinefelters syndrome	Mental retardation genetically determined
Knees	The knees that will not bend e.g. to the Lord in prayer

Knock-on effect	"Visiting the sins of the fathers to the third and fourth generation ... but blessings to thousands of generations of those who love Me and keep my commandments"
Knuckles	The clenched fist of an angry fighter. Osteoarthritis in the suppressed fighter who subconsciously wants to punch so holding in spasm

L

Laying on of hands	At time of private prayer. A spiritual gift of love and concern can be healing. After birth an infant needs the continuity of contact. Helps orientation in the fevered or hallucinated
Leukaemia	Over-production of protective white cells, seen in deep generational resentment, witchcraft, curses
Leucotomy	A drastic severing of nervous connections in the frontal lobe of the brain to bring maniacs under control. Now more selective methods used
Listen	A deliberate decision to listen to other people and to put time aside to listen to God, best in the early morning
Lying	A deliberate decision is needed with restitution

M

Malaria	Tropical disease carried by mosquito, can recur over long periods. Some have continued to mimic the shivers when back in Britain, responding to healing of memories and phobias
Manic depressive	Many are acting out the possession syndrome, when "visited" they are depressed, when not "is-tied" they are elated. Some are so affected they become chemically disturbed and need treatment with drugs; many cured by the Eucharistic approach
Masons	Began as a BC secret society. Within membership loyalty is strong. Secrecy has broken families and some occult ceremonies have

	denied Christians their personal freedom as children of God
M.E.	A post-viral syndrome with prolonged debility and muscle pain, often thought to be neurotic.
Memories	Can be explored by the truth drug or under the guidance of the Holy Spirit. Some need healing by a deliberate act of replacing with positive thought
Migraine	Paroxysmal headache, sometimes with visual disturbance. Interpersonal disruptive relationships can precipitate it. Honest apology is one healing route
Miners	The lost souls in mine disasters have become manifest in services around Cornish mines. Many seen as children
Miscarriages	The human soul has been created before conception; every miscarried baby needs to be loved, named and committed to God
Mother	"Smother." In state of loneliness some overcompensate in controlling their child, usually one. The child never learns to make its own decisions. Some develop schizoid type illness in adulthood. A deliberate spiritual decision, whether the mother is dead or alive, has brought release
Multifactorial	Most disease states may have a variety of basic causes, often more than one. Each may need attention
Munchausen syndrome	A continuous faking of illness to gain attention and free hospital living
Murder	Can cause disturbance in succeeding generations until the perpetrator or victim is offered acceptance and forgiveness

N

Name is of utmost importance	Within a family a chosen name should be one to inspire our lives. Never use a family name which has disastrous connotations. A baby aborted, miscarried or born dead, having been named, should keep that name as giving it to another can cause severe disturbance

Narcolepsy	Uncontrollable tendency to sleep. Maybe escape from subconscious family traumas
National characteristics	Accepted as normal in the place of origin can present problems for refugees to foreign countries. Because of hurried departure, dead relations may not have been buried. Alcoholism, depression, diabetes, schizoid symptoms may result
Neck pain	May result from physical causes, pride, resentment, narrow mindedness, refusing to alter one's opinions, "a stiff-necked generation
Negativism	Impatient negative decisions are easy. To wait for a positive alternative needs faith. The wider paradigm of spiritual exploration is waiting
Nerves	A common diagnosis applied to the hyper-sensitive or self- centred. Commonly used as an "escape" label
Neuritis	Inflamed nerves needing rest and megavitamins
Nose	Deluded patient complained of mishaped nose, unresolved family secrets or previous wrong family decisions, may precipitate possession syndrome

O

Obesity	Familial glandular fault, indulgence, dissatisfaction, loneliness, possession syndrome, e.g. by victims of Irish potato famine, unmourned siblings
Objectify	Taking a list of symptoms and looking at them as evidence of external origins
Obsessional	Unreasonable repetitive ideas or actions, can originate in family or personal guilt
Occult	Deliberate disobedience to God's laws revealed over thousands of years on witchcraft, necromancy etc. (see Deuteronomy 18) ending in disasters, madness or death
Oral satisfaction	Unfulfilled in infancy, narcissistic nipple-sucking as in cigarette smoking. We need to remember to delight in our palate with gratitude

Organ language	Symptoms related to specific organ may indicate source of disease, "How beautiful are the feet of them who walk in the paths of peace"
Orphan	Can ultimately take responsibility for parents' demise
Out of body	A temporary awareness of Eternal dimensions while suspending earthly consciousness of time and space

P

Paranoia	Delusional insanity, imagined persecution usually familial
Pain	The body's message system to inform central thought process that there's something wrong
Pellagra	Vitamin B3 deficiency causing depression, diarrhoea and dermatitis
Phantom limb	Painful sensation of a limb still present after amputation
Plague pits	Pain disappeared after Eucharist held for comrades blown up at the time the patient had lost his arm. Sites of mass burial of plague victims, usually in quicklime
Praise	A deliberate and essential ingredient to life to be given and received for our well-being
Prayers for the dead	Ancient custom in the Church. As God is our Father we may talk to Him about anything we choose. We may pray *for* the dead, not *to* them
Probation	Our temporary training time on earth
Psoriasis	Irritable circumscribed areas of thickened flaking skin. May occur over whole body. The site may give the clue to the underlying emotional trigger, e.g., behind knee or elbow may indicate repressed anger
Psychosomatic	A subconscious thought or emotion leading to physical disease, cf. somatopsychic, a physical condition leading to inappropriate thoughts or explanations

Q

Quiet time	A time in silence with God, essential for our spiritual health and growth. A time to listen to Him to find the positive, create alternative

to man's way of doing things. Can happen at any time, but first thing in the morning is most important

R

Relaxation	Rest and/or compensatory activity
Reincarnation	A theory to explain the possession syndrome, cancelled by the life and teaching of Christ
Rejection	A common symptom in families who ignore the unborn
Respect	For every conception within the family brings peace
Rhythm	Essential to conform to nature's rhythms, time, sleep etc. Case histories reveal rhythms, e.g. family anniversaries may be hidden only to appear as recurring unease or disease
Ritual mourning	The funeral service. A loving ceremony in which there may be proxy confession for the dead ancestor followed by committal to God

S

Sacrifice	Primitive man's concept that the life of the victim was in the blood and that through the shed blood, the strength or character of the victim could pass into those making the sacrifice. The need for this was ended by Christ's offering of Himself
Sadism	Cruelty for pleasure frequently with sexual perversion. Often ancestral in origin. Needs ending by deliberate spiritual decision
Schizophrenia	Chemical disorder of the brain. Can be controlled by drugs. High percentage precipitated by possession syndrome. Search of family tree usually reveals origin
Schizoid	Condition mimicking true schizophrenia, history of abortion, suicide or other violent death in the family
Shrive	To submit oneself to being humbled by confession of wrong or to hear someone else's confession
Singled	Isolated by death or divorce of partner, more vulnerable to emotional trauma

Skin	The largest organ in the body, covers our conscious relationship with the outside world, whether to the elements or to other people. See Eczema
Specific	Detailed events in the family history at the time of onset of disease may be the key to the answer. Prayer for healing needs to include specific details of family problems
Smoking	Narcissistic nipple sucking. Insecurity
Sorrow	"The sorrows with their unshed tears make other organs weep." Kidneys, bowels, bronchi, sinuses may be affected
Spiritualists	Those who seek communication with the dead thus disobeying the law in Deuteronomy. We may safely talk to the Lord *about* them
Spontaneous	About 10% of all conceptions end in abortion, abortion frequently unrecognised
Stealing	Is sometimes an attention-seeking cry for help. Can be from ancestral bondage
Stammer	Fear in childhood, blasphemous ancestor, suicide shot through the mouth
Stress	Caused by resistance to normal challenges of life. We are here in temporary learning environment. If we fail to learn with our own volition then transmarginal stress causes breakdown
Swallowing difficulties	If physical cause excluded, may be due to inflicted situations which are difficult to "stomach" or "swallow"
Sweating	Trigger memory of pirate ancestor who died of tropical fever and probably had no funeral
Sweaty palms	In anxiety
Synchronicity	Term coined by Carl Jung for positive coincidences

T

Teamwork	Begins in family life, an essential for growth and development all through our lives
Temper	A defensive, adrenaline-producing state. When excessive and out of control, may be due to possession syndrome especially in children

Thumb	When painful may represent interference in other's business
Thyroid	Gland in the neck which helps to control metabolism. May become overactive in disturbed relationships
Transference	One person's guilt projecting symptoms on to another. May follow a curse. Easy to blame ancestors or other people instead of facing one's own guilt.
T.M.	Self-centred form of meditation of Hindu origin. Christ-centered meditation transforms self and leads to out- going unselfish living
Transvestists	Obsession of the emotionally underdeveloped who seek satisfaction through wearing clothes of the opposite sex
Trigger	The event which prompts the onset of disease
Twin	Disturbed behaviour, possible with unaccountable rages and destruction, in children has been cured by recognition of the possible existence of a twin which failed to develop. Child unaware of parental therapy.

V

Voices	See Schizophrenia

W

War	Family tree needs to be searched for ancestors dying in war without formal burying. Often no body left to be buried or circumstances of death unclear
Washing	Of hands can be obsessional as an expression of guilt
Water	Aquaphobia-fear of water-can be subconscious reaction to hidden family drowning or torture
Weeping	A necessary physiological reaction to grief or hurt. If repressed other organs of the body may "weep"
Witchcraft	The cause of much disturbance. Covens all need breaking with the blessing of God